AMSTERDAM'S CANAL DISTRICT

AMSTERDAM'S CANAL DISTRICT

ORIGINS, EVOLUTION, AND FUTURE PROSPECTS

Edited by Jan Nijman

UNIVERSITY OF TORONTO PRESS

Toronto Buffalo London

ISBN 978-1-4875-0034-4 (cloth)   ISBN 978-1-4875-1079-4 (EPUB)
ISBN 978-1-4875-1078-7 (PDF)

Library and Archives Canada Cataloguing in Publication

Title: Amsterdam's Canal District : origins, evolution,
and future prospects / edited by Jan Nijman.
Names: Nijman, Jan, editor.
Description: Includes bibliographical references and index.
Identifiers: Canadiana (print) 20200228803 | Canadiana (ebook) 20200230166 |
ISBN 9781487500344 (hardcover) | ISBN 9781487510794 (EPUB) | ISBN 9781487510787 (PDF)
Subjects: LCSH: Grachtengordel (Amsterdam, Netherlands) | LCSH: Historic districts –
Netherlands – Amsterdam. | LCSH: City planning – Netherlands – Amsterdam. |
LCSH: Historic buildings – Netherlands – Amsterdam. | LCSH: City planning – Netherlands –
Amsterdam – History – 17th century. | LCSH: Canals – Netherlands – Amsterdam. |
LCSH: Amsterdam (Netherlands) – History. | LCSH: Amsterdam (Netherlands) – Buildings,
structures, etc. | LCSH: World Heritage areas – Netherlands – Amsterdam.
Classification: LCC DJ411.A59 A47 2020 | DDC 949.2/352 – dc23

Title page image: Henk Meijer/Alamy Stock Photo
Part opener image: Bardocz Peter/Shutterstock.com

This book was supported by the Centre for Urban Studies of the University of Amsterdam
and by Stadsherstel.

This book has been published with the help of a grant from the Federation for the Humanities
and Social Sciences, through the Awards to Scholarly Publications Program, using funds provided
by the Social Sciences and Humanities Research Council of Canada.

University of Toronto Press acknowledges the financial assistance to its publishing program of the
Canada Council for the Arts and the Ontario Arts Council, an agency of the Government of Ontario.

ONTARIO ARTS COUNCIL
CONSEIL DES ARTS DE L'ONTARIO
an Ontario government agency
un organisme du gouvernement de l'Ontario

Canada Council   Conseil des Arts
for the Arts   du Canada

Funded by the   Financé par le
Government   gouvernement
of Canada   du Canada

Canada

This volume is dedicated to the memory of Leon Deben,
scholar and passionate citizen of Amsterdam.
Without him, this book and the conference that led up to it
would not have happened.

Contents

PART II: EVOLUTION

PART III: TWENTY-FIRST-CENTURY CHALLENGES

Figures

Maps

Tables

Preface

Amsterdam's Canal District was named a United Nations Educational, Scientific and Cultural Organization (UNESCO) World Heritage Site in 2010, a declaratory gesture that affirmed the importance of preservation of the area and at the same time fuelled the already growing stream of tourists. The area's seventeenth-century design is without historic precedent in Europe in terms of scale, mixed use, and the blending of ecological and aesthetic principles; its subsequent survival for four centuries is a testament to its ingenuity. If the area's original design was special, so are its present-day challenges. The Canal District today is an extraordinary example of resilient historic design and cultural heritage in a *living* city, but there can be no doubt that in the last two decades or so its urban ecology is subject to severe pressures.

This edited volume brings together a number of top-flight scholars to debate questions about the origins, evolution, and future of the Canal District. They bring different approaches and varying arguments and perspectives. Together, their contributions render a volume where the whole is much more than the sum of the parts. The book breaks new ground in our *understanding* of the Canal District's historic design and how it has fared for over four centuries, but it also highlights some fundamental issues in strategies and policies towards the future. While the main focus is clearly on Amsterdam, the discussions have an important bearing on urban historic preservation everywhere and on questions about enduring urban design.

The production of this book was made possible with generous support from the Centre for Urban Studies of the University of Amsterdam (www.urbanstudies.uva.nl), one of the largest research units of its kind in the world; and by Stadsherstel (www.stadsherstel.nl), a foundation that has played an invaluable part in the preservation of historic Amsterdam during the last sixty years.

AMSTERDAM'S CANAL DISTRICT

Origins, Evolution, and Future Prospects

chapter one

Introduction:
Amsterdam's Canal District in Global Perspective

JAN NIJMAN

Amsterdam's Canal District stands out as an exceptional urban design in early modern Europe in terms of scale, the combination of aesthetics and functionality, and, not least, its unprecedented bourgeois rationale. Its origins alone are of great historical interest. However, it is the survival of the Canal District for well over 400 years that makes it an unusually compelling case study of enduring urban design (Map 1.1). Of course, other European cities, some older than Amsterdam such as Bruges or Venice, also display iconic parts of their historic built environments, but these are not living cities – their preserved historic cores are more akin to open-air museums. Amsterdam's Canal District appears to have been remarkably adaptive but, at the beginning of the twenty-first century, its resilience is being put to the test like never before.

The initial discussions for this book, around the time of the Canal District's 400th anniversary in 2013, tended to emphasize either the district's historic origins or its present-day challenges. Obviously, both are important, and they are connected. The first part of the book would be largely historical, the second part would focus on the present and future, and a couple of chapters in the middle would serve to bridge the two parts. However, as this bundle came to fruition, it became evident that perhaps the most important lessons were to be learned from the ways in which the area *evolved* over time, between that moment of creation in the seventeenth century and the present day. In some ways, it turns out, the Canal District has changed more than is generally appreciated.

In other ways, the predominant framing of the area, by locals and visitors, scholars and policy makers, seems to have turned a blind eye to more contentious readings of the district's history, particularly those relating to the age of imperialism. The Italian architect Aldo Rossi (referenced in chapter 6) suggested in his 1966 book *L'architettura della città* (*The Architecture of the City*; Rossi, 1982) that understanding the city can be as complex as studying the biography of a human being: true identity lies in development, growth, and change. Surely, it is the evolving identity of the exceptionally resilient design of the Canal District that must feature prominently in any future strategies of management and preservation.

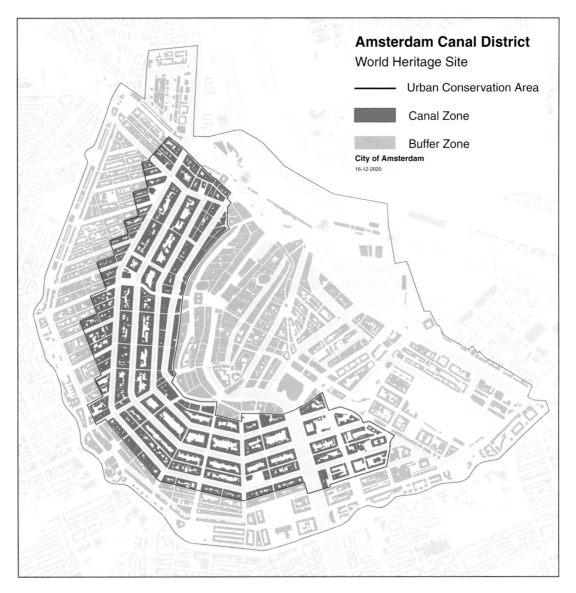

Map 1.1 | The old city of Amsterdam (built pre-1700), showing the UNESCO designated World Heritage Site of the Canal District in blue. The yellow areas (the older historic core and the outer surrounding area) are considered "buffer zones." Source: City of Amsterdam.

Overview of This Volume

The book's three parts focus, respectively, on the historic origins, evolution, and present-day challenges of the Canal District. Part I (chapters 2, 3, and 4) addresses the historical origins and context of the district's design in terms of urban planning, the broader social, political, and philosophical transformation that took place in the Dutch Republic at that time, and Amsterdam's highly unusual political economy and geopolitical position in the seventeenth century. Amsterdam has always been a highly international city, a place in the midst of flows of commerce, capital, migrants, and ideas. The creation of the Canal District, the principles of design, its meaning, and its finances must be understood in the context of these connections. Amsterdam was, not coincidentally, the richest city of its time, and urban planning reflected *and* helped facilitate the city's workings and the accumulation of riches.

In chapter 2, Jaap Evert Abrahamse traces the growth and expansion of Amsterdam since the late sixteenth century and during the seventeenth century. He argues persuasively that the extensions resulting in the Canal District were at once highly functional and necessary, and provided an unprecedented urban aesthetic. It is a critical observation, beautifully illustrated throughout, because this ingenious combination of art and expediency is what helped sustain the district through the ages. The successive four extensions of the city between the 1580s and the 1660s responded to very rapid population growth and overcrowding in what was, until the third quarter of the sixteenth century, a small and compact medieval city. The city's population grew from 30,000 in 1585 to 105,000 in 1622, at which time it ranked as the third largest city in Europe, behind London and Paris. The city's area increased fivefold between the 1580s and the 1660s.

The Canal District itself was constructed in two phases, during the city's so-called Third and Fourth Extensions, in the 1610s and 1660s, respectively. It was initially planned to be built in one single extension, but the challenge proved too difficult, both in terms of engineering and financial capabilities. The design itself was highly functional in terms of water management (much of the area was below sea level) and water transportation, with the crescent-shaped canals "embracing" the port. And it was by and large designed as a highly prestigious residential area for the upper merchant classes (especially so the Fourth Extension, comprising the southern part of the district). A critical innovation in the Third Extension, to the west, concerned strict zoning of residential and industrial functions, with upscale residential areas located on the canals and small-scale industries situated in the Jordaan to the west of the three main canals. The Fourth Extension was largely residential, and prices were higher still. As Abrahamse points out, "anyone desiring to build a state-of-the-art urban *palazzo* had to get hold of four adjacent plots: two at the canal and two more at the backstreet." Apart from innovative urban design, the Canal District embodied new frontiers in urban development, real estate, finance, and the management of urban space in the historical context of early modern capitalism.

Russell Shorto, in chapter 3, probes deeper into this early modern capitalist mindset, which was, he implies, more developed in Amsterdam and the Dutch Republic than anywhere else at the time. The Canal District was, says Shorto, a very early urban development project designed *for the city's residents*. "The canals were like arms that the city sent out to reach around the globe and gather its plenty back to it." Amsterdam breathed the early spirit of liberalism. The new district served no princes or popes but merchants and tradesmen. The role of princes, popes, and potentates in the late sixteenth and early seventeenth century was far less significant than elsewhere in the continent, and some of this change, both Abrahamse and Shorto surmise, was related to the fact that so much land was new, that is, reclaimed from below sea level by local communities. Water management boards were vital to the workings and security of this nascent society. Shorto refers to the "peculiar combination of individualism and communalism" that defined this society. To a remarkable extent, the Dutch farmers of the sixteenth and seventeenth centuries owned their own land.

The liberal spirit emphasized individual freedom, but the real "genius" of Amsterdam was that its organization and developing institutions provided, better than anywhere else, for stability and a measure of predictability in economic life. "In fact, the city's rise – its coming role not only as the world's economic entrepôt but as a centre of scientific learning, art, shipping, and much else – can be seen as the antidote to the frightful vagaries of life." Some of this securitization was created in the stock market, insurance institutions, and the organization of the Dutch East India Company as the first limited liability company. The city was, one might say (and arguably still

is, today), bourgeois to the bone. Shorto describes the reaction of the Grand Duke of Tuscany, Cosimo III de' Medici, upon a visit to Amsterdam in the mid-seventeenth century. "His gushing observations suggested an awareness that Italy's own grandeur, that of the High Renaissance over which his grandfather and namesake had held sway, was a thing of the past and what he saw in this city of business was the future." The Canal District epitomized all of this new spirit: Amsterdam had few if any grand public buildings, and it lacked iconographies of political rulers. Instead, it had the canal houses, which symbolized entrepreneurial success and individualism.

Chapter 4 rounds out Part I in perfect complementary fashion by presenting a treatise on the particular geopolitical constellation in which the First Golden Age came to be, with the Canal District as an intricate and central component. Herman van der Wusten directs our attention to the unusual and symbiotic relationship between city (Amsterdam) and state (the Dutch Republic). One could not do without the other: the city as a fabulously successful economic growth machine with the indispensable political (and military) protection from the republic. It was a remarkable moment in the evolution of city-state relations in early modern Europe.

In delightful detail, the author narrates some examples of individuals and families who had important roles in the city as well as the state. These wealthy merchant families often lived in the Canal District and had big economic stakes in Amsterdam as a centre of global trade, but they also had important roles as "regents" or other political functions at the level of the republic in The Hague. These dual roles were especially clear in the leadership of the Dutch East India Company: the board members of the company were sometimes also burgomasters and/or were representatives in the States General, the "parliament" of the republic. The importance of the Canal District, from this angle, was its centrality to Amsterdam, to the Dutch Republic, and to emerging global economic networks, all at once.

The Canal District, van der Wusten suggests, was the most striking and enduring testament of Amsterdam's political economy in the seventeenth century. "Contrary to the Venetian elite, who lived in urban palaces inhabited by extended families across the different parishes of the city, the Amsterdam elite came to congregate, largely, in a single part of the city that housed for the most part single families." At the same time that the Canal District was constructed by and for the upper merchant class, imperial and royal administrations in Vienna and Paris designed projects motivated by the presumed requirements of court life.

Just because the Canal District endured through the centuries does not mean that some of its constituent parts were not subject to change. The overall design has remained intact for over four centuries, but the uses of the area shifted over time, as did the inhabitants and the classes they represented. Moreover, the individual structures did not always survive, and some of the architectural styles evolved too. Part II (chapters 5, 6, and 7) focuses on key evolutionary trajectories of the Canal District from the seventeenth to the early twenty-first century, with an emphasis on the cultural and socio-economic composition of the residential classes, architecture, and the place of the district in city-wide urban planning trends.

In chapter 5, Jan Hein Furnée and Clé Lesger provide an intriguing and creative discussion of the urban residential ecology of the Canal District. The authors map and analyse the spatial distribution of the 250 wealthiest residents of Amsterdam from the early seventeenth to the early twentieth century. They show how the bourgeois elite moved from the old core of the city to the Canal District after the Third and Fourth Extensions, yet how they remained in close proximity to the economic functions of the old core of the city (for example, the stock exchange, the port, and so on). Further, some elite households actually remained in the old core and only gradually shifted to the Canal District. At any rate, by the early 1700s, the Canal District was almost exclusively the domain of the affluent.

While there is no doubt that the most prestigious parts of the new Canal District were meant to provide an agreeable and luxurious home to the city's elite, considerable variation in socio-economic status actually existed across the entire district (from the ultra-rich, particularly around the Golden Bend, to solid upper-middle-class households further east and west). This variation led the authors to investigate social networks of Canal District residents that did not necessarily overlap with their geographic locations. The authors' analysis is based on membership in elite social and cultural associations that were prevalent during the nineteenth century. These associations played a substantial role in both affirming and bridging fiscal and occupational class divisions, even for neighbours living in the same canal blocks.

Some of the civic associations (especially the "marriage markets") were much more homogeneous than the residential geography of the Canal District. Others were more inclusive and could function to bridge the social distance to immediate neighbours – "even if a formal house visit or a play date for the children was out of the question." The chapter paints the elite milieu of the Canal District and shows its centrality in the leading social networks from the seventeenth through the nineteenth centuries.

Freek Schmidt contributes another key chapter to this volume in the form of a survey of the Canal District's architectural history, while framing an important perspective on the district's future preservation. The essence of this unique monument, says Schmidt, lies in its "multilayered evolution and multiple architectural idiosyncrasies." By the end of the Third and Fourth Extensions, the district may have looked briefly like a new town or new suburban development *avant la lettre*, just completed, and quite uniform. But soon this image was replaced by one of continuous architectural change. In 400 years, the author points out, there has not been a single generation that did not leave behind new buildings in a variety of facades across the district. These imprints ranged from "traditional and harmonic interventions to utterly disharmonic innovations, while nondescript and mediocre works of architecture were also inserted." Indeed, one could argue that, by the 1770s, the district had morphed, in some parts, into a predominantly eighteenth-century classicist cityscape. The late eighteenth and nineteenth century also saw the introduction of office buildings, adding to the mixed use of the district.

It was only by the latter part of the nineteenth century, during the city's Second Golden Age, that historical awareness and appreciation for the Canal District came to the fore. Amsterdam acquired renewed fame as the "Venice of the North." It is worth noting that such increased awareness and re-identification with a glorious past seems to be invoked especially at times of revival – the present-day economic success of Amsterdam and the listing of the Canal District as a World Heritage Site are very much a part of the current Third Golden Age. Schmidt astutely observes that this multilayered evolution can be hard to read in the existing landscape because, at times, fashionable architecture was a throwback to earlier periods. For example, many structures acquired their "eighteenth-century" architectural appearance in the 1950s. The fundamental issue here is that the Canal District retained its overall aesthetic and functions despite these continuing changes. The key to future policies and interventions, says Schmidt, lies in the "vital importance for any monument of a living culture that the outward appearance of its architecture be linked to the identity of the people who created, used, and maintained it and still inhabit it, in order to prevent it from becoming a memorial to a lost culture."

In chapter 7, Len de Klerk examines the ways in which the Canal District has featured in urban planning through the centuries. Amsterdam has, of course, a long and well-known planning tradition, and the Canal District reflects its early modern roots. But, as de Klerk points out, it was not until 1988 that the city council of the time designated the entire inner city of 679 hectares a conservation area (the area comprising the medieval core and the Canal District). Through the seventeenth century, the emphasis of the Canal District design was on functionality, water management, access to the port and major institutions in the old core, and zoning through pricing and through the exclusion of industrial activity. As chapter 6 indicates, there was considerable change to individual lots and structures from the beginning, but the integrity of the district's design was not really tested until the nineteenth century.

It was the industrial age, and very much the revolution in transportation technologies over land, that brought momentous changes. For instance, the central railway station that was constructed in the 1880s was located on the waterfront (!) north of the city centre. It effectively suggested that Amsterdam had turned its back on the historic port. The city's population expanded from 317,000 in 1880 to 714,000 in 1925, and Amsterdam became the largest industrial city in the Netherlands. Development plans around this time emphasized better and more housing (with major outward extensions), maintenance of the city centre as the main concentration of economic activity (office and shopping facilities), and, increasingly, the need for accessibility by private car. The latter goal had to involve the Canal District to allow overland transportation to the centre.

Planning from the 1850s onward very much embraced the free market order as a successor to the state-controlled mercantile order, which had prevailed earlier and had formed an important context to the creation of the Canal District in the first place. By the mid-twentieth century, automobile and sanitation challenges together posed an existential threat

to the Canal District. Various plans were put forward to fill in canals for roads and parking spaces; some of them actually materialized in the Jordaan area, the part of the seventeenth-century Third Extension zoned for industrial use and working-class residences. Perhaps, says de Klerk, it was inspired by "Henry Ford I, who, during his Amsterdam visit, declared that he could not understand why the authorities did not fill in the canals to create wide boulevards for the coming motor age." The sanitation challenges, too, were profound. It is worth noting that the last houses in the Canal District were not connected to underground sewerage until the 1970s. The canals caused an unbearable stench and posed health hazards, so it is hardly surprising that some planners suggested fill-in as an obvious, quick, and cheap solution, while creating more space for cars along the way.

Fortunately, most of these "modern" redevelopment and traffic plans did not survive the nascent civil protest movements (in favour of preservation) in the 1970s. It also implied something of a reverse shift from free market planning to greater state involvement. De Klerk suggests that the lack of proper planning law instruments during the free market era had been something of a mixed blessing: "on the one hand, planning authorities were unable to halt the creeping CBD [central business district] process of piecemeal functional change and small-scale replacement. On the other hand, the lack of instruments disallowed a full-fledged development plan that [by the mid-twentieth century], most likely, would have destroyed the inner city as we know it." The designation of the entire inner city as a preservation zone in 1988 marked the end of a long period of "muddling through" and a turn to a more conscious policy of balancing economic and conservation values. The imminent designation of the Canal District as a World Heritage Site in 2010 solidified this direction.

Part III comprises the four final chapters of the book (chapters 8, 9, 10, and 11) and concentrates on the present challenges and future prospects of the seventeenth-century city. The different chapters focus on a comparison of the preservation strategies of Amsterdam and Barcelona; the new place of the Canal District in the city's economic restructuring; the contested framing of the district's glorified seventeenth-century past vis-à-vis its role as a centre of imperialism and the slave trade; and the impact of seemingly unstoppable tourism on the district and its resident population.

In chapter 8, Melisa Pesoa, Mark Warren, and Joaquin Sabaté provide an insightful comparative discussion of the shifting fortunes and preservation challenges of Amsterdam and Barcelona. In doing so, they lay bare some important aspects of the Canal District that have in the past determined, and will in the future likely determine, its course. First, the comparison with Barcelona's Ciutat Vella (Old City) underscores the extraordinary origins of the Canal District as a total design realized over a relatively short period of time. The Ciutat Vella, by contrast, evolved more gradually and "organically" from the late Middle Ages onward. Barcelona's Ciutat Vella, one might say, was in its development and ecology more comparable to Amsterdam's old core prior to the extensions. Second, while the Ciutat Vella comprised an evolving mix of functions (residential and

economic), the Canal District was constructed primarily as a residential area with notable exclusionary zoning of industrial activity. Third, the Canal District, from the moment of the completion of the Third and Fourth Extensions, was considered an urban planning and architectural feat, widely acclaimed at home and abroad, as is evident, for example, in paintings from that period. No such moment of early admiration took place for the Ciutat Vella. The first signs of public appreciation for the latter did not emerge until the early twentieth century and were driven more by general awareness and interest in historic preservation.

Since the 1980s, urban planning in Barcelona has sought to balance preservation and modernization. Across the Ciutat Vella, interventions have emphasized both the former and the latter. This kind of "eclectic" approach would hardly apply to the Canal District, defined as it is by a common integrated design. The United Nations Educational, Scientific and Cultural Organization (UNESCO) World Heritage Site designation pertains to the entire Canal District, not any of its constituent parts. Barcelona's World Heritage sites, on the other hand, are both inside and outside the Ciutat Vella, and the list is topped by the architectural achievements of the Catalan modernist architect Antoni Gaudi. The Canal District was and is today an elitist residential quarter, whereas the Ciutat Vella is home to a range of classes, demographic cohorts, and mixed use. Today, the latter is perhaps more versatile and resilient in that regard. The Canal District owes a good part of its fame to its exclusive aesthetic, which narrows the options for uses and future preservation.

Robert C. Kloosterman and Karin Pfeffer, in chapter 9, focus on the rise of cognitive-cultural economic activities that emerged as a major part of the city at large, and of certain parts of the Canal District in particular. They argue that, partly as a legacy of the particular seventeenth-century design with its pre-industrial mix of functions (both residential and trade-oriented, with retail and services along some of the secondary streets), today we can find "a dense, fine-grained mix of functions – residential, work, and urban amenities." Generally, the present-day cognitive-cultural urban economy is dominated by a range of high-end producer services (accounting, consulting, advertising), cultural industries (for example, design and the arts), and educational institutions. The authors point out that Amsterdam started this new economic trajectory in the late 1980s; arguably, this sector gave a new vibrancy to the urban economy and played a part in the arrival of the alleged Third Golden Age. The fine-scaled mix of economic activity, and the combination of production and consumption, is an essential driver of agglomeration in the new economy. It is further enhanced by the attraction of highly skilled workers to an amenity-rich environment (shops, cafés, restaurants, theatres, museums, galleries, and so on) and, last but not least, by the aesthetic quality of place. The Canal District scores high on all these indicators, even if the availability of space is a limiting factor in some parts, particularly in the prestigious and ultra-expensive southern part. The beauty of it, of course, is that this 400-year-old design appears to function so well in the urban economy of the early twenty-first century.

In terms of the urban economic ecology, the authors observe the following trends over recent decades, sometimes playing out differently in different parts of the district. First, the finance industry has declined in terms of office presence in the southern part. The pendulum may currently be swinging back, partially in relation to Brexit, but most new activity in finance is very likely to be at the so-called Zuidas, a high-density high-rise cluster just south-central of the ring road, an area sometimes compared to Paris's *La Défense*. Indeed, the southern part of the Canal District has over the last couple of decades lost economic activity and employment altogether, suggesting that the residential function, reportedly fuelled in no small part by foreign private real estate investors, has increased. Growth in sectors other than finance has been strong, though, and has compensated well for the decline of finance in the Canal District. Second, there is a clear trend towards very small firms (one-person firms) setting up shop in parts of the Canal District. These businesses include many start-ups and sole proprietorships, and some have actually grown very quickly in a matter of years. Many of the one-person firms are effectively freelancers, who play a big part in the cultural-cognitive economy. The growth of small firms has been especially salient in the western and eastern parts of the Canal District.

The emergence of this fine-scale new economy could provide a key to adaptation *and* preservation, but it is essential to acknowledge that the Canal District is not homogeneous in this regard. The eastern stretch of the district seems to have thrived the most in this new economy, and the western part has also witnessed rapid growth. But pricing in the south has been prohibitive for these small companies. There, preservation likely needs a continued focus on living rather than working.

Susan Legêne and Tessa VerLoren van Themaat take a radical look, in chapter 10, at the ways in which the history of the Canal District tends to be framed. They argue, compellingly, that the district today is mainly narrated as a seventeenth-century historical legacy. It celebrates ingenious design and innovative urban development in close association with the Golden Age and the riches it brought. The authors, for the most part, don't contest that particular history – rather, they point to the relative *absence* of reference to the age of imperialism in the nineteenth and early twentieth century in which historic Amsterdam held a similarly central place. Such references are conspicuously absent, for example, in the World Heritage Site dedication, but also to a large degree in local discourses and in the ways the city is presented to tourists. The authors' view on the evolutionary nature of the district aligns closely with those presented in Part II of this volume.

What is the imprint of the Second Golden Age? Two centuries after its construction, the Canal District came to embody one of the control centres of European imperialism; it became a place of articulation for a worldwide imperial/colonial network. Construction in the district at this time reflected the new-found prominence of trade houses, finance, and production. Mansions on the canals were refurbished or built entirely new (see chapter 6), sometimes funded through the slave trade. The residency of the Amsterdam mayor today, located at the Golden Bend, was owned by a well-known merchant in the slave trade. The name of the 1883 World Fair, held on Museum Square adjacent to the Canal District, leaves little to the imagination: it was called the International Colonial and Export Exhibition. More than one million people visited the fair, mainly from other European imperial countries. It was the largest single "celebration" in the city's history up to that point. Yet, the average Amsterdammer today is likely to be completely oblivious of the event. The authors do acknowledge that some progress, be it incidental, has been made. An example of a relatively new reference to the imperial past, located where the Canal District and the old city centre meet, is the 1987 sculpture of Multatuli (Eduard Douwes Dekker), author of the famous satirical novel *Max Havelaar* (1859) that sharply critiqued colonial administrative practices in Java.

The authors also make an interesting argument that, even though the Canal District is now inscribed on a *World* Heritage map, the city's "self-presentation is characterized by a one-way historical narrative of 'place making' through references to a specific [seventeenth-century] Dutch colonial past in which Europe is absent." In other words, there would seem to be salient similarities in the built environment of leading imperial cities, including not just Amsterdam but also London, Paris, and Brussels, and this similarity could be emphasized in relevant European World Heritage sites. It would expose imperialism as a European political phenomenon and indirectly also expose the network to the colonies. This reality is a long way from the romantic, glorified idea of place making in the Canal District that still prevails today.

The authors advocate future preservation of the Canal District through active engagement with the traces of the Dutch and European imperial past, which could be made visible all over the historic city of Amsterdam. It would provide a vital added dimension to broad-based historical awareness. It would also "strengthen the historical understanding and cultural awareness among the current diverse population of Amsterdam" and of visiting tourists. The authors suggest that Amsterdam could take the initiative by creating a European shared imperial history.

The final chapter deals with the proverbial elephant in the room: the overwhelming impact of tourism on the old city of Amsterdam, including the Canal District. Willem Boterman and Fenne Pinkster report on a series of interviews with long-time residents of the western part of the district. Most of them are middle-class earners, who moved into the area on average about thirty-five years ago, at a time when prices were much lower as was the condition of most houses. These residents played a vital part in the area's upgrading. They invested in their homes, financially and emotionally, but, the authors point out, recent years have brought stress, conflict, and feelings of "paradise lost."

The authors deploy the humanistic geographical notion of "dwelling," which transcends the private home and refers to "an embodied knowledge of and familiarity with [the] neighbourhood, which comes from having lived in the area and experienced place over a long period of time." They find that the residents express a strong emotional attachment to, and deep personal identification with, the Canal District,

even if their overall time-space routines are wider in scope. In recent years, however, their experiences of home are threatened by the acutely felt, growing, pressures of tourism.

The chapter contains a series of statements from the interviews that indicate an "under siege" experience of the residents. The statements pertain to matters of daily nuisances and disruptions but also to a more permanent sense of loss of place. A "normal" living is no longer possible, many suggest, because of the densities of the tourist crowds, the noise levels, and "low-brow" or vulgar tourist behaviours (loud stag parties, "beer bikes," and the like). Another complaint of the residents refers to the replacement of ordinary shops with tourist attractions. Increasingly, residents leave their home (and the city) during big events, such as King's Day or the Gay Canal Parade. In the interviews, many residents say they are thinking about moving out of the area altogether, something they emphasize would be a painful decision.

The role of local government in the tourism onslaught is, so far, perceived as largely taking the side of business. The revenues in Amsterdam from tourism are estimated to have increased by 25 per cent between 2010 and 2016, well exceeding the growth of the rest of the economy. In 2018, the city did issue new and more stringent rules for Airbnb rentals – reducing the general cap from sixty to thirty nights per year per rental unit – but it is no secret that enforcement is challenging. Tourism is expected to grow even more in the years ahead. The fear among many residents is that a point of no return has already been reached.

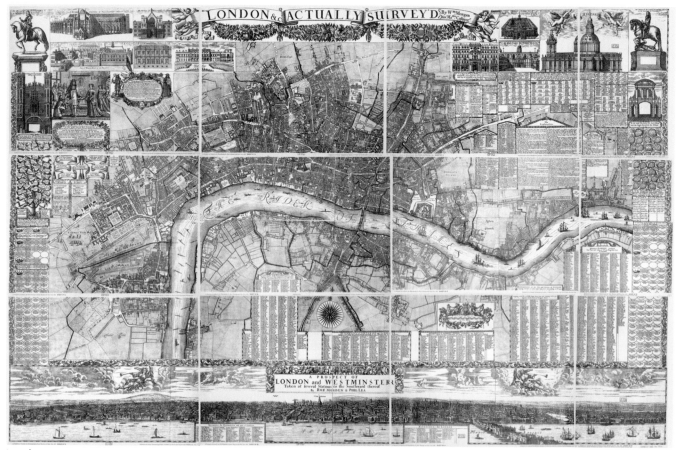

London

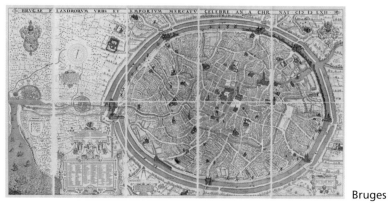

Bruges

Venice

Amsterdam

(Opposite and above) Map 1.2 |
A comparison of the urban spatial fabric of the old cities of London, Venice, Bruges, and Amsterdam, shown at roughly similar scales. The maps illustrate the exceptional design of the Canal District and the level of intervention in the urban landscape compared to the more "organically" evolved geographies of its contemporaries.
Source: US Library of Congress, Geography and Map Division. London map by William Morgan, 1682; Venice map by Lodovico Ughi, 1729; Bruges map by Marcus Gheeraerts,1520; Amsterdam map by Erben Homann, 1727.

Intersections

The chapters all contain valuable insights in their own right, but it is important to point briefly to four important intersections and connections among them, which shed light on the Canal District's origins and evolving history along with pointers for future planning and governance.

First, the actual creation of the Canal District, during the half-century between the 1610s and 1660s, very likely could not have materialized anywhere else in Europe, nor would it have been possible in Amsterdam either before or after this period. During this half-century, Amsterdam and the Dutch Republic represented a unique moment in the European history of city-state relations (Part I of this volume; Tilly, 1992; Nijman, 1994; Taylor, 1995). Amsterdam had the backing of a new state with a very considerable navy, but the city often dictated the rules of engagement. Amsterdam was not the kind of city state that prevailed in Italy or in the Hanseatic League in earlier times. It had evolved beyond that form and could wield much more power through the republic. This period was Amsterdam's "moment." The Dutch Republic was not yet a fully fledged modern European state; perhaps, this played a part in its undoing in the rivalry with England in later times.

This political economy, where political and military means generally served economic ends, was at the basis of the substantive design of the Canal District: the crescent-shaped canals and lining roads, along with radial arteries, hugged the port and old city with its key economic institutions (the stock exchange, banks, and insurance companies) and functioned to support trade and warehousing. The residences were meant for the elite, to be sure, but in Amsterdam the elite meant the wealthy merchants, who, in important cases, were also burgomasters or members of the States General that governed the Dutch Republic in The Hague. Elsewhere in Europe's cities, the bourgeoisie did not come near to that kind of influence (see, for example, Girouard, 1985). Before this particular half-century, the pressures for expansion had not been sufficient to force the Third and Fourth Extensions, nor would the funds have been available. Afterwards, the Dutch Golden Age petered out, the republic gradually morphed into a regular modern European state, and Amsterdam became less exceptional. More extensions followed in subsequent centuries, but they carried no semblance to the logic behind the Canal District design. Map 1.2 provides four maps that allow visual comparison of the urban spatial fabric of the Canal District with that of the old cities of Venice, Bruges, and London – all contemporaries but the exceptional, deliberate, urban design of Amsterdam stands out saliently.

Second, the unusual logic behind the design, and for whom it was intended, raises a deeper question about the philosophical underpinnings of Amsterdam's society during this time, about norms and values, social hierarchies, religion, and individual versus communal responsibilities (see chapter 3 of this volume). It is tempting to view Amsterdam at that time as, in some ways, picking up where ancient Athens left off: a place not run by kings (or popes) but by groups of citizens, a place designed according to planning principles to serve the citizens (see, for example, Benevolo, 1980). The Dutch Republic, and Amsterdam in particular, was home to two foundational philosophers of the early enlightenment and ethics in the seventeenth century: René Descartes and Baruch Spinoza (Figure 1.1). Both were entangled in conflicts with, respectively, the Catholic Church and Jewish religious authorities. Neither played a formal part in the Canal District design – that is not the point; rather, their presence in Amsterdam (and, presumably, their wanting to be there, both from immigrant families) suggests some of their ideas were reflective of the society at large. The Dutch Declaration of Independence against Spain in 1581, an important source for the American version two centuries later, already articulated these notions of free will, individual rights, and individual responsibilities. The importance of these convictions implied a significant distance from Catholic dogmas of the time.

Depictions of Amsterdam in the form of a virgin goddess on seventeenth-century paintings, or a present-day statue at the main entrance of the Vondelpark, emphasize the connection with pre-Christian ancient Greece in a visually tantalizing way (Figure 1.2). Neither aristocracy nor religion would dictate the interests of the Amsterdam citizenry, which is not to suggest that the merchant elite were all that compassionate with the travails of the lower classes. It is well documented that poverty and inequality were rampant. The inaugural lecture at the creation of the University of Amsterdam in 1632, by Caspar Barlaeus, was titled "Mercator Sapiens," in which he argued that a "wise merchant" maintains a healthy business in part by contributing to a healthy society. It was a hint at social entrepreneurship *avant la lettre*.

Third, the evolution of the Canal District during its 400 years of existence has been considerably more profound than is generally assumed. The static notion of the district, which prevails in popular discourse and permeated the World Heritage designation, derives from its exceptional moment of creation and close association with the "glorious" Golden Age. In reality, change and adaptation have been defining characteristics through the ages in terms of architecture, economic uses, and the social composition of the residential population. Such change rarely, if ever, applied generally across the district, implying differential developments across the district as a whole, which, it should be remembered, was differentiated from the very beginning in its design.

The appreciation for the Canal District evolved as well: from widespread recognition and admiration in the seventeenth century; to near-obscurity in the eighteenth century; to renewed glorification in the nineteenth century's Second Golden Age; to partial dereliction and near-demolition around the middle of the twentieth century; to revival in the late twentieth and early twenty-first century in what some have termed the Third Golden Age. It is at times of exceptional growth and prosperity (during the three "golden ages") that appreciation for the Canal District has been the highest. These periods are typically times of rising real estate investment and prices, as is shown in research on long-term real estate values in the Canal District (Eichholtz, 1997). Between 2013 and 2019, average home values in all of Amsterdam rose an astounding 76 per cent, more than anywhere else in the country, with the Canal District among the most expensive areas in the city (Trouw, 2019). Put differently, the public appreciation and general framing of the Canal District is also reflected in the market

DANS CETTE MAISON HABITA PENDANT L'ÉTÉ DE L'ANNÉE 1634 LE CÉLÈBRE PHILOSOPHE FRANCAIS
RÉNÉ DESCARTES
À SA GLORIEUSE MÉMOIRE CETTE PLAQUE A ÉTÉ CONSACRÉE PAR L'ALLIANCE FRANÇAISE DES PAYS-BAS LE 16 OCTOBRE 1920

IN DIT HUIS WOONDE GEDURENDE DEN ZOMER 1634 DE BEROEMDE FRANSCHE PHILOSOOF
RÉNÉ DESCARTES
TER EERE VAN ZIJN ROEMRUCHTIGE NAGEDACHTENIS IS DEZE STEEN GEPLAATST DOOR DE ALLIANCE FRANÇAISE IN NEDERLAND OP 16 OCTOBER 1920

"QUEL AUTRE PAYS OÙ L'ON PUISSE JOUIR D'UNE LIBERTÉ SI ENTIÈRE
(LETTRE DE DESCARTES À BALZAC, 1631)

(Opposite and above) Figure 1.1 | The residence of René Descartes from 1629 to 1635, Westermarkt 5, located in the western part of the Canal District. The plaque above the centre window was added by the Alliance Française in 1920 and contains an excerpt of a letter from Descartes to fellow philosopher Jean-Louis Gueze de Balzac in 1631: "Quel autre pays, ou l'on puisse jouir d'une liberté si entière?" ("In what other country can one enjoy such utter freedom?"). (To read the full letter, see R. Decartes [1631, 5 mai], À Jean-Louis G. dit Balzac, *Les petits classiques*, retrieved from http://www .homme-moderne.org/textes/classics/dekart/balzac.html.)
Source: Author

and in investments in renovations and upgrading. Interestingly, the residents interviewed in chapter 11 were mostly middle class and moved into the district before the Third Golden Age gathered momentum. Today, they find themselves in the company not only of massive numbers of tourists but also of high-wealth investors.

Fourth, the chapters in this volume hold out some important lessons and suggestions for the present and future governance of the Canal District. These can be summarized in three observations. Most fundamentally, the chapters underscore evolution and adaptation as key characteristics of the district through the ages. While the overall urban design is largely intact,

the Canal District today looks quite different and certainly functions differently from the ways it did in the seventeenth century. Indeed, if it looked exactly as it did during the Golden Age, one would imagine oneself in a theme park or at some other surreal venue, not in a living city. The implication is that efforts at *conservation* would be misdirected as they would halt this natural process of evolution. The essential value of the Canal District, surely, lies in its adaptive ability, which is what should be at the heart of planning policies today and in the future.

In addition, several chapters underline the considerable spatial variation within the Canal District of economic functions and residential populations, partly reflected in varying land and real estate values. For example, long-term middle-class residents are concentrated in the western parts, high-income long-term residents are traditionally clustered in the south, and the eastern part is dominated by a more recent gentrifying (upper) middle-class population. The eastern and western parts also show more significant clustering of small-scale economic activity in the creative sector. Governance of the Canal District at large should be sensitive to these variations; it should also be sensitive to the interstitial spaces that connect public and private domains throughout the district: chapters 9 and 11 in this volume, especially, point to the integral experiences of private and public space, both in living and working.

Finally, there is the essential notion that a living, adaptive, urban environment is meaningful only if it is an integral part of the local culture and the daily lives of the resident populations. This theme is developed in lucid terms in chapters 6 and 10, especially. It is, one might say, the indispensable connection between building and dwelling (Sennett, 2018). This connection is what made the Canal District such a feat upon its creation in the first place, its essence defined by its daily uses and for whom it was intended. Clearly, this notion is always a matter of political contestation and policy choices; it was then, and it is today. Whose city is it? Which histories of the city are celebrated or slighted? If it is too late for Venice or Bruges, there is still hope for Amsterdam. Arguably, some parts of the old city of Amsterdam have already witnessed a severance of building and dwelling through excessive and persistent commodification, particularly so the Red Light District (Nijman, 1999). The most flagrant expressions of that process have been contained in that area and steered away from the Canal District. Lefebvre's (1968) original ideas about the "right to the city" were quite wide ranging: they emphasized not only rights of habitation but the very right to produce the city through daily urban life (see also Attoh, 2011). It is the latter, it seems, that is at stake in the historic city of Amsterdam today, and particularly in the Canal District, as is so adeptly described in the final chapter. When the vital connections between design, architecture, and local culture are at risk of disappearing, so is the living historical city.

(Opposite) **Figure 1.2** | Gerard de Lairesse, *De Stedenmaagd van Amsterdam* (*City Virgin of Amsterdam*), c. 1675. The painting shows the virgin goddess seated at the centre, her arm resting assuredly on the globe, flanked by the Roman god of trade, Mercator, and with goods from afar distributed at her feet.
Reproduced with permission of the Amsterdam Museum.

PART I

HISTORIC ORIGINS

chapter two

Between Art and Expediency:
Origins of the Canal District

JAAP EVERT ABRAHAMSE

In the Dutch Golden Age, Amsterdam developed from a small trade town on the Amstel River into a mighty merchant metropolis. Between 1585 and 1672, Amsterdam became a world power and one of the largest European towns. The geographer H.J. Keuning proposed renaming the Dutch Golden Age to the "Age of Amsterdam" (Keuning, 1979: 147–95). Looking at an overview of town development in the Dutch Republic, this suggestion might be a sensible one: Amsterdam became the one dominant town in Holland from the end of the sixteenth century, as Holland itself had grown into northwestern Europe's economic centre (Abrahamse & Rutte, 2016). The seventeenth century saw the construction of Amsterdam's famous Canal District, which was the central element of two huge town extensions, realized in 1613 and 1663 (Map 2.1). To be able to understand this spectacular urban development, we need to look at the basis of Amsterdam's growth. First, we will look into the circumstances around 1600; then we will go further back in time and consider the rise of Amsterdam from different perspectives, such as state formation, infrastructure, and landscape.

After a relatively long build-up in the fourteenth, fifteenth, and sixteenth century, Amsterdam reached a population of around 30,000 inhabitants in 1585, the year in which Antwerp, Brussels, and Mechlin surrendered to Spanish troops. Ghent had fallen the year before. This dramatic turn of the Dutch Revolt resulted in a true exodus from the southern Netherlands to the upcoming Dutch Republic. Many thousands of people moved away from Flanders and Brabant. Whenever Spanish troops took over a town, its Protestant residents were given the choice: convert to Catholicism or leave. Many of them chose to move to the relatively tolerant north (Van Deursen, 2006: 108). The population of Antwerp decreased from over 100,000 to fewer than 45,000 inhabitants (Asaert, 2004: 136–7). The shift of the economic centre from the south to the north took place during the Dutch Revolt. Holland took over the position of economic core area from Brabant and Flanders; instead of Antwerp, Amsterdam became the central staple in the Netherlands. Together with a number of other towns, it formed a network of trade and industrial towns in which the contours of today's Randstad Holland are clearly discernible (Brand, 2012: 59–92).

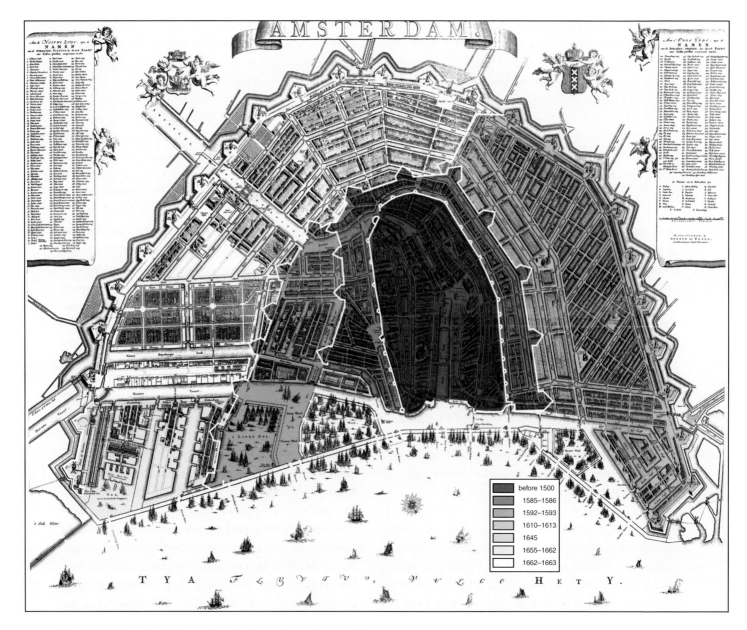

Map 2.1 | Growth of Amsterdam in the early modern period.
Source: Cultural Heritage Agency of the Netherlands/ Menne Kosian.

Amsterdam was the last town in the province of Holland to join the Dutch Revolt in 1578. Until that moment, many Protestant citizens had left their hometown. Many of them returned after 1578. By 1600, Amsterdam's population had grown from 30,000 to around 50,000. The first census in 1622 counted 105,000 inhabitants; we have reasons to assume that this number was adjusted downward, as towns were taxed per inhabitant (Kuijpers, 2005: 82–3). In 1680, after the expansions, Amsterdam's population is estimated to have been at 220,000 or even 240,000 (Van Leeuwen & Oeppen, 1993; Lourens & Lucassen, 1997: 55–7; Nusteling, 1985: 234–6). Amsterdam's territory increased fivefold between 1585 and 1663. This population explosion was entirely caused by immigration; all larger towns had a death surplus and did not grow naturally (Kuijpers, 2005: 9). In the second half of the seventeenth century, Amsterdam took position among the great European capitals, right behind London and Paris; it tied for third place with Naples, at that time the capital of the Kingdom of the Two Sicilies.

From Frontier Society to Dutch Golden Age: The Reclamation and Urbanization of the Dutch Peatlands

The urbanization of the coastal areas in the west of the Netherlands took off during the Middle Ages. As early as the fourteenth century, the urbanization level of Holland surpassed that of northern Italy; it has remained the highest in Europe ever since (Rutte & IJsselstijn, 2016).

This remarkably rapid and lasting urbanization cannot be understood without some knowledge of the landscape, its occupation history, and settlement patterns. Three aspects seem to have been essential: the physical landscape itself, the political organization (or rather the lack thereof), and the shifting of the economic centre from the south to the north under the influence of international developments. Urbanization was brought about by a range of interconnected phenomena resulting in fundamental changes in the landscape. To understand these changes, the method and results of the peatland reclamations and their lasting effects have to be explained first.

The marshy peatlands in the west of the Netherlands were a large, practically impenetrable wilderness until around AD 1000. In the following two centuries, this landscape went through a drastic transformation as it was reclaimed and turned into agricultural land – by digging the typical patterns of drainage ditches that are still visible in today's landscape and in many town patterns. This period is generally called the "Great Reclamation" (Abrahamse, Kosian, & Schmitz, 2010; Abrahamse, Kosian, & Schmitz, 2012; Borger et al., 2011). The western provinces consisted of new land, the ownership of which was transferred to the private cultivators. The religious and secular authorities never really managed to get this frontier society under control. The bishops of Utrecht and the counts of Holland sent their ministers into the new territories, but instead of securing control, many of these figureheads tried to wriggle out from under the constituted authorities and establish their own territory. When successful, they often got into conflict with each other. The influence of the aristocracy and feudal structures in Holland was therefore weak and fragmented. This decentralized and relatively weak power structure – and the relative lack of regulations and weak guild system related to it – created a situation in which non-economic impediments for development were largely absent (Van Bavel & Van Zanden, 2004).

Another element causing the urbanization of the western Netherlands was the transformation of the landscape set off by human intervention. By dehydrating the peatland, more than 80 per cent of which consisted of water, its new owners caused a rapid and irreversible subsidence of the soil. The resulting rising water tables had a profound influence on agriculture. Farmers were forced to switch to summer grain on their squidgy land – and to cattle breeding at a later stage as the soil subsidence progressed. This less labour-intensive agricultural activity led to a shrinking demand for labour, pushing people towards other branches of activity, such as peat extraction, fishery, and shipping, or causing them to move to the towns, speeding up urbanization. Another result of the soil subsidence was the construction of systems of dykes and drainage canals, both of which could also function as traffic infrastructure. Within a short period of time, an intricate infrastructural network was created as an unintentional side effect of the soil subsidence.

The tight relations between the towns and the countryside were economic in nature and not so much the result of the towns laying claim to the territories surrounding them, although lots of land and means of production were owned by urbanites. The urban pattern in Holland as it came about between 1100 and 1400 was formed by market and trade towns (Map 2.2). The distribution of towns over the land was a result of shifting trade flows that found their way by the rivers, the canals, and the sea. The

network of commercial exchange and the shifts within this network facilitated the rise of towns.

The frontier society resulting from the reclamation of the land has in part formed the basis for the polity of Holland, not only in the Middle Ages but also during the Dutch Republic (see chapter 3 in this volume for a perspective on the particular political culture that evolved accordingly). Within the province of Holland, the towns were in charge of matters. The system was based on the autonomy of towns and therefore on economic power. Unlike the Italian city states – northern Italy was the other highly urbanized region in Europe – Amsterdam and the other towns in Holland were created in a new territory, while Italian cities had a long and often continuous occupation history since Roman times and functioned as administrative centres of a region. In many cases, such as Mantua and Ferrara, noble families chose a town as their base of operations, from where they ruled the surroundings. Huge palaces and castles of the ruling families dominated their skylines. Amsterdam's castle, if it may carry that name at all, was only a small structure that maybe even was left unfinished. The same goes for Leiden Castle – a hardly relevant remnant, not even worth demolishing.

(Opposite) **Map 2.2** | Towns in the Dutch landscape, **1100–1400.**
Source: Cultural Heritage Agency of the Netherlands/ Atlas of the Dutch Urban Landscape, map by Marcel IJsselstijn and Yvonne van Mil.

Urbanization and landscape context:
Seven groups of towns originating in the eleventh to fifteenth centuries

+ Oldest urban settlements

▲ Flemish-Zeeland ports (twelfth to thirteenth centuries)

★ Products of land lord urban politics and planning (c. AD 1200–AD 1270)

■ Other thirteenth-century towns

◆ Western ports (c. AD 1270–AD 1400)

● Late-medieval new towns (c. AD 1270–AD 1400)

▼ Other fourteenth-century towns

  Dunes/beach ridges

  Marine clays

  River clays

  Peat

  Sand

  Loess

  River terraces

Appingedam

Dokkum

Groningen

Leeuwarden

Harlingen Franeker

Bolsward

Workum Sneek

Hindeloopen IJlst

Stavoren Sloten

Medemblik Steenwijk

Enkhuizen Coevorden

Alkmaar Hoorn Vollenhove

Purmerend Genemuiden Hardenberg

Kampen Hasselt Ommen

Edam Zwolle Ootmarsum

Beverwijk Monnickendam Elburg Hattem Almelo

Haarlem Amsterdam Muiden Rijssen Delden Oldenzaal

Weesp Naarden Harderwijk Goor Enschede

Leiden Woerden Utrecht Deventer Lochem

The Hague Oudewater Montfoort Amersfoort Zutphen Groenlo

Delft Gouda IJsselstein Arnhem Doesburg Bredevoort

Vlaardingen Schoonhoven Vianen Wijk bij Duurstede Wageningen Doetinchem

Brielle Rotterdam Nieuwpoort Leerdam Rhenen 's-Heerenberg

Geervliet Schiedam Heukelum Buren Tiel

Goedereede Gorinchem Asperen Zaltbommel Megen Nijmegen

Brouwershaven Dordrecht Woudrichem Ravenstein Batenburg

Zevenbergen Heusden Grave

Zierikzee Geertruidenberg 's-Hertogenbosch Gennep

Veere Sint-Maartensdijk Steenbergen Breda

Middelburg Tholen

Vlissingen Goes Bergen op Zoom Helmond

Oostburg Eindhoven Venlo

Sluis Hulst Weert

Aardenburg Axel Roermond

Montfort

Echt

Nieuwstadt

Sittard

Valkenburg

Maastricht

0   km   50

The relation of mutual dependency between towns and lords soon turned into a situation in which the towns were no longer bound to any higher authority. Amsterdam was the power base of no other entity than Amsterdam itself. In Amsterdam and most other Holland towns, the merchant elite formed the town government. Without much effort, the urban elites took over power from the weak nobility. The Holland towns engaged in what was sometimes tough economic competition but weren't at all interested in acquiring each other's territories. Rivalry between towns was economic in character, which resulted in a relatively stable system of towns with all kinds of economic relations within a loose federative association.

Particularism was the obvious result of urban autonomy and remained a dominant force in matters of state formation – it was the basis for the Dutch Republic's administrative system – and a system change on a higher level, from the Duchy of Burgundy to the Spanish Kingdom to the Dutch Republic, only further reinforced the position of towns. Economic integration was fuelled by the development of infrastructural and trade networks and by competition between towns. The combination of the rapidly changing peat landscape – with cheap energy in abundance and the emergence of an intricate web of infrastructures – and a relatively weak administrative system functioned as an incubator for the towns of Holland. The essence of the republic was not the formation of a unified state, but quite the opposite: its main goal was the preservation of acquired rights of smaller entities, the provinces, and the cities. Urban particularism and self-interest, not nationalism, were the main forces behind its formation. The power relations were

and remained based on local interests. The republic was governed more or less bottom-up: the provinces were sovereign – they could choose their own stadtholder, the substitute for the king.

The Rise of Amsterdam

Amsterdam was the town to profit most from this situation, due a large extent to its location on the northern end of the "route binnen dunen" or "route within the dunes." This passage was the safe shipping route from the Zeeland ports across Holland to the Zuiderzee, avoiding the dangerous North Sea coast.

Amsterdam expanded in several stages during the late Middle Ages. In the thirteenth century, a series of terps were connected to become the first dykes and roads along both sides of the Amstel River. The dam that gave the town its name was built to close off the estuary to prevent the low-lying peatlands from flooding and, as a result, joined the banks of the Amstel. From these humble beginnings, Amsterdam grew rapidly on both banks. In the fourteenth century, both of the Voorburgwal canals were constructed parallel to the Amstel, soon to be followed by the Achterburgwal canals. The need for building grounds was one reason for digging these canals, and water management was

(Opposite) **Map 2.3** | Amsterdam in 1544, map by Cornelis Anthonisz.
Source: Amsterdam City Archives.

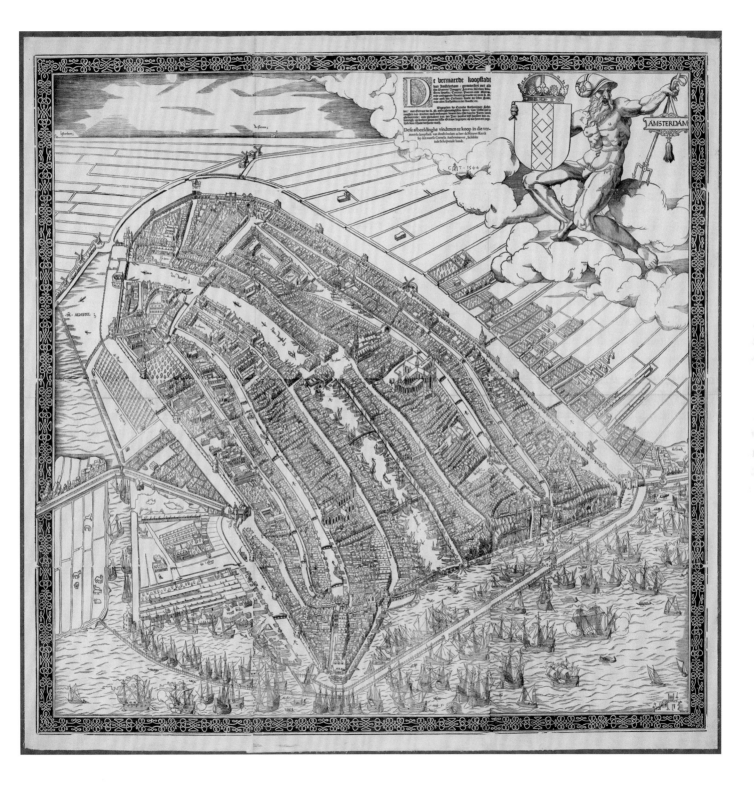

another: as the bed of the Amstel River became ever narrower because of land reclamation on both banks, an increase in the drainage capacity was necessary. The growth of the city's population led to the densification of the built-up area within this urban structure. During this process, the grounds between the canals were divided into ever smaller lots and opened up by a large number of alleyways, which followed the pattern of ditches laid out in medieval times to drain and reclaim the marshy peatlands. The medieval reclamation landscape remains visible in the urban structure of Amsterdam's core to this day.

Around the year 1425, the Singel, Kloveniersburgwal, and Geldersekade canals were dug as the new outer moats (Map 2.3). Once more, narrow strips of land were added to the town. In the years 1460 to 1490, a huge brick town wall was built and provided with heavy gates and towers, to be enhanced with roundels in the mid-sixteenth century (De Graauw, 2011). Halfway through the sixteenth century, densification of buildings in the existing urban territory again reached its limits, while the town's defence works became ineffective because of the introduction of heavy artillery as an attack weapon. Large-scale building activities started outside the city in defiance of regulations issued to maintain the field of fire around the walls. In 1550, around 550 houses and an unknown number of shipyards, ropewalks, warehouses, mills, timber yards, limekilns, and other buildings were built outside the eastern boundary of Amsterdam (Map 2.4). The town government got into conflict with the inhabitants of this area, which was called the Lastage after its naval

functions. The administration ordered the people living outside the city to move inside its walls.

Disciplinary measures, however, were not taken, and the city's already obsolete defensive system became completely ineffective (Burger, 1918). When Amsterdam entered the Dutch Revolt in 1578, as one of the last cities in the Netherlands, this problem became acute. In the years 1585 and 1586, a bastioned town wall was built, and the Lastage was incorporated into the city. This operation was called the "First Extension" of Amsterdam. In its scale, it was incomparable to Amsterdam's later, much larger, extensions. The primary goal of this First Extension was to bring the city's defences up to date. One of the consequences was the transformation of the Singel canal from defensive moat to residential canal. Shortly after 1585, the first double-wide luxury houses were built there. Unlike the previous extensions, the structure of the existing landscape was now erased to create orthogonal city blocks, and the streets were at a thirty-degree angle to the old pattern of paths and ditches. This regular pattern resulted from the design of the modern, bastioned fortifications.

Only six years later, the city was extended to the east as a result of its booming economy. This "Second

(Opposite) **Map 2.4** ⎪ Amsterdam in the 1560s, map by Jacob van Deventer (1501/2–75). West of Amsterdam, the informal settlement forming on "the paths" running through the peatlands is clearly visible.
Source: Noord-Hollands Archief/ Provincial Atlas – Maps and map books, inventory number NL-HlmNHA_560_002424.

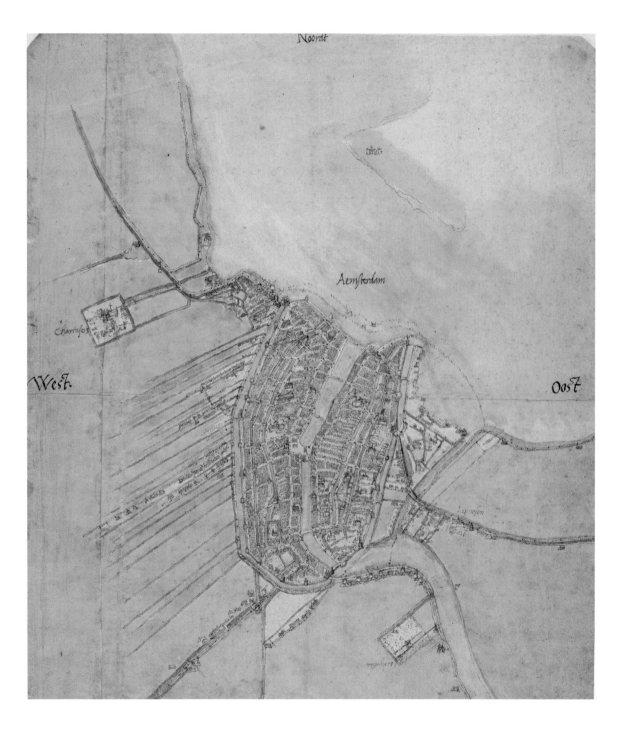

Noort

West   Oost

Aemsterdam

Chartusos

Extension" contained the new harbour islands of Uilenburg, Valkenburg, and Rapenburg (see Map 2.1). In 1600, Amsterdam had become the largest town in the Dutch Republic, and there was more to come. In the seventeenth century, Amsterdam acquired absolute dominance in the Dutch economy and the polity of the Dutch Republic, and its town extensions now would reach an unprecedented level of scale and planning. From 1610 and 1662 onward, respectively, two much larger extensions would take place: The "Third Extension," which was carried out from 1610 onward, included a new harbour area, the Canal District, and the Jordaan quarter. In the 1660s, the huge "Fourth Extension" followed, which connected the Third Extension with a newly created harbour area east of the city (Abrahamse, 2019: 111–21). The Canal District is part of these two extension projects.

Trial and Error: Amsterdam's Third Extension

As mentioned earlier, Amsterdam's population grew from around 50,000 in 1600 to 105,000 in 1622. Within one generation, the population grew by a factor of 3.5. In the seventeenth century, both town and country people were mobile. They moved to places where work or education was supplied and stayed there for short or longer periods. Some towns, like Leiden (Van Maanen, 2003: vol. II, 20–7; Smit, 2001: 44–5) and Utrecht (Abrahamse, 2011: 447–9), actively promoted immigration, for instance by offering newcomers free burghership (citizenship) or fiscal benefits. In Amsterdam, there was no need for such policies, as more people came in than it could handle. Chain migration caused more and more people from certain groups and regions to come to Amsterdam. Economic growth, but also fortification works and town extensions, had a flywheel effect because they offered work to thousands. The growth of the population was a self-perpetuating process. The wave of immigration from the south, and the economic impulse that it caused, led to more immigration from inside the republic, but also from the German lands.

A large and growing part of the newcomers settled outside the town wall. The first houses were built along the arterial roads, just outside the town gates. In the years to follow, urban development spread over an ever-wider area. Already before the turn of the century, fewer than ten years after the last extension, informal settlements were again booming outside the Haarlemmerpoort gate along the main road to Haarlem and the Overtoom canal. At a later stage, thousands settled in the polder area west of the city, further away from the main roads. The polder was divided into elongated agricultural fields, separated by drainage ditches. Such a field, called a "weer," was opened up by a path laid out through the field lengthwise. These paths were gradually heightened, paved, and extended as more people settled there. The settlements west of Amsterdam were therefore known as "de paden" or "the paths." In the years 1602 to 1609, the council, the burgomasters, and the treasurers did not take any decisions relating to urban extension. Without a doubt, the pros and cons were discussed, but, as time passed, an intervention in these developments would become more expensive and complex.

Several maps "concerning the enlargement and extension of this town" were discussed by the council on 6 February 1610.[1] An extension plan was at that time designed by Hendrick Jacobsz. Staets, the town carpenter (Abrahamse, 2019: 53–70). He had drawn up a plan for an extension all around the town. Probably, it was not just a fortification plan, but a design of the complete urban structure: it is described in the *Kroniek van Staets*, or "*Staets Chronicle*" as "the pattern of the whole work, with all its canals, its streets, its walls, forts, bastions" (quoted in De Roever, 1969: 34). However, some poetic licence might have been taken, as this rhymed chronicle about the life and times of Hendrick Jacobsz. Staets was commissioned in support of a request for an extra allowance. Anyway, Staets's plan seems to have simply ignored the unplanned development outside the town walls, reasonably assuming that the problem would be dealt with in due time – which didn't happen.

The only part of the plan that was to be "taken in hand immediately and be finished as soon as possible" was a new harbour area on the shores of the IJ, west of the town (Abrahamse, 2019: 53–9). Together with the harbour, space for shipbuilding yards, repair yards, housing, and storehouses was ordered. The area was to be surrounded by a ring of fortifications that was to be extended up to the Carthusian monastery (Map 2.5).

Remaining empty grounds within the fortification owned by the authorities were leased out as pasture in the summer of 1612.[2] The remaining part of the extension work came to a standstill, due to multiple causes, including a conflict with the Rijnland water board about the sea dyke, which was incorporated in Amsterdam's extension, and a scandal involving several leading figures of Amsterdam's government buying land in the extension with the evident goal of speculating at the expense of the town. In the meantime, the situation outside Amsterdam's gates had become unmanageable. A frenzy of illegal construction was going on outside the city. Amsterdam seemed to be drowning in these informal settlements. It took years to finally come to a solution, and by then the plan made by Staets had gone out with the trash.

On the 5 March 1613, the council took an important decision: the whole plan was to be divided into two parts. The extension of Amsterdam would not be around the town, but only on the west side. This western extension was to be attached to the old town near the Heiligewegspoort. The gate was at the present Koningsplein, where the Overtoom canal reached the town walls. No exact location was prescribed; the commission had to find a convenient way to tie the new town to the existing one. The council records, which rarely motivate decisions, state that cancelling more than half of the project was inevitable because the administration couldn't handle "the scale and complexity of the works" (Noordkerk, 1748–78: vol. I, 13).

---

1. Vroedschapsresoluties (Council Resolutions), Amsterdam City Archives 5025–9, fol. 448.
2. Rapiamus, Treasurer's Archive, Amsterdam City Archives 5039-298, fol. 104vo.

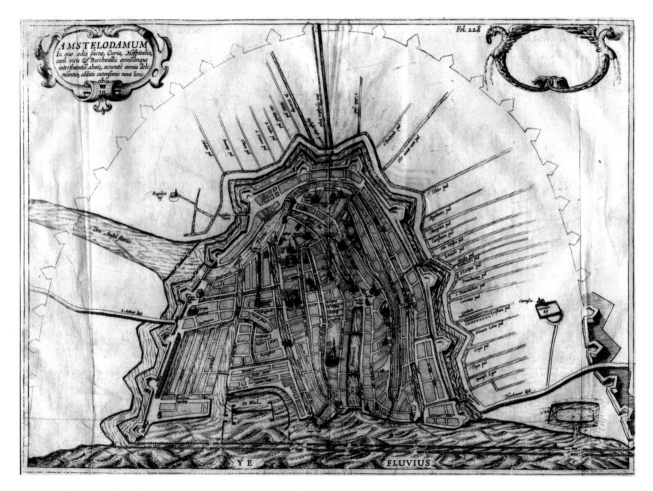

Map 2.5 | Amsterdam from I.I. Pontanus's *Rerum et urbis Amstelodamensium historia* (1611). The Carthusian monastery is clearly visible just within the new town walls.
Source: Amsterdam City Archives.

Thus, the extension plan of Amsterdam was cut in half and would simply halt at what is now known as the Leidsegracht canal. This way, the Overtoom canal, the fifteenth-century waterway towards the Haarlemmermeer, Leiden, and The Hague, was kept outside the new town walls. That decision had clear practical advantages. It was not necessary to expropriate the high-density area along the canal and to solve the complex infrastructural problem of connecting the Overtoom canal to the canals in town. These problems were passed on to the next generation (Van Gelder, 1925: 374). By leaving the east side of the town unaffected, a large part of the fortification could be cancelled.

After the project was cut in half, the internal structure of the remaining part of the extension was to be designed. Two canals were to be created near the old town; the rest of the area would remain more or less as it was. Its urban structure could not be changed because of the unplanned developments outside the town walls; people who were forced to move out due to the construction of the new canals were offered new plots in the area that we today call the Jordaan; this part of the seventeenth-century extensions kept its pre-urban structure.

It was obvious that the street plan of the extension needed to be adapted to its new outline as the project was cut in half. A council commission presented a proposal for the layout of the canals in August 1613. The records do not give any details, but from a later resolution we can gather that it was a three-canal plan, with a church square between the present Reestraat and Berenstraat, and a marketplace in the location of Westermarkt Square.[3] This plan was approved unaltered. No other plans for the canal plan were discussed later, so this one must have formed the basis of the famous three-canal plan. An extra canal, called Keizersgracht, was inserted as compensation for shortening the Herengracht, which was the result of dropping the eastern part of the extension.

The construction of the Herengracht canal started in November 1613; in January, the plots along it were put up for auction. Three days after the auction had started, 24 January 1614, the continuation of the extension project was on the council's agenda. The layout of the "second and third canals," the later Keizersgracht and Prinsengracht, was now discussed. It was decided to first dig the Prinsengracht, the third canal, and then proceed with the canal in between. Planning in phases was inevitable, not least because of dependence on supplies of materials. Demolition dates were set for the current inhabitants. The people living on the location of the future Prinsengracht were ordered to leave before 1 May 1614. The first of May was the traditional "verhuisdag" or "moving day," on which most lease contracts ended, and many people had to move to new housing. For the Keizersgracht, the date was set one year later, 1 May 1615. The authorities wanted to start with the third canal as soon as possible, so Prinsengracht was constructed in 1614 and Keizersgracht in 1615.[4]

---

3. Vroedschapsresoluties (Council Resolutions), Amsterdam City Archives, 5025-10, fol. 263–4.
4. See note 3.

The design fell apart into very different fragments: the Jordaan area was an adapted informal development; the Herengracht and Keizersgracht canals were planned as residential canals; while the Prinsengracht, dividing these two areas, was a main traffic route with dwellings, industrial buildings, and warehouses on both sides. The Prinsengracht was also the divide between the rich canals and the much poorer Jordaan area. The form the Third Extension eventually acquired was the result of emergency measures. The crucial innovation was the creation of a luxury residential area. All other activities were excluded from the main canals to the area outside the Prinsengracht, where spontaneous urban development in the medieval reclamation landscape was transformed into an urban area. In this fragmented constellation, the different quarters varied significantly in terms of urban structure, architecture, and activities. The Herengracht and Keizersgracht were the most successful, prestigious, and prominent elements. These were to be the standard for the next extension project.

Amsterdam's Fourth Extension: Mastery of Urban Planning

As early as 1618, no empty plots were left on the newly constructed canals (Von Zesen, 1664: 165). Thousands of new houses had been built at unprecedented pace, partly as prefabricated structures, since many shipyard owners threw themselves into house building (Abrahamse, 2019: 131–3). Population growth continued, now mainly fuelled by immigration from German lands, where the Thirty Years' War raged. A new shortage of building lots arose shortly after the realization of the Third Extension. Parts of the city were restructured, and new streets and quarters were created by filling in sections of the Amstel River and the IJ. However, despite these efforts, haphazard urbanization again took over. New fortification and extension plans were drawn up after stadtholder William II's failed attack on Amsterdam in 1650 – the result of a conflict between Amsterdam and the stadtholder about spending cuts for the military – but none of these were realized.

In the years 1654 to 1660, after the First Anglo-Dutch War, a new harbour area was laid out on the east side of Amsterdam. It consisted of three different islands, of which Kattenburg was mainly used for the Admiralty, Wittenburg for private shipyards, and Oostenburg for the Dutch East India Company. The Admiralty's and East India Company's rope yards were built on a separate island, east of Oostenburg (Abrahamse, 2019: 161–71). Just like half a century earlier, this harbour area would be the first part of a much larger town extension. This "Fourth Extension," which took place in the 1660s, reflected lessons learned from the Third Extension. The problems, and the context and conditions within these extensions, needing to be resolved were identical: Amsterdam needed to expand in a peat polder landscape in which rapid unplanned urbanization was taking place. The crucial innovation of the Third Extension was the exclusion of industry from the main canals, thus creating a luxury residential area. In the Fourth Extension, the concept of the Canal District was elaborated within a consistent plan.

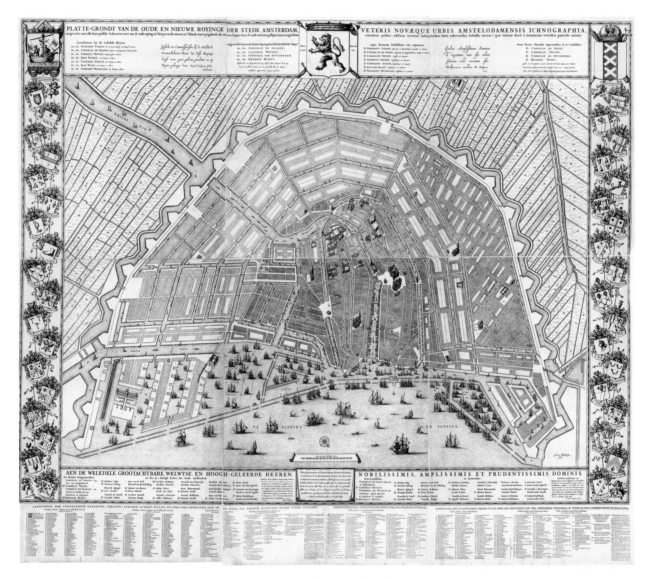

Map 2.6 │ Amsterdam with the 1662 extension plan, map by Daniel Stalpaert.
Source: Amsterdam City Archives.

In 1662, a plan was approved for the area between the Leidsegracht and the Nieuwe Vaart (Map 2.6). Previous experiences – and possibly ideas from contemporary treatises on architecture and urban planning – were brought to this plan, which led to a well-considered, coherent scheme. The plan was rooted in the further elaboration of the successful concept of the canal belt. To facilitate the execution of this scheme, all of the necessary land was expropriated in order to be able to level all informal settlements in the area and create the space needed for the realization of the extension project. These land policies were a necessary condition for success.

The Fourth Extension was created on the basis of a meticulously elaborated masterplan, in which a well-planned superposition of land and water traffic systems, functional zoning, and well-designed blocks with different plot forms and sizes were combined to solve all the problems Amsterdam was dealing with. The system of plots was adapted to the traffic system: large residential plots were located at the Herengracht and Keizersgracht canals, with smaller plots at the backstreets (see Map 2.6). These plots could be sold separately, but anyone desiring to build a state-of-the-art urban *palazzo* had to get hold of four adjacent plots: two at the canal and two more at the backstreet. This way, it was possible to erect a double-wide canal house with annexes, such as a coach house, stable, and staff residences at the back (Abrahamse, 2019: 196–201). This system provided clients with maximum choice, while at the same time maximizing the town's land revenues. Although Keizersgracht was further away from the centre and had less stature, it was, like Herengracht,

an exclusively residential area. In the Fourth Extension, Kerkstraat was the borderline between the canal belt and the outlying mixed-use areas. Beyond Kerkstraat, industrial activities were tolerated to a certain degree. As the blocks were located closer to the edge of town, more – and more polluting – industries were allowed. From the inner part to the outer edge, one moved from a luxury residential neighbourhood to a mixed-use zone with ever more industry.

Conclusion

In the early seventeenth century, Amsterdam was confronted with an unprecedented population growth and the urgent need to extend its built-in surface and create new building plots. As Amsterdam's population boomed, its administration was faced with a series of seemingly unsolvable problems. It had to create large numbers of building plots in the marshy peatlands of the Amstel estuary. Extensive informal developments had to be cleared. Budgets were tight, and, besides, a number of the city's burgomasters and council members were involved in ground speculation. The necessity to recover the costs of development from the proceeds of ground sales was another complication. The number of newcomers was so large that drastic measures were needed. Instead, the town government manoeuvred itself in a situation that can best be described as an administrative infarct. At first, Amsterdam was planned to be expanded all around, but, as the speculation scandal led to conflict in the administration, the project was held up, while immigration and informal settlements continued in the polders around the city. It took years before the Third Extension could be realized, causing the whole project to be cut in half; Amsterdam was extended to the west side only. This remaining part eventually fell apart into different fragments, causing severe traffic and water management problems at a later stage.

The Third Extension was not only scaled down but also restructured, as the luxury residential district was laid out at the side of the old city and the Jordaan district was created within the framework of the existing medieval peat reclamation landscape to house the people who had to move out from the Canal District. This way, a fragmented urban structure was created. A city of great functional and architectural contrast arose: along the tree-lined canal embankments, large houses with gardens were built, while the area outside Prinsengracht (now called Jordaan) was a mixed-use neighbourhood, where cheaper living was combined with various branches of industry. The residential canals proved to be a big success, not only aesthetically – they were admired by many foreign visitors – but also functionally and financially, as the revenues of ground sales on the west side of Herengracht only were over a half million guilders and prevented the city from going into bankruptcy. The scale and character of the canals, especially the Herengracht and Keizersgracht, was caused by their location in the infrastructural network, their layout, and their strict zoning regulations. Amsterdam acquired a new functional profile. The residential canals near the centre provided luxury housing in an urban environment without the usual inconveniences such as pollution, noise, and congestion. The canal belt was clearly distinguished from the busy, largely medieval centre and the mixed-use and industrial areas beyond Prinsengracht. The plots along Herengracht were the most desirable in the city. Anyone who could afford it could live in luxury at the wide, tree-laned canal in a town house – a Dutch version of the Italian *palazzo* – with a huge garden, within walking distance of the economic and administrative centre located around Dam Square.

The next extension project was handled in a very different way. The government adapted the legal and organizational frameworks to optimize the conditions for planning and realizing the project. Having learned from experience, all grounds were expropriated and all buildings razed.

A rapid professionalization of the administration and civil service had taken place in the preceding period. The Fourth Extension was designed based on rapidly evolving insights into urbanism, real estate, and the management of urban space. Town architect Daniel Stalpaert was the central figure. He had been hired in 1648 as a supervisor for the new city hall, but was involved in town planning and all the problems connected with it: water management, land division and sales, traffic planning, and fortification. This overview resulted in a plan that was designed to the right level of detail, but also offered a maximum freedom of choice to the buyers of building plots. Real estate strategy was a central element of urban planning. With the generation of skilled designers, builders, and administrators of which Stalpaert was an exponent, scientific methodology made its entry into many fields of civic life, in government, water management, and urbanism. A commission of learned governors and the city architect drew up a masterplan for the "Fourth Extension" of Amsterdam. This plan was the result of a rapid development in the methodology of urbanism, in which functionality and aesthetics were combined with the maximizing of ground revenues. An urban structure was designed in which canal and road systems were integrated with the arrangement of building plots for various urban functions. The new Herengracht, especially, with its rows of double-wide canal houses, gave Amsterdam a cosmopolitan character. New policies in the field of expropriation resulted in the possibility of actually realizing the extension as planned, the elimination of private interests meddling in public affairs, and, eventually, much higher revenues.

After the 1672 "Year of Disaster," the development of Amsterdam stopped dead in its tracks. Amsterdam gradually lost its position as the main trade hub in northwestern Europe to London. Urban development and land sales reached a standstill. The part of the extension east of the Amstel River was in danger of remaining completely empty. The government stimulated development there by granting substantial pieces of land to charitable institutions for free and by creating the Plantage, a large garden park where Amsterdam citizens could lease a pleasure garden. This way, it prevented a too dramatic dichotomy between the rich Canal District and the almost empty eastern part of town. The garden park remained in place until what is generally called the Second Golden Age of Amsterdam, when the North Sea canal opened in 1876 and urban development once again took off.

chapter three

Designing the World's Most Liberal City

RUSSELL SHORTO

Imagine you are a trader living in Amsterdam during its seventeenth-century Golden Age. You make your home on the Prinsengracht, one of the city's newly constructed canals, in a gabled canal house. Now imagine yourself saying goodbye to your wife and children and travelling halfway around the world with a commercial fleet in which you have an interest – all the way to the East Indies, where you oversee a purchase of spices. Eventually, you make the long voyage home, arriving, typically, two to three years after you left. On entering the IJ, Amsterdam's waterfront, with its fabled "forest of masts," you transfer, along with your goods, to a smaller vessel. Then you sail up the Prinsengracht to your front door. There are your wife and children on the stoop, waiting to greet you. Your house is much like those on either side of it, narrow but deep, three stories high (Figure 3.1). As you step inside, workers fasten a rope and pulley to the hoist beam that protrudes from the top of the house and begin hauling the carefully packed, sweet-smelling purchases you made, so long ago and far away, up into the top floor, which is both the attic of the house and your company's warehouse.

You have just done something remarkable: you have travelled around the world and brought the riches of a distant land into your home, and you have done it without needing to set foot on dry land.

The point of this hypothetical voyage is to underscore what exactly Amsterdam's Canal District was in the seventeenth century: an urban development project designed for the city's residents, and designed in particular to enable those residents to do nothing less than exploit the world. The canals were constructed in part as a way of controlling water, but they were more than that: they turned the problem of water into an advantage. They empowered individuals and were therefore both a means towards and a metaphor for the age of the individual, which dawned in the seventeenth century and continues today.

Roots in the Water

In the family of European capitals, Amsterdam is one of the younger siblings. Even if we set aside Romulus and Remus, archaeological evidence suggests that Rome started with herders and farmers settling the cluster of hills along the Tiber around 900 BC. Athens goes back staggeringly farther than that, into the Neolithic predawn. Amsterdam, by contrast, with its inhospitable geographic position discouraging human settlement, began life c. AD 1100, when, in an effort to stop the sea from remaking the shoreline every year, a few hundred farmers set to heaping up earthen dykes along the edge of the marshy wilderness they had chosen to call home.

Indeed, early humans, in their migratory roaming, sensibly stepped around the whole corner of Europe known as the Low Countries. Looking at the planet not from the perspective of human beings but merely in terms of its own processes, one might say that this region was meant to be purely for drainage purposes, for what is today the Netherlands is one vast river delta. Three of northern Europe's largest rivers – the Rhine, the Meuse or Maas, and the Scheldt – having variously swept down from the Swiss Alps, rolled across German plains, and twisted through northern France and the forests of the Ardennes in Belgium, reach here to meet the sea. In its natural course, this drainage is a complex process that keeps the boundary between land and sea constantly shifting. Starting sometime before AD 1000, the early inhabitants of what became the province of Holland began to interfere with nature. The peaty land was good for farming, provided the peat, which is essentially spongy decayed plant material, could be drained. The inhabitants built up dykes to keep out the sea, then cut channels in the peat bogs, which allowed the water contained in them to flow down

Figure 3.1 | Amsterdam canal houses, photographed by Tim Killiam.
Reproduced with permission of the photographer.

into rivers. That strategy led to further difficulties, since once the peat loses its water, it begins to sink. Eventually thepeat level falls below the water level, whereupon the land is once again in danger of flooding, which necessitates more dykes as well as pumps. Medieval Hollanders – and their neighbours in Zeeland to the south and Friesland to the north – thus set off a never-ending struggle against nature, one that continues today. These circumstances – the water, the perils, the bravery, the absurdity of the geographic position, and the development of complex communal organizations to cope with the situation – explain much of Amsterdam's history, including the creation of the Canal District (as laid out in the previous chapter), and provide as well a backdrop to the development of liberalism, a philosophy based on individual freedom, which is the hallmark of the modern era.

The situation of the Low Countries ensured that they would develop in a crucially different way from the rest of Europe (De Vries, 1974). One of the defining elements of medieval Europe was the top-down structure of society, called the manorial system, which had a lord who oversaw an estate and peasants who worked the land and paid rent in the form of labour or produce. The lord provided protection and served as the court of law for his peasants, so that the manor was a complete economic and political unit. The lord, in turn, owed fealty to both a greater lord and the Church.

The Dutch provinces did not become manorial, and the reason, as with nearly everything else, related to water. Since much of the land was reclaimed from the sea, neither Church nor nobility could claim to own it. It was created by communities (hence the Dutch saying "God made the earth, but the Dutch made Holland"). Residents banded together to form water boards that were responsible for the complex, non-stop task of maintaining polders (reclaimed lands), dams, dykes, and watermills to keep the water at bay. The boards – "waterschappen" – are still very much a part of Dutch life and have exerted an enormous influence on the culture, in particular on the peculiar combination of individualism and communalism that helps define "Dutchness."

In this system, people bought and sold their own plots of land. Many Amsterdammers owned land just outside the city, which they farmed or rented out for extra income. The striking feature of this land ownership is that it was individuals, of all levels of society, who were invested in the land. Whereas the land was controlled by noblemen and/or the Church in other parts of Europe, in the province of Holland, c. 1500, only 5 per cent of the land was owned by nobles, while peasants owned 45 per cent of it (Israel, 1995: 108–9).

This situation meant that ordinary Dutchmen were less inclined to adopt the posture of obedience that serfs and peasants elsewhere were forced into. Instead of owing fealty to lords, people paid rent to one another or bought and sold property.

Impulse to Innovation

Sometime around the year 1200, then, in order to control flooding, the inhabitants of a region of marshy soil at a juncture of two bodies of water – the spot where a river flowed into a vast bay that connected with the North Sea, about 50 miles (80 kilometres) away – built a dam on the Amstel River. The dam would ever after mark the centre of the city, and it gave the community a name: Amestelledamme. Cornelis Anthonisz.'s bird's-eye view, c. 1557 (Map 3.1), clearly shows the river and the dam, with the medieval city built up around it.

One might expect that, perched on the far northwestern flank of the continent, soaked by rains, beaten by winds, ravaged by tidal currents, Amsterdam was destined to remain a distinctly minor urban hub, home to farmers who grew barley and rye to make their porridge and bread and to fishermen who caught pike, eel, and carp in the marshy inlets, all of them continuing to live in wooden huts with straw roofs and clay floors sloped to let rainwater flow through rather than puddle.

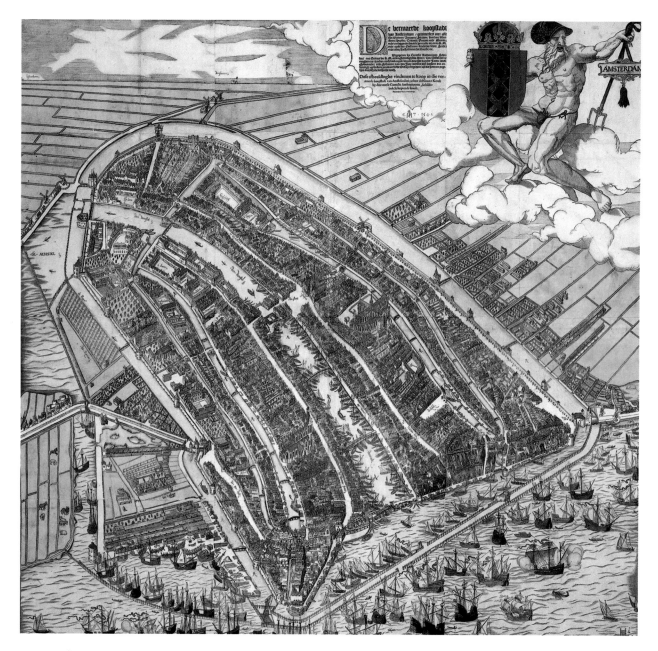

Map 3.1 | Cornelis Anthonisz., *Bird's-Eye View of Amsterdam*, print, c. 1557.
Source: Collection of the Rijksmuseum; image source Wikimedia, https://commons.wikimedia.org/wiki/File:Cornelis_anthonisz_vogelvluchtkaart_amsterdam.JPG. Public domain.

But the struggle against water had given rise to an innovative impulse, which would set them apart from people elsewhere in Europe. Where the manorial system kept people locked in a certain socio-economic stratum, medieval Amsterdammers began buying and selling plots of land, farming it, exploiting it, and in so doing came to realize that by innovating and seeking opportunities they could make life better for their children.

This innovative impulse helped the Dutch to race to the forefront of a succession of industries. One example: Dutch fishermen had for centuries plied coastal waters for herring (Unger, 1980, 1978; Carasso-Kok, 2004: 135–7). The fish were caught, hauled ashore, gutted, and packed in brine to preserve them. The Dutch had no monopoly on the herring trade – it was a common activity in many northern European lands, and the Dutch for a time were regular customers of Swedish-caught herring.

But, through a series of innovations, Dutch fishermen cornered the market on herring. It began with what was probably an accidental discovery. Fish such as herring have little pouches in their stomachs called pyloric caeca, which contain enzymes that aid digestion. If, instead of gutting the fish entirely, you leave these pouches, as well as the pancreas, in the brine mixture, the result is fish that keeps for a much longer period of time and, as a bonus, has more flavour.

This discovery gave Dutch fishermen – theoretically, at least – the ability to move away from the coastlines and into the deep, icy, impetuously heaving waters of the North Sea to the north of Scotland and west of Norway. There, far from land, lay Dogger Bank, a broad and relatively shallow region of sea that held a mother-lode, for it was thick with the muscular, silvery bodies of shoaling herring.

But such a journey required a new kind of vessel. In 1416, shipbuilders in the town of Hoorn, to the north of Amsterdam, developed a long, stout, eminently seaworthy boat with bulging sides and a cavernous interior. Along with it came modifications that made it possible to do the gibbing (the technique of gutting and curing herring) aboard ship. Thus, the herring buss – essentially a factory that could plough through rolling seas – came into being. Instead of immediately needing to get caught fish ashore, where they then had to be quickly processed and shipped off, the Dutch boats were able to stay at sea for five weeks or more at a stretch, fishing, gibbing, and fishing some more, and when they returned to port their hulls were packed with market-ready barrels of cured herring – lightly salted, or "soused," in the terminology of the Elizabethan period – which would last for a year and which, to boot, were tastier than fish that had been cured in the old manner.

Within a few decades the Dutch led the market. They shipped tons of herring to Poland, to France, up the Rhine into Germany, even as far afield as Russia. Dutch artists made etchings of herrings wearing crowns, and writers spoke of "our noble herring."

Transforming the herring industry could happen only if there was an unusual degree of cooperation among different people. Here Amsterdam's tradition of water management, which by this time had a couple of centuries of history behind it, served the city well. Building up dykes and dredging canals were massive communal activities in which everyone concerned had to see a common as well as an individual interest in order to take part. Fishing the coastline required little more than a father and son and a few hands, but moving into deep waters meant a commitment of capital and a complex support infrastructure. The ships were larger, and they had teams of specialized workers: sailors, gutters (a skilled team of gutters could process 2,000 herring an hour), packers, and officers. Since a herring fleet had such a recognizably valuable cargo, it needed a naval escort for defence. Ship chandlers had to supply linen, hemp, tar, tallow, netting, barrels, salt, and other products.

To make all of this work, herring merchants pushed for local government to get involved. The government sent warships to protect the fleet, and over time it developed regulations covering every aspect of the netting, processing, and sale of herring. This was done with one purpose in mind: to keep the quality high. As more money came into the province of Holland, the provincial government required that herring casks be of regulation size and manufacture and that they be stamped not just as Dutch but as Holland Herring, a very early and stunningly successful instance of branding.

At the height of the industry, fishermen of the province of Holland caught about 200 million herring per year. New wealth came to Amsterdam. And dominance in one field led to success in others (Israel, 1995: 116–19). In order to build herring busses, Amsterdam bought timber from Germany and processed it into planks. The city's sawyers (and later sawmills, after a farmer from nearby Uitgeest patented a crankshaft, which turned the circular motion of a windmill into the back-and-forth motion of a sawing blade)

produced so efficiently that England's burgeoning shipbuilding industry bought processed wood from Amsterdam and the surrounding area. Meanwhile, the city's own shipyards expanded, producing barges for working the region's rivers as well as seagoing vessels. And the city's merchants in turn became savvy international traders; they paid top dollar for information about faraway events that they could earn money on and adjusted their cargo accordingly. When harvests in southern Europe failed, the city's vessels returned from their herring runs to the Baltic port of Danzig laden with rye and wheat, so that Dutch vessels provided Polish grain for tables in Spain and Italy. The ships likewise carried wine from France to the Baltic and brought beer from Germany for Dutch consumption.

All the while, merchants kept alert for new business opportunities. When they discovered that rapeseed, hempseed, and potash, the main ingredients of soap, could all be got cheaply in the Baltic ports their ships frequented, they carted the raw material home and created an industry. At one point, there were twenty-one soap works along Amsterdam's canals. Once again branding became part of marketing: Amsterdam's unique "green soap" became famous throughout Renaissance Europe, and for all we know could have been the preferred brand of Leonardo da Vinci or Queen Elizabeth.

Company Town

All of this furious innovation came to a head with the advent, in 1602, of the Dutch East India Company

(VOC), whose fortunes were inextricably tied to those of Amsterdam and to the development of its canal grid. The VOC transformed the world in a way few companies have. It practically invented global commerce. It shuffled the world's ecosystems. It advanced cartography and shipbuilding, fostered slavery and exploitation. Little appreciated, however, is the fact that its activities were all about consumerism. The VOC was devoted to procuring goods that individuals craved and to making money for its individual investors. And all of its activities benefitted the city of Amsterdam. As the company rose, the city grew into its Golden Age self.

One way this growth occurred was through the development of Amsterdam's stock exchange, which began almost the moment the VOC did, with the trading of shares of VOC stock. The first selling of shares took place in the open air on the New Bridge, which separated the city from the harbour and thus was a way station of information from ships that had just arrived. By 1611, construction was complete on this first purpose-built stock exchange (Figure 3.2).

But Amsterdam's stock exchange was not an end in itself. The pieces of paper that changed hands were valuable because they represented other things. Indeed, over the course of the next few decades they came to represent, as it were, everything. Europe was in the early stages of its infamous period of exploitation of the wider world. The image we have of Europeans of the seventeenth century – semi-medieval peasants rooted to their villages, their entire lives, including all they consumed, comprised of what was available within the few miles of their homes – is in need of updating. Europe was

exploring the world with vigour, and Europe was ready to exploit, to consume. And the Dutch were on their way to becoming the greatest shipping nation the world had ever seen. The genius of Amsterdam in particular – the economic foundation of its liberalism – lay in its identifying and solving the problem that Europe's would-be consumer culture faced: Life was staggeringly unpredictable. Fate was swift and could blindside anyone. Plagues swept in on a sudden wind. A returning fleet could be swallowed by a storm. Life was carried on perilously close to its natural state, which Thomas Hobbes would famously describe a few decades later as "nasty, brutish, and short." Nobody could count on anything, and therefore business suffered. Price and availability were wildly variable.

Security was what was needed, and Amsterdam's stupendous rise can be seen as a result of the awareness that, if you provided security, virtually everyone would thank you for it. Your enemies, your competitors, would be grateful to you for giving them a small foothold of safety and would repay you over and over, even if they hated you at the same time.

One step in achieving this security was providing a central stock exchange. Another was having insurance offices and other services, as well as hotels and facilities for travelling merchants. All of these services came into being and were clustered in the buildings laid out around the exchange. Another part of the plan was the concept of a central storehouse. Shortly after the founding of the stock exchange, Amsterdam went about making itself into the Amazon.com of the seventeenth century, a place where everything was available to everybody. But,

Figure 3.2 | Claes Jansz. Visscher, *Byrsa Amsterodamensis (Amsterdam Stock Exchange)*, print, c. 1612.
Source: Stadsarchief Amsterdam, Beeldbank 010001000620, public domain.

of course, it was an analogue emporium: nothing was virtual; everything was real, in all its bulky, aromatic, or reeking glory. That meant an unfathomable amount of hard work. And it meant that the city – a city with barely a foundation, which had been tenuously built on marsh and swamp and for which inundation was a constant threat – would have to transform itself to hold all the goods of the earth.

Amsterdam's physical self as it developed in the seventeenth century, and as is largely still evident in the city centre today, was a product of this awareness and this decision. The city morphed itself, carved itself, flooded itself, dammed itself, built itself up brick by brick around this idea, which is part of the foundation of liberalism. For individual freedom can come about only, can be conceived only, if there is some sense of security to life. In fact, the city's rise – its coming role not only as the world's economic entrepôt but as a centre of scientific learning, art, shipping, and much else – can be seen as the antidote to the frightful vagaries of life.

If you wander around Amsterdam's fabled canals, especially the Prinsengracht, the outermost central canal, which was specifically designated for commerce, you'll note that a lot of the gabled brick buildings that line them have shuttered windows right in the middle of each story. These were warehouses. Indeed, in a sense the whole city became a warehouse. A trader kept his office on the ground floor of his house, the room that connected to the street. His family lived behind. And the upper floors were packed with whatever goods he dealt in. Particularly in the case of spices, being able to store quantities kept prices from fluctuating wildly.

How vast an enterprise was this? In 1625, VOC warehouses in the Netherlands contained almost 4 million pounds of pepper. The year after, thanks to especially successful voyages, there were nearly 6 million pounds of pepper packed into the quaint little canal-side buildings of middlemen, not to mention warehouse upon warehouse filled with cinnamon, stockfish, tea, whale oil, sugar, salt, soap, sail cloth, silk, beer, tobacco, and other goods waiting to ship out again (Bastin, 1996: 287). A generation later, when Cosimo III de' Medici travelled to Amsterdam, his gushing observations suggested an awareness that Italy's own grandeur, that of the High Renaissance over which his grandfather and namesake had held sway, was a thing of the past and what he saw in this city of business was the future: "Greater trade is done in Amsterdam than in any other city in the world. Foreigners are astounded when they first see it, and it appears that the four-quarters of the world have despoiled themselves to enrich her and to bring their rarest and most curious treasures into her port. Anyone who considers the present state of Amsterdam ... will be amazed that the city with such small beginnings and in such a short time has become enriched to such a degree of greatness, beauty, and magnificence" (quoted in Sutton, 2006: 12).

Urban Development

Before this transformation could happen, before the city could become the world's emporium, it had to grow. The Amsterdam in which the VOC had been founded was a small medieval city hunkered inside its walls, surrounded by a moat. Its size had been restricted by legal decree. The war with Spain was on, and it was feared that any outlying buildings could be taken over by the enemy and used as bases for attack. Thus, it was against the law to build outside the city walls.

But as the city grew, people wantonly ignored the law. Look at any of the many maps and paintings that date from before 1610, such as the Anthonisz. view (see Map 3.1), and you will find dozens if not hundreds of buildings of various types beyond the walls, along with neatly laid-out gardens and fences. Despite potentially putting themselves in harm's way, people were defying the city ordinance for the oldest of reasons: it was cheaper. Land was cheaper, and, crucially, beyond the city walls you didn't have to pay city taxes.

By 1610, the old way of doing things had completely fallen apart. The city needed to expand and to raise the money for its expanded urban infrastructure by selling off parcels (Elias, 1963: liv–lxxvi; Abrahamse, 2010: 42–88; Lesger, 2006: 174–80; Brugmans, 1973: 207–10). The man most responsible for the great expansion of the city in its Golden Age – for the physical manifestation of Amsterdam's commitment to liberalism – was Frans Hendricksz. Oetgens.

Oetgens can perhaps be said to have had some ambition for the city, but it is beyond doubt that his greatest ambition was reserved for himself and his fortune. As fabrieksmeester (city builder), he urged the city's panel of four mayors to give up the long-standing policy of barring building outside the defensive walls. They acquiesced, putting him in charge of the expansion project. Oetgens worked with the city carpenter, Hendrick Jacobsz. Staets, to map out precisely where the city would expand. Meanwhile, he won an appointment as one of the four mayors and from there got several friends appointed to positions in the city government. Most notable of these was a nephew named Barthold Cromhout. Together, Oetgens and Cromhout oversaw the expansion of Amsterdam. One of their first achievements was to have committee meetings held in secret. Next, they proceeded to buy much of the land that they had targeted for inclusion in the city. This land was mostly swamp, which Oetgens and Cromhout got for next to nothing, since, of course, the owners of the land were ignorant of the secret expansion agreement. Their plan, then, was to wait for the value to rise. One example, cited by Clé Lesger: a stretch of land just beyond the western walls of the city that Oetgens, Cromhout, and two of their cohorts purchased for 16,179 guilders in 1611 was valued in 1615 at 122,247 guilders (Lesger, 2006: 175).

Oetgens and other speculators orchestrated dozens of such deals. Eventually the land was divided into lots. The flagrant corruption of Oetgens, Cromhout, and others was met by one of Europe's first systematic attempts at regulation, but by and large it can be said that the speculators got their way. While the speculation battle raged, work was going on to develop the new districts. And despite all the corruption, the care and foresight that went into the overall development was remarkable. In one swoop, the surface size of the city was increased fivefold. The development took the form of three new canals that would wrap in a semicircle around the medieval centre. The sensibility behind it all was strikingly modern. Each of the new canals was given a fancy name to attract the nouveau riche merchant class to build gracious homes: Prinsengracht (Prince's Canal, named in honour of Willem, the Prince of Orange), Keizersgracht (Emperor's Canal), and Herengracht (Gentlemen's Canal). The original plan also included the idea of renaming the canal called the Singel, which had served as the moat surrounding the city, the Koningsgracht, or King's Canal, but the Dutch republicans had a particular aversion to kings so the name never took; the Singel is still the Singel, though the attempt at fancifying it remains enshrined in one small square along it, which is called the Koningsplein.

Before building could happen, the swampy terrain needed to be pumped. First, the perimeter fortifications had to be built. Then mills had to be erected. Then the new canals had to be dug and a system of locks constructed so that the canals would be flushed daily. Try as one might, it is impossible to imagine the effort all of this took. For, of course, it was done without machinery. One can get the gist from the occasional print or painting that shows wheelbarrows and shovels, men's legs planted in thick mud, boards laid down for the barrows to traverse the glop. Nevertheless, the American architect Tim Killiam calculated in the 1970s (Killiam & van der Zeijden, 1978) that, in the span of a single lifetime

* six miles (9.6 kilometres) of canal were dredged by hand and foot (using waterwheels powered like stationery bicycles);
* twelve miles (19 kilometres) of canal-side land were built up, with mud from where the canals were dug

out and sand hauled in via barges, to raise the ground level enough above water to build on;
* somewhere around one hundred bridges were constructed;
* a dozen miles of canal-side road were laid brick by brick.

And then came the houses: upward of 3,000 of them, every single one built, with outrageous improbability, on shifting marshland, requiring the back-breaking work of pile driving by manual labour (Killiam, 1978: 7). This project in itself was such a supreme effort that the Dutch word for pile driving, "heien," is the root of a number of sayings, songs, and folktales. A single house required maybe forty pairs of piles, each a stout, straight log of Scandinavian pine, to be jammed 40 or 60 feet (12 to 18 metres) into the sand, peat, and clay. The grandiose City Hall (today known as the Royal Palace), built on Dam Square in 1653, required 13,659 piles. Were you to travel to Amsterdam in its glory days, probably the sight you would have been most struck by would have been that of the triangular "trees" of support posts dotting the landscape, each with a block of iron weighing maybe half a ton poised above the pile. Teams of thirty or forty men, keeping time by chanting songs and fuelled by ready barrels of beer, simultaneously pulled ropes to heave the "heiblok" into the air; then, on the call from the "heibaas," they would let loose and the weight would slam down, hammering the log a little deeper into the ground (Figure 3.3). The Scandinavian logs are still there: the canal houses you see in Amsterdam's central ring today (except for those that have had foundations replaced) rest on piles that were rammed into the earth in the 1600s. That they are still holding up so much of the city is the result of a bit of seventeenth-century genius. The engineers knew that the logs would not rot once they were below the waterline. The problem was the tops had to rest in the air, where masonry fixed them to the bricks in order for the mortar to harden. The solution was to dig ditches where the piles would be driven to a point below the waterline and then temporarily pump water out of them. Once the mortar had dried, the water could be let back in the ditch, and the pile, safely under water, remained preserved from the ravaging effects of oxygen.

This process went on throughout much of the century. Joan Blaeu's 1649 map of Amsterdam (Map 3.2) shows the expansion project in progress, with work complete on the new canals only on the west side of the city. When it was complete, Amsterdam's canal ring was the greatest urban feat of the age, a model for cities from England to Sweden. Peter the Great set himself up in the city for a time, studying its engineering and urban planning techniques, and then put them into practice in constructing St. Petersburg, which was likewise built on marshland. For four

Figure 3.3 | Tim Killiam, *Seventeenth-century pile drivers*, drawing.
Reproduced with permission from the artist.

(Opposite) Map 3.2 | Amsterdam, map by Joan Blaeu, 1649.
Source: Wikimedia, https://commons.wikimedia.org/wiki/File:Map_of_Amsterdam_-_Amstelodami_Celeberrimi_Hollandiae_Emporii_Delineatio_Nova_(J.Blaeu,_1649).jpg. Public domain.

AMSTELODAMI CELEBERRIMI HOLLANDIÆ EMPORII DELINEATIO NOVA.

Ae mstela fluvius

YA FLUVIUS

centuries, Amsterdam's canal ring has been a wonder, worthy of tourism and imitation, for reasons that UNESCO identified when in 2010 it named the district a World Heritage Site: "It is a masterpiece of hydraulic engineering, town planning, and a rational programme of construction and bourgeois architecture" (UNESCO, 2010). In other words, the reason early modern Europeans marvelled at Amsterdam's Golden Age urban core was that it served people extraordinarily well. And the people it served were not princes or popes but merchants and tradesmen. As Europe lurched towards secularism, democracy, modernity, a society based on the individual, it became intrigued by this city that had remade itself to serve the ordinary individual and his or her upwardly mobile aspirations. The new city Amsterdam became brought the world to one's doorstep. The canals were like arms that the city sent out to reach around the globe and gather its plenty back to it.

The infusion of wealth led to innovations in other arenas. In art, the city pioneered a new secularism, which focused on ordinary individuals rather than religious subject matter. Rembrandt became the chief example. Today we know him as a multifarious genius, but his first fame came from painting portraits of the city's powerful merchants. These people were fascinated with themselves – their inner lives, their individuality – in a way previous generations had not been. Rembrandt did not just paint what they looked like (many Dutch painters of the period could do that); he seemed to be able to portray who they were, to reach their essence.

At the same time, the city was rising to become a centre of science. This development involved scientific observation, but it also included the rise of science as an industry, as Amsterdam's fabricators turned out lenses and other scientific equipment. At the same time, Amsterdam came to dominate European publishing. By one estimate, over the course of the seventeenth century the Netherlands produced one-half of all books published worldwide (Sprunger, 1994: 29), and Amsterdam's printers led the way.

The development of these fields – art, science, publishing – signalled the arrival of the era of the individual, in which the world would become available to individual exploration. The revolutionary new shape that Amsterdam gave itself made it uniquely suited to that task.

chapter four

A Privileged Site in the City, the Republic, and the World Economy

HERMAN VAN DER WUSTEN

The Canal District has been one of Amsterdam's most distinctive features since its emergence during the Golden Age of the Dutch Republic. With the new town hall and the completely restructured waterfront, the Canal District came to dominate the city plan. During that time slot of about a century, the city of Amsterdam was a major force in shaping the republic's prominent presence within the emerging European state system and in the European expansion across the globe. Subsequently, the prominence of the Canal District in Amsterdam's cityscape has fluctuated along with the prominence of the city's reputation. The district regained its former fame as the city entered its Second Golden Age towards the end of the nineteenth century (Vroom, 2008: 23). And it is happening yet again in the early twenty-first century as the "Third" Golden Age of the city is declared, and the Canal District acquires the global seal of approval as it is placed on UNESCO's World Heritage List.

Even if the Canal District was historically an internationally significant site in its own right, much of that significance was dependent on the district being part of Amsterdam. The Canal District came about at the initiative of the city's government, and it was part of the city's jurisdiction. In turn, the international role of the city of Amsterdam was mediated by its incorporation in the Dutch Republic. Amsterdam was undoubtedly the leading city within the republic, but it was not its all-powerful single centre. In the case of Venice – often compared with Amsterdam (Burke, 1974: 45–53) – the reign of that city extended across the terra firma. Amsterdam even in its heyday was not a city-state like Venice, though some of its leaders occasionally behaved as if it were.

This chapter focuses on the international setting in which the Canal District arose and assumed a degree of centrality. It concentrates on the international conditions that affected the timing and helped shape the plan and morphology of the Canal District, as well as on the district's function as a social site in international networks and its significance in Amsterdam's international representation. Seen from Amsterdam, the world and the international sphere were quickly expanding during the Golden Age, thanks to the bold initiatives of local merchants and the personnel of the merchant marine.

The Golden Age is a constituent element of the Dutch Republic's history, but its precise demarcation in time is somewhat opaque. In Dutch, it is in fact called the Golden Century, but according to most accounts it did not last quite that long. The fortunes of the republic improved quickly from 1590, and its brilliant image gradually tarnished from 1672 onward. Israel (1995a) distinguishes between an early (1590–1647) and a later Golden Age, and stretches the later period three decades beyond 1672. It is perhaps an irresolvable question. Gold, after all, comes in different carats.

Politics and Territory

To refer to "international" Amsterdam in the Golden Age is in fact an anachronism. The modern state system only emerged during this period. Those speaking and acting on behalf of a few emergent territorial states (such as the Dutch Republic) were competing for sovereignty with religious authorities, empires, city leagues, and city states. Exclusive state authority in matters of political order gradually gained the upper hand and saw its example emulated across Europe (Tilly, 1992).

Within this emergent state system, the political entity in which Amsterdam was located was a special kind of state (Israel, 1995a: 276–306; Prak, 2002: 183–203). Amsterdam played a special role within that state, and the political elite of Amsterdam, in turn, largely resided in the Canal District. The "stateness" of the Dutch Republic has long been questioned, initially even by its founders. The republic was the eventual outcome of an insurrection in the Low Countries as a whole against its overlord, the apex of the feudal pyramid. He was the Spanish king, a member of the House of Habsburg, who had inherited the titles of the Dukes of Burgundy in the Low Countries. Eventually, the northern part of the Low Countries seceded.

The government of the fledgling republic was originally called the Generality. It lacked a steady, permanent agency in charge of foreign affairs with exclusive coercive capabilities. These powers gradually coalesced in the hands of two functionaries whose positions had already been established during the reign of the Burgundian dukes: the "stadtholder" (a noble man) and the "advocate," later called the "pensionary" (a jurist in charge of an incipient civil service). The functionaries of the most prominent province, Holland, became central figures in the politics of the Generality as a whole. The advocate/pensionary primarily concentrated on civil affairs, diplomacy (Israel, 1995a: 290), and the economy, while the stadtholder's authority concerned military matters in particular. The position of the stadtholder became hereditary within the House of Orange, while the advocate/pensionary tended to represent the particular interests of the cities.

The major internal political conflicts of the period pitched these two figures against each other during the Golden Age and reflected that, while the relationship between city and state was critical to the rise of Amsterdam and the Dutch Republic, it was certainly not devoid of tension. The conflict resulted in a judicial execution of one advocate/pensionary (1618) and the murder of yet another (1672). A principal factor in the 1672 incident was a long conflict about the stadtholder function. The Amsterdam political elite were deeply involved in these episodes, and most of the time they tended to oppose the stadtholder on the issue of military policy and, in particular, military expenditures. Most of the members of the elite also tended to be in a different camp from the stadtholder as regards religion. While the stadtholder stayed in tune with the more orthodox creed of the official Reformed Church, most but definitely not all of the Amsterdam elite during this period had more latitudinarian views and a more tolerant attitude towards religious diversity.

The political influence from Amsterdam in the republic was considerable, and the city's political elite were almost indistinguishable from its leading merchant class. Formally, the republic was a confederacy of seven provinces and had in fact a considerable body of shared powers, to an extent operating as a federal state. The province of Holland was surely the most important of these seven provinces, and Amsterdam was by far the largest city in that province and in the country. Decisions concerning the republic as a whole had to be made in the States General, where each provincial delegation had one vote. To reach a decision, votes formally had to be unanimous, but in practice they often were not. Provincial decisions for Holland were prepared by a standing committee and finalized by the provincial assembly consisting of nineteen delegates (one from the nobility and eighteen from the different cities), each of them acting under strict instructions from the body of nobles and the respective local councils.

In the city of Amsterdam, the government consisted of a small college of four burgomasters annually selected from the "vroedschap," a body of high-standing citizens, mostly merchants, with interests in long-distance trade but also financially invested in local production or more risky ventures like land reclamation in still submerged parts of Holland. Stadtholders during crises enforced some say in selection and co-optation. Positions in these bodies were increasingly occupied by a small ever-more closed group of families called the "regenten," the rulers. They and their family members and trusted followers also occupied the board positions in the local charitable institutions and the rare staff positions in the different administrations. They were the delegates to the state assemblies, sat in the governing councils of the republic, and acted as diplomatic representatives.

Many regent families came to live in the Canal District as it was constructed. This elite also acquired fashionable summer residences away from the city. From the tax returns of 1742, some generations after the end of the Golden Age, we know that 600 Amsterdam households had such summer houses and 60 per cent of them lived in the Canal District. This entire group had an annual income in the order of twenty times the minimal income on which a family could supposedly survive. The "regenten" households came from their midst and tended to have even higher incomes. At the same time, about half the entire population of Amsterdam lived in households with incomes of less than twice that survival level (Diederiks, 1987: 48–9).

From 1585, the States General and the States of Holland sat in The Hague at Binnenhof, a number of buildings around the courtyard of an old castle belonging to the Count of Holland traditionally used for judicial proceedings. The stadtholder had his official residence in the same complex. Gradually, he acquired an additional number of residences with royal allure close to the Binnenhof and across the country. The core of the state-wide political establishment was part of the small town of The Hague. One of the reasons for this choice for the republic's political centre was precisely The Hague's lack of city rights. In this way, jealousies among different cities had been prevented. Close to Binnenhof appeared a high-class residential environment for people connected to the central government institutions. Its central tree-lined broad boulevard (Lange Voorhout) was seriously considered to be an attractive example to follow instead of one of the three canals when the first plans for the Canal District were drawn up in Amsterdam (Abrahamse, 2019: 83).

Figure 4.1 suggests the hesitant recognition of this part of the state system and its territorial form in the popular imagination. It shows the lion as a heraldic emblem used to underline the identity of the province of Holland as the republic's most important province (with the profiles of its cities added). During this period, the same lion had been used to represent two different political entities: the seventeen provinces of the Low Countries as part of the Habsburg Empire and the Dutch Republic as a secession of its northern part (with a number of the political leaders involved in the struggle on both sides of the map). These three different representations were produced by two publishers of the main atlas, map, and newsprint publications in Amsterdam. The lion as representation of the seventeen provinces had been earlier introduced as the Belgian lion and much later also became part of the heraldic emblem of the Kingdom of the Netherlands.

Taylor (1996) has called this Generality a polycentric city-region state. It was a vibrant core of many cities, on the land side surrounded by a defensive frontier of fortifications. The vibrant core was, of course, widely open to the sea. The cities were initially united by a common defence against the centralizing and taxing efforts of its distant overlord. At issue at its origin was also the pacification of violent religious conflict and the resistance to the introduction of an inquisition aiming to restore the monopoly of the Catholic faith. All these relatively local conflicts were part of all-European struggles in which the modern state system was born. The opponents of the Spanish king in the Low Countries were materially supported by monarchs who also felt threatened (French, English) and by nobles and Protestant cities in Germany. In the early stages of the insurrection, they received intellectual and diplomatic assistance from French lawyers, diplomats, and administrators, often Protestants, who were in the process of formulating new notions on popular sovereignty, justifications for the right to resist, and foundations for the position of the law in politics. These people were influential in legitimating the unusual republican state that was

(Opposite) Figure 4.1 | The Low Countries, Holland, the Dutch Republic, and its leading cities. Claes Jansz. Visscher, *Comitatus Hollandiae denuo forma Leonis...* [etc.], 1648.
Source: Courtesy of Allard Pierson, University Library, University of Amsterdam, HB-KZL I 1 A 1 (10).

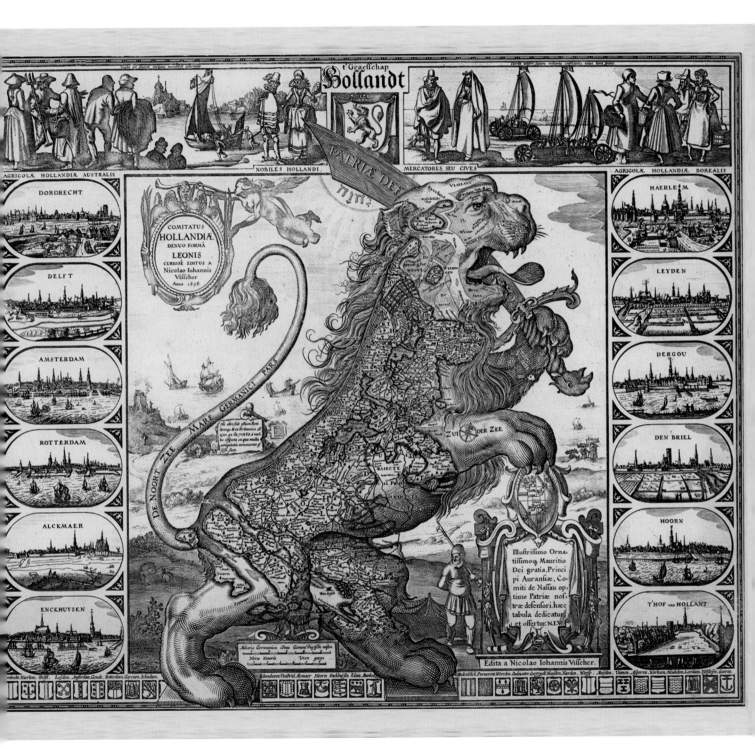

t'Graefschap **Hollandt**

COMITATUS
HOLLANDIÆ
DENUO FORMÂ
LEONIS
CURIOSÈ EDITUS A
Nicolao Iohannis
Visscher.
Anno 1648.

PATRIÆ DEF

AGRICOLÆ HOLLANDIÆ AUSTRALIS

NOBILES HOLLANDI.

MERCATORES, SEU CIVES

AGRICOLÆ HOLLANDIÆ BOREALIS

DORDRECHT

DELFT

AMSTERDAM

ROTTERDAM

ALCKMAER

ENCKHUYSEN

HAERLEM

LEYDEN

DERGOU

DEN BRIEL

HOORN

T'HOF van HOLLANT

DE NOORT ZEE   MARE GERMANICI PARS

ZUIDER ZEE

Illustrissimo Orna-
tissimoq Mauritio
Dei gratia, Princi
pi Auransiæ, Co
miti de Nassau op
timo Patriæ nos-
træ defensori, hæc
tabula dedicatur
et offertur. N.I.V.

Edita a Nicolao Iohannis Visscher.

proclaimed just before Amsterdam's phenomenal rise (Kriegel, 2011).

Demographic Growth, Economic and Military Power

Holland, more generally the seaward part of the northern half of the Low Countries, had from long before 1590 been a region of partially reclaimed lowlands cut through by waterways, with a pasture-based agriculture – a host of small trading towns dependent on riparian and overseas trade and fishing. There were not many signs of feudalism, but Holland was not completely devoid of a nobility. Longer distance trade was primarily concerned with grain and wood from the Baltic, and, where possible, salt and herring were offered in return. Dutch vessels also called frequently at French, Portuguese, and English ports. The seaports in Holland, Amsterdam one of them, had established themselves as dominating centres in the networks concerned with these particular trades. It was so far not intimately implicated in high-value, rich trades as the cities of Flanders were (Israel, 1989).

In the course of the sixteenth century, Amsterdam (as the only one of these northern towns) started to grow quickly, a sure sign of immigration in a period when the difference between births and deaths for urban populations tended to be negative. Most cities grow mainly for economic reasons, but sometimes politics is the main driver of population growth (as with many capital cities). During the first half of the sixteenth century, Amsterdam was the sixth-fastest growing city in Europe for mainly economic reasons;

from 1550 to 1600 it was second; and from 1600 to 1650 it was first. Similar growth, though not quite as steep as in Amsterdam, was recorded in other Dutch cities such as Haarlem, Leyden, and Rotterdam (Taylor, 2013: 265). The Hague grew just as quickly for political reasons. In 1570 (growth was already well underway), Amsterdam was still a small city with 30,000 inhabitants. Its spectacular population growth came to an end around 1672 at 200,000 inhabitants. In other words, population growth – and by implication economic growth – in Amsterdam had started well before the beginning of the Golden Age. The acceleration coincided with the start of that period around 1590. The Canal District was created, in large part, to accommodate this growth and particularly those who were leading merchants or in charge of administering this extraordinary development and its consequences.

The polycentric city-region of the Dutch Republic knew a high level of economic interdependence between its different parts. All the cities in the provinces of Holland and Zeeland along the North Sea coast had their own niche in international trade. All cities in the region were nodes in a dense infrastructural domestic network of waterways and roads. And the whole region was externally connected by the seaports, major rivers, particularly the Rhine, and some important overland roads.

From 1590, the tide for the emergent Dutch Republic turned favourably as a result of the sacking of Antwerp by Spanish troops in 1585 and a shift in the politico-military priorities of the Spanish king to his interests in France (Israel, 1989: 38–42). The military pressure on the north decreased. Antwerp's merchants left for Amsterdam as they saw the opportunities

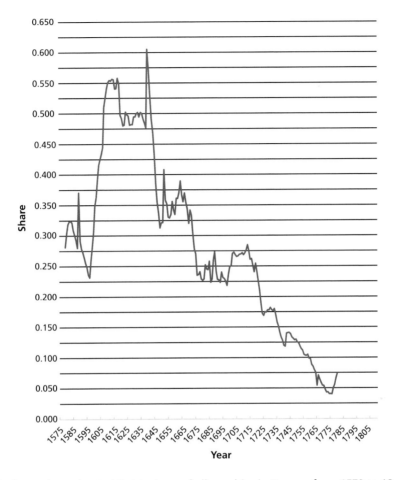

Figure 4.2 | The graph shows the estimated Dutch share of all warships in Europe, from 1579 to 1810.
Source: Modelski & Thompson, 1988: 194, with the permission of Professor W.R. Thompson.

opening up in the northern Low Countries. In the following decades, Dutch primacy in world trade was firmly established.

At the same time, the Dutch navy became the strongest in the world (Modelski & Thompson, 1988: 194). A principal part of the naval force had Amsterdam as its home port. Still, the republic's navy could only maintain its predominant position for a few decades. When political independence from Spain was finally agreed in 1648, the peace dividend was immediately collected. England and France emphatically asserted themselves as naval powers, and the long-term relative decline of the Dutch navy could no longer be countered (see Figure 4.2).

The Dutch Republic embodied the essence of early modern capitalism as a partnership of governors (the regents) and merchants that blended the power of both. In this particular case, governors and merchants to a large extent were one, or, in any case, the governors had merchant forebears. In another version, individual merchant capitalists in cities involved in long-distance trade became the bankers of and were provided with protection from kings and emperors (Howell, 2016). In early modern capitalism, big money was made by buying cheap and selling dear in different markets. Monopolies were crucial for success, and states helped to secure them. In the republic once formed, the cities quickly developed as staging posts and organizers of rich trade of various kinds, where prices per unit of volume and weight in the sellers' markets could be high and potential profits soared on account of the huge gaps in prices in the different markets. At the same time, risks were pronounced on account of the forces of nature during long ocean journeys and the possibilities of violent encounters. Such risks were mitigated by private insurance and state protection.

From 1590, the traditional Baltic, English, and French trade that continued to thrive was accompanied by quickly expanding "rich trade." It consisted of all kinds of luxury items (exotic goods and produce; rare, fashionable materials; precious minerals and metals) and stimulated new warehousing, different forms of manufacturing, further ship building, the increase and further specialization of business services (banking, insurance), and the collection of global information. The Dutch commercial centre,

which started to dominate global trade from 1590 onward and came to be concentrated in the Canal District, became a linchpin in all the regional trading networks in the world. The Dutch merchants connected these networks to each other and dominated their interfaces. Amsterdam and other ports acted as entrepôts where goods were imported, stored, and exported. This domination was brought about by a class of merchants and other entrepreneurs consisting of recent immigrants from Antwerp and elsewhere, but also by local merchants widening their perspective. It was often backed up by state support to enforce monopoly conditions or to enable daring initiatives.

The capturing of the East Indies and the general expansion of the Dutch presence in the Far East resulted from a uniquely successful public–private initiative to acquire an important role for Dutch traders. The Dutch East India Company (VOC) was for a long time the most successful of a series of European-controlled chartered companies. It was organized by the advocate/pensionary on behalf of the States General in 1602, involving a series of city governments and with merchants as shareholders in a joint stock company. Monopoly rights for the Dutch trade in the East Indies and elsewhere in the Far East were granted along with the power to establish forts and make agreements with indigenous rulers, using armed force if necessary. Its commercial and military powers were expressed in the distribution of its Asian strongholds across Asia. The States General, in The Hague, had rights of approval ex post facto. The company was administered by a board of seventeen directors, of which

Amsterdam supplied eight. At the same time, Amsterdam put up 57 per cent of the initial capital. The remainder of the seats were divided among other participating cities, finely balanced across the provinces of Holland and Zeeland. The resulting subtle overall balance was carefully maintained and enabled Amsterdam, where headquarters were established, to have a highly influential position. The VOC realized in the following years a monopoly position in some branches of the spice trade, which made a significant contribution to Dutch trade dominance (Nijman, 1994).

As trade flows through the republic increased, the opportunities for manufacturing also grew, much of it destined for abroad as the home market remained relatively limited. There was already some industrial base in a few branches as the expansionary drive started. The Dutch got the upper hand in the production of copperware and certain textiles; the processing of dyes, tobacco, and whale oil (for soap and lighting fuel); the cutting of diamonds and the grinding of lenses; and the refining of sugar. This industrial development progressed steadily during the Golden Age.

In the first decades following 1590, the city of Amsterdam was provided with a whole range of professional specialists and new institutions to facilitate trade. Most of them had emerged in previous trading cities like Venice, Genoa, and Antwerp, and to some extent also in London, but in Amsterdam they reached a new scale and further levels of sophistication. The number of brokers who could bring buyers and sellers together increased quickly and was organized through a system of licencing by the city gov-

ernment. Brokers started to specialize in certain trades, and, by 1612, there were 300 of them. In 1598, the city had also started a civic chamber of insurance to regulate the proceedings in those contracts. In 1609, the Amsterdam Exchange Bank started to provide reliable exchange facilities. In 1611, a bourse building (close to the Dam Square, pictured fully operational in Figure 4.3) was opened where commodity deals and insurance could occur under one roof in the city centre and also where shares in the East India Company (and later on the West Indies Company as well) were traded. In 1614, the Amsterdam Loan Bank was launched to ensure the availability of commercial credit.

Amsterdam thus became the site of an "information exchange," a focal point for international information flows. In Smith's (1984) view, the global expansion and increasing complexity of markets from the fifteenth century gave rise to a centralization of information networks. The information exchange was an informal cluster of individuals and institutions acquiring, transferring, analysing, and disseminating economic and economically relevant political information, notably on exchange rates, commodity prices, and politics hindering or facilitating trade, mainly across Europe.

There were different channels through which this information was acquired, with their relative importance changing over time. Originally, the information exchange concerned mainly the correspondence between private merchants and the reciprocal visits between Dutch businessmen and others sharing information face to face. Then there were the reports of Dutch consuls stationed in other trading places

Figure 4.3 | Job Adriaensz. Berckheyde, *The Old Stock Exchange of Amsterdam*, c. 1670.
Source: Museum Boijmans Van Beuningen, Rotterdam/ Photographer: Studio Tromp. Reprinted with permission.

(mostly locally prominent merchants of Dutch origin). These reports were stored with the Amsterdam city government and available to the merchants. Dutch diplomatic representatives sent reports from political capitals to The Hague, which were also available to the merchants as these diplomats were recruited from the same circles and other family members occupied positions in the central administrative councils. Finally, and increasingly important, were special channels that the different chartered companies maintained between their principal offices in Amsterdam and elsewhere in the republic and their agencies abroad. These channels were exemplified by the practices of the VOC but applied also to the West Indies Company, the Directorate for the Levant, and others.

The Dutch exchange provided superior information, and it was widely used across Europe. Since about 1650, an international market for this type of information emerged, which gave rise to early "newspapers" printed in Amsterdam in different languages and sold across the continent. The accumulation of ever-longer time series on economic variables also gave rise to early efforts at long-term analysis concerning inflation and business cycles that was used by VOC directors to plan their market behaviour. These efforts were not always very successful (they are hardly flawless today), but they pointed the way to later capitalist practices where market research and forecasting call the tune. As Russell Shorto argues in chapter 3 of this volume, information and regulation played critical parts in the stabilization of emergent markets in early modern Europe. Amsterdam (and the republic) provided an unrivalled business climate at the time.

The Canal District and the International Realm

The construction of the Canal District, and its subsequent functioning, was part of this overall story. Key protagonists performing roles briefly sketched earlier came to live there, and the district housed essential parts of the warehouse and transport infrastructures that were inserted so firmly at the heart of the global economy. As a distinctive part of the cityscape and its representation on imagery of Amsterdam, the Canal District also became an important element in the external perception of the city.

In the course of the seventeenth century, there was an outpouring of imagery (maps, drawings, paintings) related to the city. This cultural production was, on the one hand, facilitated by better cartographical technique and superior printing; on the other hand, it was driven by increasing interest and local pride of citizens about their own expanding cities and a demand to learn about foreign places elsewhere. The Dutch cities, and Amsterdam in particular, were frequently portrayed in this period and therefore relatively well known (van Lakerveld, 1977; Bakker & Schmitz, 2007; Schmidt, 2008). Maps prominently displaying the Canal District played an important part in spreading this imagery.

The genre was exemplified by Joan Blaeu's book *Theatre of Cities* (Blaeu, 1649–52), first published right after the end of the secession war. This work was a large collection of city descriptions by Amsterdam's master cartographer with illustrative city maps, initially of the cities of the Netherlands that had remained under the Spanish king and then also of

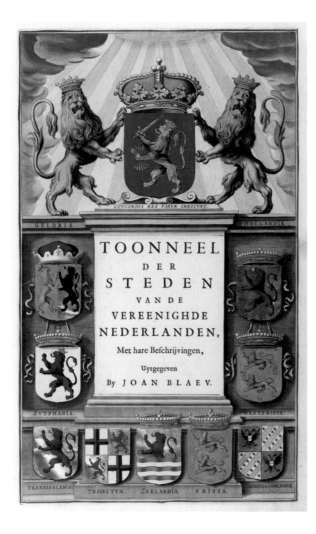

Figure 4.4 | The cover of Joan Blaeu's *Toonneel der Steden (Theatre of Cities)*, Amsterdam, 1649–52.
Source: Statendeel, titelpagina. Allard Pierson, University Library, University of Amsterdam, HB-KZL Blaeu kast.

those in what Blaeu called the United Netherlands under the States (Figure 4.4 shows its cover). In following years, further instalments on other parts of Europe were published and finally one volume encompassing the earth.

Amsterdam also became a planning and management model for other cities (Figure 4.5). Its system of street lighting and firefighting was copied, notably in Northern Germany and the Baltic area, as were its provisions to control the quality of medical doctors and apothecaries (Israel, 1995b). The city's plan was also to some extent guiding Russian czar Peter the Great as he re-entered the Baltic region and founded his new capital. But Amsterdam itself had also looked elsewhere. The Dutch version of classicist architecture used for the plan of the town hall or some of the designs of the mansions along the canals had been inspired by the rediscovery of the Romans and the Greeks in Italy (Burke, 1998: 115–21). The bourse building had been modelled after the examples of Antwerp and particularly London, first visited for that purpose by the city architect of the time.

The creation of the Canal District was a major part of the four extensions that the city achieved during the Golden Age (Bakker, 2004: 17–101; see also chapter 2 of this volume). The first two extensions predated the district. They aimed to extend the port and to bring already existing storage and production facilities inside newly constructed fortifications. They took shape between 1578 and 1600, and are clearly depicted on a 1597 map by cartographer/painter Pieter Bast, one recent migrant from Antwerp. Most of the newly incorporated city is on the east side of the old town, much of it on recently reclaimed land.

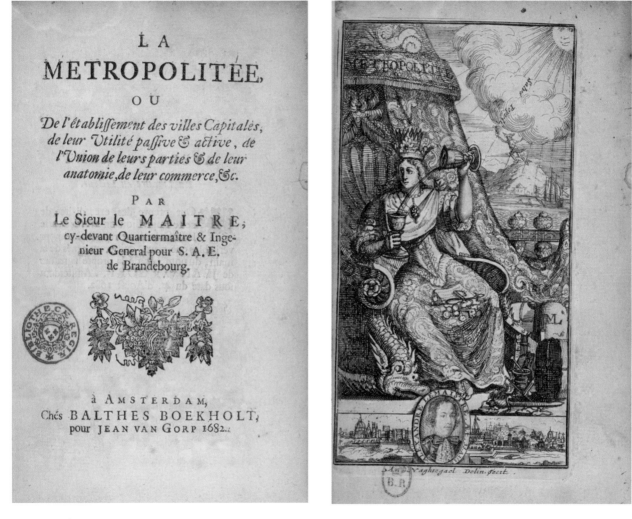

Figure 4.5 | A very early primer on the planning of capital cities as metropoles by sovereign rulers, published and printed in Amsterdam (1682) and based on classic literature and contemporaneous experience repeatedly referring to Amsterdam – non-capital in a republic – as ideally equipped and governed for commercial development.
Source: gallica.bnf.fr (Bibliothèque national de France).

The Third and the Fourth Extension (which started in 1610 and 1656, respectively) resulted in the Canal District, with the three new main canals jointly semi-circling the old city (Abrahamse, 2019). The western part of the Canal District was constructed during the Third Extension, and the remaining part of the crescent was realized during the Fourth Extension (1656–1662). Daniel Stalpaert's map of 1657 (see chapter 2 of this volume) shows the Third Extension realized and the plan of the Fourth.

The three main canals – the more central ones around the old inner city on the map – were from the inside to the outside called Herengracht, Keizersgracht, and Prinsengracht. The Herengracht (Gentlemen's Canal, referring primarily to the upper crust of the merchant class), the most prestigious one, was named after its intended residents, the patrician local families. The name of the Keizersgracht referred to the emperor of the Holy Roman Empire who had bestowed the city with an imperial crown, sign of his protection, in return for the support of the city in regional conflicts late in the fifteenth century. It is interesting that this gesture was still underlined in this way more than a century later, some decades after the Generality, of which Amsterdam was now a part, had stated its independence. The Prinsengracht was named after the Prince of Orange, the noble title of the stadtholder. It is a curious name in light of the disputes and varying relations between city government and stadtholder.

The canals had slightly different functions, and there was also some variation in the activities that took place alongside the waterways and the adjoining streets. The Herengracht and Keizersgracht were particularly used for pleasure boats, their sidewalks planted with trees. All this contributed to a pleasant residential milieu, although there was a continuous, major problem with sewage and stench from the water. The Herengracht held the highest status, with the Keizersgracht a very respectable second. The most prestigious part of the entire Canal District was the bend around the south (later called the Golden Bend) and particularly the addresses on the two sides of the Herengracht. Many sites here consisted of two adjacent standard plots with lush gardens at the back. A few stretched even to the next canal, with another structure perhaps for business purposes built there.

The members of the elite residing in the houses along the canals, particularly the Herengracht, were very close to the city centre (see Figure 4.6): from a few hundred metres to about a kilometre (from around 109 yards to about half a mile) to Dam Square, the town hall, the bourse, and all the financial services and major commercial establishments. Burgomasters, other regents, and merchants went there on foot. A bit further at the eastern edge of the old town was the local headquarters of the Dutch East India Company; the local headquarters of the West Indies Company was initially at the northern edge of the Canal District itself.

(Opposite) **Figure 4.6 | Gerrit Adriaensz. Berckheyde (1638–98),** *The Town Hall on the Dam,* 1693.
Source: Collection of the Rijksmuseum, Amsterdam, object number SK-C-101. Public domain.

The Prinsengracht had a direct connection to open water (ships had to pass a lock due to different water tables), so transport of goods and warehousing played a larger role there. This canal was somewhat less luxurious than the other two, with some more modest houses, warehouses, and also other functions like an orphanage. Place was also left there for churches (at the northern edge, in the west, and close to the Amstel River) and their adjoining public squares. This arrangement had a financial background, as the most expensive space with the highest profits for the city along the other two canals was reserved for sale as private residential properties to maximize the returns for the city.

Just as the timing of the first two extensions was related to Amsterdam's changing position in the international economy and its consequences in terms of new economic activity, so the timing of the Third and the Fourth Extension was connected with the evolution of the Dutch international position that clearly also affected Amsterdam's policies. The Third Extension started a year after a general ceasefire with Spain was concluded, which in the end would remain intact for twelve years. In these first domestically quiet years, long-established and recently arrived merchant families with thriving businesses were ready for more and better equipped residences than so far were available. Many such new houses were built in the Canal District. Contrary to the Venetian elite, who lived in urban palaces inhabited by extended families across the different parishes of the city, the Amsterdam elite came to congregate, largely, in a single part of the city that housed for the most part single families (Burke, 1974: 39, 41–2, 85).

The Fourth Extension came under consideration after the War of Independence finally ended in 1648. The ongoing work on another major public project, the new town hall, delayed its prompt realization. The Fourth Extension included the second (southern and eastern) part of the Canal District and was prepared and started to be realized in the years between the short-lived Dutch-Anglo wars of the 1650s and 1660s. They were about matters of trade policy and the dominance of the respective navies on the high seas.

An impression of the kind of people who lived in the most luxurious part of the Canal District – the Golden Bend at Herengracht from 1660 on – can be gleaned from a collection of fourteen of its residents during its first decades. Seven had acted as burgomaster. Most of them simultaneously held a range of other positions, such as membership on councils in The Hague, regent in the Dutch East India Company, board member of the *Atheneum Illustre* (twice); there was also a cartographer and a writer. Three of the group were merchants, one with several warehouses, one who had visited China and India, and one who traded with Spain and was also engaged in the slave trade. In addition, there was an admiral in the navy marine, a medical doctor who also performed as an actor in the nearby theatre, an artist painter, and a famous international art dealer. Quite a few had studied, mostly at Leyden University, and at least two held law degrees from the universities of Orléans and Poitiers (founded in 1306 and 1431, and provisionally abolished during the French Revolution). Some had quite long family histories in Amsterdam, but there were also people whose family had migrated from Antwerp and elsewhere around 1590 or later.

One of the burgomasters who lived in the Golden Bend was from a prominent family of traders who had lived mostly in Amsterdam for five generations. His grandfather, already one of the richest merchants in the city, had resided at Damrak, the main entrance to the city from open water. Ships landed there close to Dam Square. The family had Protestant sympathies and moved (as did many others) temporarily to Emden, northern Germany, as the city remained committed to the Spanish king until 1578, when they returned. His grandfather then played a key role in the new city government as an ally of the first stadtholder of Holland in the Dutch Republic who preached tolerance and aimed to reconcile Protestants and Catholics. As an adult, his father first lived in the old town close to Damrak and then moved to a new property at Herengracht in the first part of the Canal District. He had two sons: one, the burgomaster who possessed the house in the Golden Bend; the other – his older brother, also a burgomaster – who took over the house at Herengracht where his father had lived. Both brothers studied for longer periods in France and travelled extensively. Both were actively involved in the East India Company and managed their quite considerable fortunes, partly invested in various estates around Holland. As art collectors, they had an active hand in the procurement of the paintings and ornaments for the new town hall (Faber, Huisken, & Lammertse, 1987) and also acquired considerable numbers of objets d'art themselves. They played key roles in Amsterdam's and the Dutch Republic's politics of the 1650s and 1660s until 1672, when the political tide turned and the political influence of the family ended.

On the ceiling of the house in the Golden Bend, there was a painting made by a famous artist of the late Golden Age consisting of three parts, allegorical representations of the notions of Unity, Freedom, and Security (Figure 4.7). Apparently, they were meant to indicate the ideal state of Amsterdam as hopefully largely realized at the time. It remained an unfulfilled dream. In the first years of the twentieth century, the paintings were sold to the board of the Peace Palace in The Hague, where the three segments now hang on another ceiling as an allegory of the Triumph of Peace, another still unfulfilled dream, now for the international realm at large. In the seventeenth century, the burgomaster also had other artworks in his house. One sculpture, prominently displayed, showed him as a consul of the Roman Republic, a reference that was repeatedly used by the Amsterdam elite (Vis, 2010). Several residents also had cabinets of curiosities and arts at home that referred to the distant places where they traded. Another burgomaster, who was an expert in cartography, had a collection of materials on Russia and Siberia where he had earlier travelled. In this way, the Canal District reflected the globe, appropriate context for its cosmopolitan population.

A Place of Power through the Ages

Fernand Braudel, long-time doyen of studies of the world economy, saw its emergence as the fruit of the organizing power of a succession of temporary

Figure 4.7 | Gerard de Lairesse, *Triomf der Vrede, Allegorie van de Handelsvrijheid (The Triumphant Victory of Peace, an Allegory of the Freedom of Trade)*, 1672. An Amsterdam burgomaster commissioned these paintings for his private residence on the Herengracht to express his political philosophy. From left to right, they represent Unity, Security, and Freedom.

Source: Photograph by Erik Smits, property of the Carnegie Foundation, Kunstcollectie Vredespaleis, reprinted with permission.

dominant cities, one of them Amsterdam. But, in the specific case of Amsterdam, he also emphasized the importance of the republic as a whole. He saw "this quarrelsome and jealous bunch of cities" as subject to the law of the beehive, which obliged them to combine their efforts and cooperate in commercial and industrial activity. Together, they formed a power bloc (Braudel, 1984: 180).

The Dutch "city-region state" was, in the end, an internationally recognized covenant between provincial delegates of clusters of cities and some nobles. Cities were mutually related economically through links between local clusters of investors, merchants, and manufacturers and through cooperative institutions to acquire common material benefits in domestic and international markets. Politically, cities were participants in the production of agreements through exhaustive negotiations on common domestic and international aims and the division of obligations (mostly taxes) needed for their realization. Economically, the republic's main aim was continued dominance as a commercial centre. All this needed sufficient military capability to guard the territory and to enforce economic interests. Amsterdam was by far the most important city of the Dutch Republic, and its voice weighed heavily in the republic's decisions.

The Canal District was primarily a very privileged residential milieu for the well-to-do in Amsterdam. It was situated in the immediate vicinity of the sites where vital political and business decisions were made: the town hall, the bourse, and also the headquarters of the East India and the West Indies Companies. Residents of the Canal District were frequent visitors to all these institutions. But major decisions for Amsterdam were made in The Hague as well, and inhabitants of the Canal District or their family members were present there also in their numbers.

The Canal District was, therefore, a prominent location in the beehive. Here was an unusually large concentration of rich and influential people who retained a bourgeois character, originating as they did from a merchant class. There was a nobility present in the republic generally and even to some extent in Holland. But its role was limited compared to what was normal in Europe. Nonetheless, noble status symbols, such as titles to an estate, were highly appreciated among the inhabitants of the Canal District. Still, these accoutrements did not wipe out their original merchant traits altogether (Prak, 2002: 149–50).

In the seventeenth century, the creation of a site like the Canal District, a large more or less homogeneous residential milieu for the well-to-do within an existing city, was an exceptional series of ventures at the time. The Ringstrasse in Vienna and Haussmann's boulevards in Paris were realized much later, from 1850 on (Figure 4.8). They were larger, but they were comparable with the Canal District in other respects. They also aimed to attract privileged population groups by offering spacious private residences, or the plots to realize them, and an attractive surrounding public environment close to the city centre. Projects were executed by means of careful manipulation of land ownership, high prices, and some minimal set of building rules to guarantee sufficient commonalities in appearance and preclude unnecessary hindrances.

Figure 4.8 | Gustave Caillebotte, *Paris Street in Rainy Weather,* 1877. A bourgeois living in a cityscape recently realized by Haussmann close to Gare St. Lazare.
Source: Collection Art Institute of Chicago. Public domain.

There was certainly a demand for this kind of residential environment in the city of Amsterdam at the time. But it was perhaps particularly its patrician city government that made the difference and brought the site in its new form to life. During the period that the Canal District was created, the imperial and royal administrations in Vienna and Paris mainly realized projects on the outskirts of these cities, induced by the presumed requirements of court life. New residential development on already largely occupied land for the upper bourgeois classes generally did not have a high priority (Girouard, 1985: 151–80). In Amsterdam, the opposite was true. It resulted in a relatively large, extraordinary urban design that has pretty well withstood the test of time for 400 years.

PART II

EVOLUTION

chapter five

Bourgeois Homes:
The Elite Spaces of the Canal District, 1600–1910

JAN HEIN FURNÉE AND CLÉ LESGER

Over the last centuries and up to the present, the Amsterdam Canal District has been widely known as an archetypical elite quarter. But to what extent did the Amsterdam elites actually settle there? How did their residential patterns evolve over time? Did Amsterdam's elites make up and act as a homogeneous group: spatially, economically, socially, and culturally? Although scholars have already accumulated considerable knowledge on the inhabitants of the Canal District, we are only at the start of a more systematic, spatial approach that covers the longer term.

This chapter maps and analyses the spatial distribution of the 250 wealthiest residents of Amsterdam from the early seventeenth to the early twentieth century. It will demonstrate to what extent, when, and why they moved from the old medieval part of the city via the western part of the Canal District to the famous Golden Bend and, from the second half of the nineteenth century, also settled in the newly developed quarters around the Vondelpark and Frederiksplein. For the mid-nineteenth century, when primary sources are more abundant, it takes a closer look at the residential patterns within the Canal District. By linking fiscal and occupational data on 6,000 male tax-paying electors to a recently created geographic information system (GIS) database, it is possible to visualize with greater detail than ever before the socio-economic landscape of Amsterdam in the mid-nineteenth century.

The striking variation in wealth and socio-economic position within the Canal District, to the level of individual building blocks, will lead us to the chapter's second main question: to what extent did residents of the Canal District form an integrated social and cultural elite? To answer this question, the chapter turns to the social and cultural networks within the Canal District, especially to the city's most prominent social and cultural associations where the Amsterdam upper classes could meet. The analysis will demonstrate how social and cultural associations seem to have played a substantial role in both affirming and bridging fiscal and occupational class divisions, even to the level of neighbours.

Elites, Residential Preferences, and the Construction of the Canal District

In early modern cities – as in most cities at any time in history – wealth, power, and prestige were unevenly distributed. Usually, a strong position in one respect went hand in hand with a high position in others. Economic success, for example, could be used to gain political influence, which in turn led to greater prestige and also to additional economic benefits. Wealth, power, and prestige often came together in the hands of a distinct upper class. There were some positions in society that carried considerable prestige and power but without significant economic means – clergymen are a case in point. Nevertheless, these remained exceptions. In general, wealth, power, and prestige did indeed converge in a relatively small upper class. That was also the case in Amsterdam.

This upper layer of society was obviously the best equipped to realize its residential preferences. Going down the social ladder, Amsterdam households were more and more forced to settle for homes that were left after those with more resources had made their choices. In the most general sense, we need to think of residential preferences as driven by the quest for assets that improve the quality of life. Among these is the quality of the home itself, as reflected among others in size, degree of comfort, and state of repair, but also the "externalities." Johnston (1984: 164) defines these as "aspects of the local environment which contribute to the quality of life of an individual, family or household resident there, but which are not purchased directly by them." More

specifically, externalities have to do with things like a central location, a pleasant environment, and good accessibility.

In medieval and sixteenth-century Amsterdam, the main streets were Warmoesstraat and Nieuwendijk (see Map 5.1 for the location of these streets). These levees were not only access roads to the rural surroundings, but, together with Dam Square, they also enclosed the old inner harbour of the city. The position of the Nieuwendijk was undermined when the development of a broad quay (Op 't Water / Damrak) cut it off from direct access to the water. Warmoesstraat on the other hand, until the end of the sixteenth century, continued to be the place of residence of the economic and political elite (van der Leeuw-Kistemaker, 1974). However, by that time the quality of life in the old centre of Amsterdam had seriously deteriorated. These were the years when the city's economy was booming, when tens of thousands of migrants settled in Amsterdam, and the population multiplied (Lesger, 2006). Around 1580, Amsterdam counted about 30,000 inhabitants; this number increased to more than 100,000 in 1622 and more than 200,000 in 1680 (van Leeuwen & Oeppen, 1993).

The economic and demographic growth put immense pressure on the available space. The city centre, where economic, political, and religious functions were concentrated, increasingly suffered from congestion. For the elites, the city centre therefore became less attractive as a residential area. The hustle and bustle disturbed the peace, and possibly they also wished to withdraw from the proximity of the large numbers of poor migrants who settled in the city and continued to do so during the seventeenth and

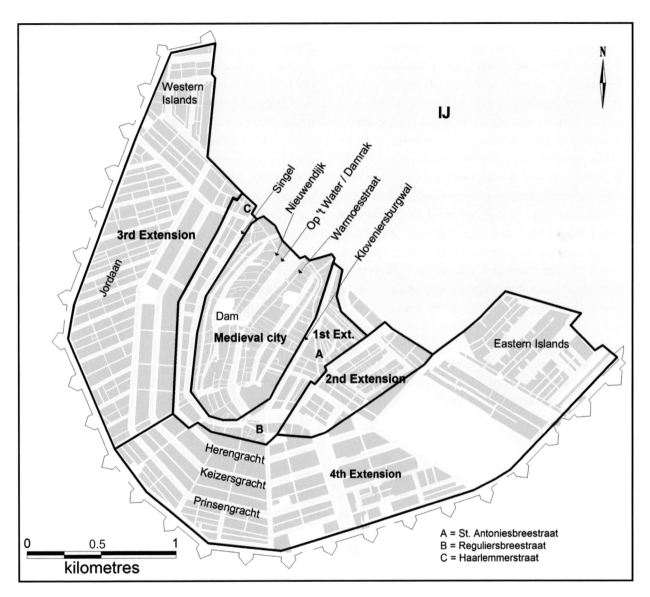

Map 5.1 | The medieval city and city extensions up to the mid-nineteenth century.
Source: Authors.

eighteenth centuries. Amsterdam, unlike many other cities in the Dutch Republic, did not bar poor migrants from the city. In the urban expansion that began in the last decades of the sixteenth century (see chapter 2 of this volume), we see the first evidence that the Amsterdam elites used their political influence and financial resources to create for themselves an agreeable and prestigious residential environment.

Thus, the three main streets leading from the old city gates into the First Extension (see Map 5.1) were meant to house wealthy Amsterdammers. The St. Antoniesbreestraat, Reguliersbreestraat, and Haarlemmer(bree)straat were considerably wider than the streets in the old city, and crafts using hammer, anvil, and fire were not allowed to settle there (Dudok van Heel, 1997: 126–8). The fact that these breestraten (literally meaning "wide streets") in the longer term did not develop into the favourite residential domain of the elite had to do with the availability of a more attractive alternative. During the First Extension (1578–86), the former moats (Singel, Kloveniersburgwal) came to lie within the fortifications. These broad canals offered space for large and prestigious town houses, provided an unobstructed view over the water, and, important in a period when merchandise was often stored in the merchants' homes, also provided easy access by both water and road (Figure 5.1). The attractiveness of these canals as a residential environment was enhanced further when the quays from the beginning of the seventeenth century were planted with trees (Abrahamse, 2019: 384–5).

In the large-scale Third Extension (1610–13) and Fourth Extension (1655–63), the success of former moats as an attractive living environment for the elite was replicated in the Canal District. This Canal District was planned as a zone of high-quality housing surrounding the medieval part of the city. Consequently, its inhabitants benefitted from the vicinity of downtown, without being too much burdened by negative externalities like crowds, stench, and other things that detracted from the distinguished and stately residential environment they wanted for themselves. In the Canal District, degradation was prevented by an ordinance that forbade filling the courtyards with buildings. In 1615, the town council explicitly decided that the Herengracht was to be built with beautiful houses for the wealthy. Finally, in 1618 a total ban was issued on the establishment of industries causing inconvenience or danger (fire hazard), not only on Herengracht but also on the other canals in the Canal District (Taverne, 1978: 165–8; Abrahamse, 2019: 78–80). There can be no doubt that the Canal District was meant to be a quiet and attractive living environment for the Amsterdam elites. In addition, ample financial resources allowed the inhabitants to construct the mansions that to this day have preserved their air of wealth and good taste.

Residences of the Amsterdam Elite, c. 1600–1910

The question that occupies us here is when and to what extent the elite found their home along the main canals. To answer that question, we determined the addresses of the fiscal elite for 1631, 1742, 1853, and 1910. Concretely, for each of these years

Figure 5.1 │ Large houses on Kloveniersburgwal.
Source: Stadsarchief Amsterdam, Beeldbank 010097011181.

Table 5.1 Number of elite households and mean taxed wealth, 1631

Location	Number of households	Mean taxed wealth (guilders)
Inner city	126	106,278
Extensions 1 + 2	50	94,929
Extension 3	76	108,092
Total	**252**	**104,573**

Source: Frederiks, J.G., & Frederiks, P.J. (Eds.). (1890). *Kohier van den tweehonderdsten penning voor Amsterdam en onderhoorige plaatsen over 1631.* Amsterdam: Ten Brink en De Vries.

we collected data on the location of the 250 Amsterdam households with the highest tax assessment.

For 1631, we have used a tax of 0.5 per cent on the total value of an individual's wealth. To put the data in perspective, it is good to know that, in the 1580s, several years after Amsterdam had taken the side of the Dutch Revolt, the richest inhabitant of Amsterdam, the mayor and merchant Dirck Jansz. Graaf, had assets worth some 140,000 guilders. Besides him, there were only four to five Amsterdammers with assets worth 100,000 guilders or more. By 1631, this number had increased to ninety-seven, and a quarter of them (twenty-four taxpayers) were even taxed for a wealth of 200,000 guilders or more. At the top of the fiscal elite, we find the heirs of the very wealthy merchant and mayor, Jacob Poppen. They are valued at 500,000 guilders. Following at the top were Guillielmo Bartholotti and Balthasar Coymans, each with a taxed wealth of 400,000 guilders (Frederiks & Frederiks, 1890; van Dillen, 1970: 310–12).

Additional information makes clear that their wealth was considerably higher than the fiscal records suggest. Jacob Poppen, for instance, had a fortune of 920,000 guilders, and Bartholotti at his death in 1658 left his heirs no less than 1.2 million guilders (van Dillen, 1970: 311; Zandvliet, 2006: xi). Since the difference between fiscal and actual wealth seems to have counted for all tax payers, the data from the 1631 tax nevertheless give a good impression of the composition of the group of richest Amsterdammers. Because the tax register provides information about their addresses, it is also possible to determine their spatial distribution over the city. This information is summarized in Table 5.1. To put the wealth of this fiscal elite into perspective, it should be compared with the nominal daily wage of about 1.5 guilders for skilled craftsmen (Soltow & van Zanden, 1998: table 3.9; Nusteling, 1985: appendix 5.1).

From Table 5.1 and Map 5.2 it is clear that the newly constructed Canal District, and especially the

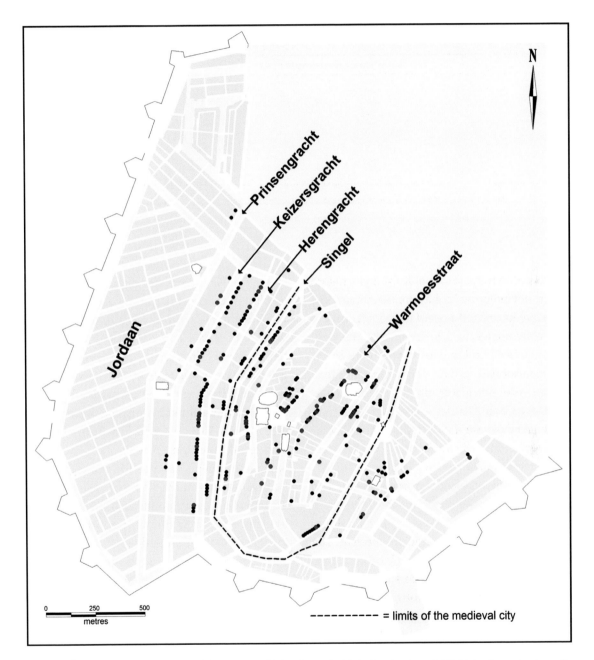

Map 5.2 | Residential geography of the 250 wealthiest households in Amsterdam, 1631 (richest quarter in red).
Source: Authors.

Table 5.2 Number of elite households and mean taxed yearly income, 1742

Location	Number of households	Mean taxed income (guilders)
Inner city	25	13,160
Extensions 1 + 2	11	15,636
Extension 3	106	15,179
Extension 4	110	17,441
Total	**252**	**15,986**

Source: Oldewelt, W.F.H. (Ed.). (1945). *Kohier van de personeele quotisatie te Amsterdam over het jaar 1742*. Amsterdam: Genootschap Amstelodamum.

spacious parcels on the east side of Keizersgracht and the west side of Herengracht, was popular among the elite. Nevertheless, in 1631 no less than 50 per cent of the richest citizens still lived in the medieval part of the city and another 20 per cent in the extensions on the east side (Extensions 1 and 2). Moreover, the mean taxed wealth in the inner city was only slightly lower than that in the Canal District. All in all, it is safe to conclude that the development of the Canal District did not pull the entire elite in one swoop to this new and coveted residential area.

Around 1660, the urban government decided to extend the city once more (the "Fourth Extension"). Part of the plan was the extension of the very successful Canal District in an upgraded form. The quality of the environment was, among other things, enhanced by the introduction of side streets allowing for the construction of coach houses and stables; it also kept through traffic away from the quays along the main canals. The famous Golden Bend of the Herengracht is part of this Fourth Extension of the

city and is reputed for being the domain of the wealthiest citizens.

Data for elite residential patterns in 1742, our next snapshot, pertains to c. 13,300 Amsterdam households assessed for annual incomes (not wealth) of 600 guilders or more. They made up the richest 23 per cent of the Amsterdam households (Lesger, 2005: table 13). The highest annual income (70,000 guilders) was registered for the widow of the eminent banker and merchant Andries Pels. Two burgomasters, Dirk Trip and Lieve Geelvinck, and the nobleman Gerardus Wassenaer were assessed for an income of 50,000 guilders, and, at the bottom of the top 252, we find 88 households taxed for an annual income of 10,000 guilders.

Table 5.2 and Map 5.3 provide information on the spatial distribution of the Amsterdam elite in 1742. There is no doubt that, in the long run, the top 250 did prefer to live in the Canal District, especially in the newest and southernmost part of it, developed after the mid-seventeenth century. But the older

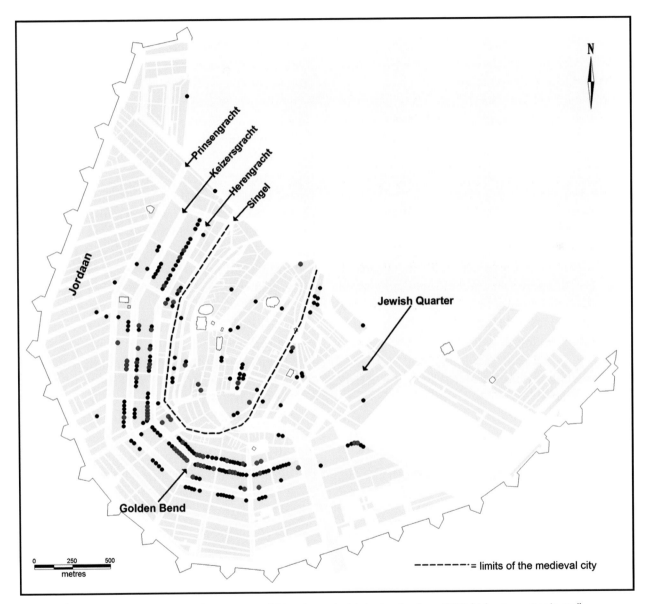

Map 5.3 | Residential geography of the 250 wealthiest households in Amsterdam, 1742 (richest quarter in red).
Source: Authors.

western section of the Canal District still housed a similar number of the richest Amsterdammers. Compared to 1631, by 1742 the inner city, along with the earliest extensions on the east side, had lost their appeal to the rich almost entirely.

Since the 1742 tax data includes information on occupations, it can be established that those actively engaged in trade, shipping, and related activities often preferred to live in the city centre and the western (older) section of the Canal District. These areas were close to the harbour, close to the tax office where merchants had to pay import and export duties, and close to institutions like the bourse and exchange bank (both on Dam Square). By comparison, the southern Canal District – and especially the famous Golden Bend – was to a large extent home to persons living off interest and members of the local government. This area was also where Dirk Trip, Lieve Geelvinck, and the widow of Andries Pels lived.

After 1742, the residential geography of Amsterdam's wealthiest classes did not change for a long time. The Dutch economy had difficulty keeping up with that of neighbouring countries, and Amsterdam went through a period of stagnation and decline. The urban economy was especially hit when Holland, in the early nineteenth century, became part of the French Empire and was all but cut off from the sea. Even after the French had left, in 1815, the economic situation remained precarious, to say the least. It was only after the mid-nineteenth century that recovery slowly set in, but until the end of the century large parts of the population lived in dire poverty.

In these circumstances, it should not surprise us that the new city extensions of the 1860s, the first ones since the second half of the seventeenth century, were meant to house the upper classes. It was only from around 1870 that property developers started to build houses to accommodate the growing middle classes, with the working classes and the poor mostly being thrown back on housing in the poor and run-down parts of the medieval and early modern city.

Since wealthy citizens could now also choose a house in the newly developed elite quarters beyond the seventeenth-century city, the Canal District lost part of its appeal. Data on the residential addresses of the 250 inhabitants with the highest taxable income in 1910 shows that the new nineteenth- and early twentieth-century elite quarters were highly coveted by the city's elite (Table 5.3 and Map 5.4). More than half of the 250 high-income households lived there. By contrast, the oldest, western part of the Canal District (Third Extension) only housed 35 elite households (83 per cent of them living on Herengracht and Keizersgracht), and the southeastern part (Fourth Extension) was home to 70 elite households (86 per cent of them on Herengracht and Keizersgracht). In terms of income, the households in the new extensions lagged behind those in the Fourth Extension (including the Golden Bend), but their income was higher than that of the 35 households in the Third Extension.

The attraction of the new elite quarters has no doubt to do with the quality and modernity of the housing and with positive externalities like the proximity of the Vondelpark for the inhabitants of Vondelstraat and Van Eeghenstraat and the Crystal Palace–like Paleis voor Volksvlijt (1864) near Sarphatistraat and Sarphatikade. But the pull of the new elite quarters had also

Table 5.3 Number of elite households and mean taxed yearly income, 1910

Location	Number of households	Mean taxed income (guilders)
Inner city	5	56,560
Extensions 1 + 2	–	–
Extension 3	35	53,831
Extension 4	70	75,903
New extensions	140	61,704
Total	**250**	**64,475**

Note: Four households in the Plantage are counted with the new extensions since that part of the pre-modern city was only developed after the mid-nineteenth century.
Sources: Bijvoegsel tot de Nederlandsche Staatscourant, 15 juni 1910, 8–14; City Archives Amsterdam, archief 5178 (Archief Secretarie, afdeling belastingen), inv.nrs. 3953–4119.

to do with the decreasing supply of bourgeois homes in the canal belt. After all, the economic expansion generated a large demand for office space. The growth of a central business district was especially pronounced in the old city, but between 1869 and 1909 the canal belt also lost almost 11 per cent of its private houses and 26 per cent of its population (Wagenaar, 1990: 148, table 5.1). Moreover, public transport, the infilling of a number of canals, and partial reconstruction of the street network greatly improved the accessibility of the central business district, especially for those living in the newly developed elite quarters near Vondelpark and the Paleis voor Volksvlijt.

In a detailed study of the early occupants of the Vondelstraat, Bruin and Schijf (1984) found no evidence that prominent Amsterdammers left the Canal District because they felt its prestige and standing were deteriorating. Instead, for the mid-1880s, the authors suggest that some of them decided to live in

these new areas because they could not afford a large house on Herengracht or Keizersgracht. Among them were the younger scions of elite families, still starting up their careers, and widows and old age pensioners who could no longer keep a large house on Herengracht or Keizersgracht. Ultimately, Bruin and Schijf argue, the Canal District remained the most desired location for the Amsterdam elites.

By 1910, however, things appeared to have changed: the wealthiest citizens no longer seemed to have a preference for the Canal District. More than half of them lived in the newly developed elite quarters, and a tentative analysis of their age reveals that they were only slightly younger than those who lived in the canal belt (on average 52.6 years as opposed to 57.5 years). Nor was the religious mix very different from the one in the Third and Fourth Extensions. Compared to the Canal District, the nineteenth- and early twentieth-century city extensions housed fewer

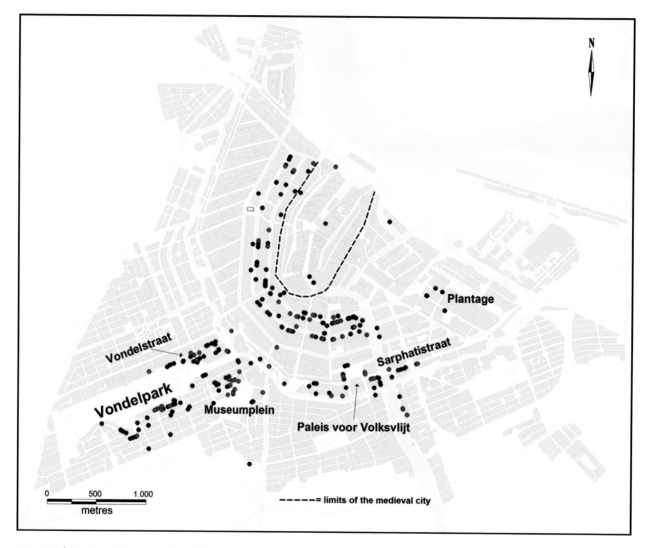

Map 5.4 | Residential geography of the 250 wealthiest households in Amsterdam, 1910 (richest quarter in red).
Source: Authors.

of the ancient families, those who during the Ancien Régime and the first half of the nineteenth century had dominated urban politics and social life. Given that many of these patricians lived in houses along the canals that were handed over from one generation to the next, this observation should not come as a surprise. Nevertheless, it is clear that by 1910 the Canal District was no longer the only habitat for Amsterdam's wealthy upper class.

Social and Cultural Integration within the Canal District

Between the seventeenth and the early twentieth centuries, the Canal District attracted Amsterdam's wealthiest citizens – even if it took a considerable time before the medieval part of the city lost its attraction – and in the second half of the nineteenth century some of them shifted to newly developed, high-end quarters. Obviously, these richest citizens did not inhabit the Canal District on their own. In most early modern cities, much more than today, rich and poor often lived quite close to each other (Sjoberg, 1960: 95–103). In Amsterdam, this socio-economic mix continued throughout the nineteenth century, in contrast to many foreign cities where suburbanization or city beautification à la Haussmann strongly increased residential segregation (Lesger, van Leeuwen, & Vissers, 2013). What were the socio-economic characteristics of the urban landscape inhabited by the wealthiest residents of the Canal District? Who were their neighbours, and to which extent did they form a socially integrated Canal District elite?

A larger database of all 6,200 male electors for the local council, tied to residential addresses and including tax assessments, allows us to visualize the socio-economic landscape of mid-nineteenth-century Amsterdam with great detail (Map 5.5). The map confirms that the Canal District attracted and concentrated most of the richest inhabitants of the city and that the average fiscal position of citizens living in the Canal District towered high above citizens living in the poorest and nearest districts: the Jordaan, the Jewish Quarter, and the Devil's Corner immediately north of the Golden Bend (for location, see Map 5.3). However, the differences in wealth *between* the four main canals are striking as well: with only a few exceptions, we find no substantial wealth on the Singel and the Prinsengracht. Furthermore, even the elitist Herengracht and Keizersgracht show remarkable differences in wealth between the west and east sides of both canals and between the northern and southern sides of the Keizersgracht. At closer inspection, we find huge tax assessments in the Golden Bend and the southern part of the Keizersgracht – the habitat of prominent aristocratic and patrician families such as Luden, Labouchère, Van Loon, Borski, and Van der Hoop (Figure 5.2). But moving further to the west of the Herengracht and Keizersgracht, tax rates tend to drop and rise quite erratically, and we find a considerable variety of inhabitants from distinct socio-economic strata.

Perhaps this relatively large variety in wealth within the Canal District should not surprise us, even if the Canal District tends to invoke an image of homogeneity. After all, if we take a walk on the canals today, or look at historical photographs or drawings, we can observe a considerable variety in house sizes and degrees of architectural splendour. It raises the question of how the richest residents of individual parts of the Canal District dealt with the often quite different socio-economic position of their immediate neighbours. What was the nature of the social networks of the elite residents of the Canal District?

In the mid-nineteenth century, social, cultural, and political life in Dutch cities was characterized by an exceptionally vibrant urban associational culture. Tracing back to the early modern period and especially to the "associational mania" in the late eighteenth century, many cities counted a large and fast-growing number of active associations (De Vries, 2006a, 2006b). In Amsterdam, with about 220,000 inhabitants in 1850, a local address book listed twenty-one social and cultural associations and fifteen religious, philanthropic, and self-help associations, while a contemporary overview of philanthropical institutions listed more than fifty philanthropic associations (*Algemeen Adresboek*, 1853; Calisch, 1851). We may safely assume that, by mid-nineteenth century, Amsterdam counted at least a hundred associations: one for every 2,200 residents and one for every 600 adult men.

Although the size of the associations greatly varied, the average level of participation was substantial. As most associations excluded females and boys under the age of twenty-one, we may conclude that about 9 per cent of the male adult population joined at least one of the twenty social clubs and cultural associations that we have studied for this chapter. Among the local electorate, the level of participation was about 36 per cent of the 6,200 electors. The importance of club life among Amsterdam citizens is

also demonstrated by the high level of double membership. About a quarter of all members (1,400 out of 5,400) participated in more than one of the selected clubs and associations, up to a maximum of seven clubs (and a total of about 7,300 memberships). Among the local electorate, the level of double membership reached 37 per cent. In the second half of the nineteenth century, the number of associations in Amsterdam accelerated: as the population expanded from 220,000 to about 510,000 in 1900, no less than 1,318 new associations were granted formal recognition, the majority of them after 1885.

How did the wealthiest citizens of the Canal District relate to these associations? To what extent did they socialize with their less affluent neighbours in these clubs and associations? The two most exclusive clubs in nineteenth-century Amsterdam were the gentlemen's club De Munt and the social ball association Casino (De Vries, 1986: 81–93). Map 5.6 shows the residential geography of the clubs' memberships. It suggests that these two clubs confirmed and firmly established the elite status of the members. For the extremely rich inhabitants on the Golden Bend and further down the Herengracht, De Munt, housed just above the Golden Bend, formed a welcome gentlemen's refuge that was much more homogeneous in composition than their residential neighbourhood. Even the well-to-do merchants living in the northwestern part of the canal belt were strikingly absent on its membership list and probably not very welcome. Just slightly more inclusive were the social balls of Casino, the most important marriage market for the top elite of Amsterdam. At these social balls, the richest inhabitants of the northern part of the

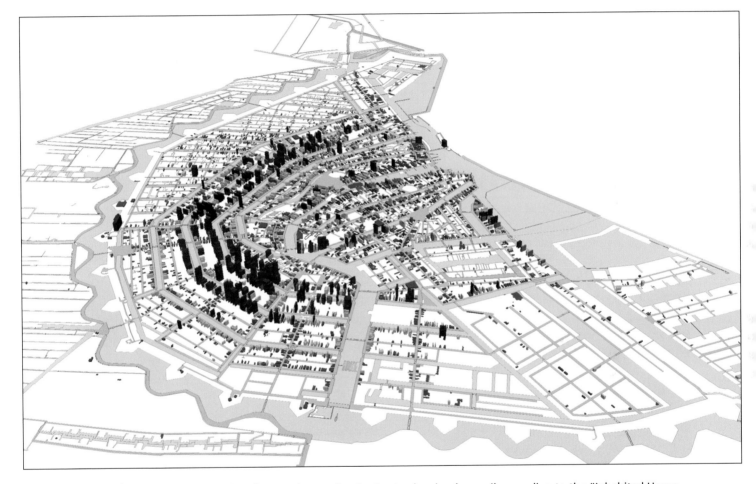

Map 5.5 | Residential geography of 6,200 electors for the Amsterdam local council, according to the "Inhabited House Duty," a tax raised on external signs of wealth, 1853. The heights of the columns correspond with the absolute tax levels, ranging from the lowest quartile in blue to the highest quartile in red.
Source: Johan Feikens and Hans Mol, Fryske Akademy, reprinted with permission.

Figure 5.2 | The Gouden Bocht (Golden Bend) of the Herengracht, c. 1850–70.
Source: Stadsarchief Amsterdam, Beeldbank 010094001536.

Herengracht and Keizersgracht happily joined the elite from the Golden Bend. And they set themselves emphatically apart from immediate neighbours who did not quite make the grade.

However, not all clubs and associations were so exclusive. Two of Amsterdam's most famous and prominent social and cultural associations at the time – Felix Meritis and Doctrina et Amicitia – were much more inclusive. Felix Meritis (Happy through Merit) on the Keizersgracht, established in 1777, was especially popular for its splendid aristocratic concerts, but also for its lecture series on commerce and literature and for its drawing school. Doctrina et Amicitia (Learning and Friendship), established in 1788 on the Kalverstraat near the bourse, offered lectures, a reading room, and other pleasures of a distinguished gentlemen's club. Based on an analysis of 1853 membership lists, Map 5.7 shows how both of these societies established and integrated relatively broad social networks of elite members, predominantly living on the canals yet with different degrees of external wealth. In some cases, it appears as if some neighbours collectively decided to join either Felix or Doctrina. Quite a few canal dwellers joined both societies, granting them a special position in their living quarter as social brokers between both elite formations. In fact, this practice also applied to most of the wealthiest members of Casino and De Munt, who also joined Felix Meritis and, in some cases, Doctrina. Evidently, they liked to set themselves apart as an exclusive elite on some occasions, but in a different context they also sought to bridge the social distance towards some of their immediate neighbours on the canals.

In general, Felix Meritis was socially more exclusive than Doctrina. But their members did not live in entirely different social networks. Several prominent cultural associations offered a platform to forge new relations on the basis of common cultural preference across social formations based on primarily socio-economic positions. This is, for instance, the case in the reading society Leesmuseum on the Rokin, established in 1800, and the art society Arti et Amicitiae, established in 1841, almost next door. In these two cultural associations, we find many neighbours living on the canal belt who did not belong to the same networks of Felix or Doctrina, but who met each other in the reading room or at the famous art events in Arti, where members exchanged their own print works on long tables. Perhaps, on the basis of shared interests in art and literature, the most wealthy and the less affluent Canal District neighbours would encounter each other in some of the more inclusive associations; they would respect each other for their cultural knowledge; and they might, occasionally, continue their conversations at their front doors on the canal – even if a formal house visit or a play date for the children was out of the question.

Conclusion

The residential history of the Canal District displays features that are common to the residential preferences of the urban well-to-do in general and also some features that are specific to Amsterdam. In times of urban economic and demographic growth, pressure on the available space in the inner city

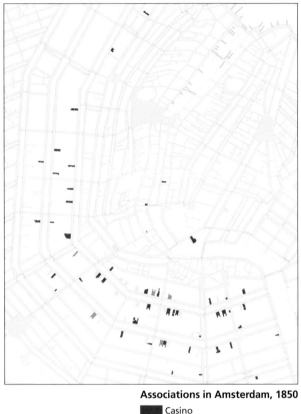

Associations in Amsterdam, 1850

◼ Casino
◼ Casino and De Munt
◻ De Munt

Associations in Amsterdam, 1850

◼ Doctrina
◼ Felix Meritis
◼ Felix Meritis and Doctrina

Map 5.6 │ Residential geography of the members of the gentlemen's club De Munt and of the social ball association Casino, 1853.
Source: Johan Feikens and Hans Mol, Fryske Akademy, reprinted with permission.

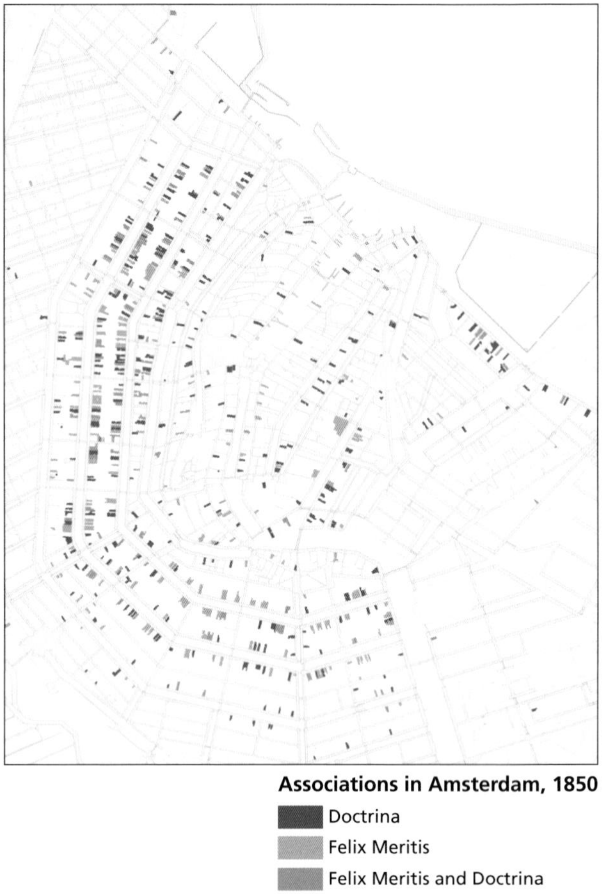

Map 5.7 │ Residential geography of the members of the gentlemen's clubs/cultural associations Felix Meritis and Doctrina et Amicitia, 1853.
Source: Johan Feikens and Hans Mol, Fryske Akademy, reprinted with permission.

increases. Elites would therefore be inclined to move to new and more pleasant surroundings. But, at the same time, the important political and economic institutions should remain within easy reach. In early modern London, for example, this resulted in a spatial separation of businessmen and patricians. The first, requiring easy access to the City, the docks, and the warehouses, both before and after the Great Fire of 1666, remained in and near the City and had to take the hustle and bustle for granted (Thorold, 1999: 18–19). The patricians, having other sources of income and closely linked to the court, moved to the suburban West End. In other European capitals, the court also formed the nucleus of elite quarters.

In Amsterdam, the economic centre of the Dutch Republic and, from the nineteenth century, capital of the Kingdom of the Netherlands, there was no court and no nobility. Business was king, and the elite drew its wealth from trade, shipping, and finance. Here, too, the elite wished to leave the inner city when, from the late sixteenth century, the economy and population entered a phase of rapid expansion. But, at the same time, their businesses required them to be near vital institutions like the bourse and the exchange bank and close to the docks and warehouses. Since there was no court in Amsterdam, a clear focal point for the new elite quarter was missing, which opened the possibility of an elite residential zone. The Canal District was a perfect solution to the demands of the elite: it allowed them to live in a pleasant and prestigious environment, but its curved shape surrounding the inner city also allowed for fast and easy access from all parts of the Canal District to the institutions and facilities located in the inner city. And those who temporarily wanted to flee the city built secondary homes in the nearby countryside, just like the merchants and businessmen living in the City of London did.

Focusing on the social context in which the top 250 wealthiest households lived in the middle of the nineteenth century, we have been able to demonstrate with much more precision than before that, in terms of external wealth, the social composition of the Canal District was considerably more heterogeneous than we had thought. These findings have raised a new and intriguing question: how did the richest residents of individual parts of the Canal District deal with the often quite different socio-economic position of their immediate neighbours? To what extent did citizens living in this area form an integrated "Canal District elite"? On the basis of quantitative research on social clubs and cultural associations in combination with GIS, we have been able to demonstrate that – also in spatial terms – social and cultural associations both affirmed and bridged socio-economic differences in the Canal District.

Acknowledgments

We are very much indebted to Hans Mol and Johan Feikens from the Fryske Akademy for linking the data on the 1853 electors and the nineteenth-century associations to their GIS database and making the visualizations. For more information, see www.hisgis.nl/amsterdam. We also wish to thank our MA students in the 2007–2011 seminars for their help in compiling the databases on clubs and societies and the 1910 income tax. Mrs. Caitlin Schouten kindly provided us with data for 1631 and 1742.

chapter six

The Architectural Essence of the Canal District: Past and Present

FREEK SCHMIDT

The "outstanding universal value" of the Canal District is specifically recognized as a seventeenth-century monument of urban design, a well-preserved "unique and complex urban landscape" (UNESCO, 2009: 106–7). Although its four centuries of history are acknowledged, along with the fact that "the series of almost 4,000 listed buildings – houses and warehouses, churches, charitable institutions and almshouses – and hundreds of historic bridges within the 'property' show great architectural diversity" (94), the protection of the original urban layout is accentuated. The Dutch Monuments Act and the Amsterdam municipal by-law, as well as additional protective measures and regulations, are in place to protect the Canal District and its buildings.

To safeguard the revered "spirit" of the Canal District, it is important to understand what defines or determines its architecture and to appreciate the character of its buildings and their transformation over time. This chapter focuses on the varied architecture of the individual buildings that together make up the Canal District's colourful palette of streetscapes as it exists today. The chapter presents a re-reading of four centuries of designing, building, and changing to uncover, out of the multilayered evolution and multiple architectural idiosyncrasies, the essence of a unique monument. It is argued that this essence provides the basis for future development and architectural projects, while respecting the district's monumental status. The vital permanence of the district owes much to the eclectic mixture of its architecture, the product of four centuries of the changing needs, uses, and tastes of Amsterdam's inhabitants. In a chronological exploration of the Canal District's architecture and how its design style was appreciated over time, this chapter stresses how the district can be regarded as an urban artefact that has evolved constantly to become the dynamic monument of a living culture it is today.

Establishing Basic Formulae

The basic facts about the creation of the Canal District are fairly well known (see also chapter 2 of this volume). The ring of canals was constructed in steps, following decisions taken by the municipal government in 1610–13 and 1662–63. The first stage of the Canal District, called the "Third Extension" because it was preceded by two smaller extensions only a few years earlier, saw the creation of the west side of the Herengracht, the Keizersgracht, and the Prinsengracht between the Brouwersgracht and the Leidsegracht, with the Jordaan developing alongside the three canals. Within a few years, houses were erected on almost all plots. The "Fourth Extension" allowed for growth and continued the three canals around the existing city, across the Amstel River, right up to the three eastern islands bordering the IJ.

The Third and Fourth Extensions had similar building regulations and distributed standard plots of slightly different widths, which were often bought in bundles and built with houses that sometimes varied from less than four to more than sixteen metres (less than thirteen to more than fifty-two feet) wide. The Prinsengracht became more of a workers' area, while the Keizersgracht and Herengracht were increasingly reserved for large and fancy houses, with crafts and industry being banned. Yet, the lavish houses built by leading families, such as those in the Golden Bend of the Herengracht, were exceptional. Most houses were constructed with basic materials like (imported) wooden beams and received rather straightforward brick facades, often built by local carpenters and masons, of whom some became influential and big contractors, while special ornaments in stone, often used to decorate gables, were crafted by stonemasons (Vlaardingerbroek, 2013). Only a few houses in the seventeenth century were built according to the designs of specialized artists and architects, a situation quite different from today, where the majority of projects are designed by professional architects or specialized engineers.

Initially, the variety of the Canal District architecture was rather limited. There were lots of brick stepped gables, decorated with stone details, while in the Fourth Extension an increase in variations of the neck-gable and bell-shaped gable appeared. One could say that the Canal District developed a specific brand of houses with a limited variety of facade types, directed by local and indigenous forces and circumstances. Through the application of ornament in stone or sometimes plaster or painted wood, often invented or copied by local craftsmen and artists, this basic vernacular could be differentiated, leading to more distinct and ostentatious facades of houses for the wealthiest inhabitants (Figures 6.1 and 6.2). With every generation during the seventeenth century, the homes in the district were upgraded. The number of vernacular facades increased, intermingled with the occasional more elaborate mansion, adding to the diversity of Canal District architecture.

When in 1625 the double house for the two sons of the original Flemish trader Balthasar I Coymans, the second richest man in Amsterdam at the time, was erected on the Keizersgracht 177 opposite the Westerkerk, it looked like nothing else in the city (Figure 6.3). It represented a break with all the characteristics of houses up to that point with its heightened cornice and its combination of Doric and Ionic pilasters. In 1625 Amsterdam, this house qualified as exotic, strange, and whimsical, both in its ordinance and its detailing. Today it is considered an important

Figure 6.1 | Keizersgracht 123, the "House with the Heads," built in 1622 for Nicolaas Sohier of French descent. This building was one of the richer detailed houses built in the Third Extension of 1610, featuring a red brick facade embellished with stone details and ornaments and a richly decorated stepped gable.
Source: Collectie Rijksdienst voor het Cultureel Erfgoed, object number 511.757. Photograph by Sergé Technau. Reprinted with permission.

Figure 6.2 | Keizersgracht 401, the "Huis Marseille," with a city view of Marseille inscribed on the gable stone based on a map of 1657, built c. 1660 after designs by the painter-architect Philips Vingboons. The sandstone facade has a richly decorated raised neck-gable with Corinthian pilasters under a segmental pediment.
Source: Author.

Figure 6.3 | Keizersgracht 177, the "Coymans Huis," built for the brothers Balthasar and Joan Coymans. According to Salomon de Bray's *Architectura Moderna ofte bouwinge van onsen tyt* (1631), the house was designed by the painter-architect Jacob van Campen in 1625. A better-known and more elaborate example of two houses built for two brothers, known as the "Trippenhuis" and designed by Justus Vingboons, was built 1656–62 on the Kloveniersburgwal in the older part of town.

Source: Collectie Rijksdienst voor het Cultureel Erfgoed, object number 511.758. Photograph by Sergé Technau. Reprinted with permission.

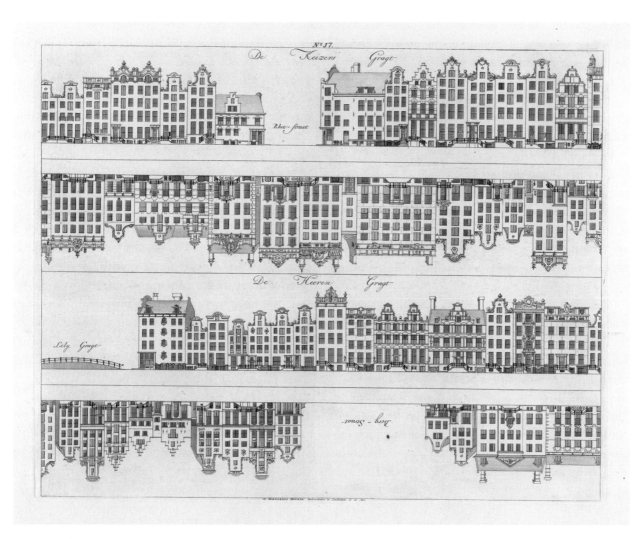

Figure 6.4 | Engraving from *Verzaameling van alle de huizen en prachtige geoubwen langs de keizers en heere-grachten der stadt Amsteldam...* (c. 1767), better known as the *Grachtenboek* (*Canal Book*), published by Bernardus Mourik after drawings by Caspar Philips Jacobsz. and others. The *Grachtenboek*, consisting of miniatures of all the street facades in twenty-four plates, shows the streetscapes of the Keizersgracht and Herengracht and their continuous transformation.
Source: Rijksmuseum Amsterdam, http://hdl.handle.net/10934/RM0001.COLLECT.337515. Reprinted with permission.

example of Dutch classicism, but in 1631 it was, according to the painter, architect, and critic Salomon de Bray, a hallmark of modern architecture (Schmidt, 2009). It displays four centuries of building activity: an eighteenth-century fenestration and a nineteenth-century mezzanine in style, with an entrance and internal organization transformed to house a school and offices in the twentieth century.

By the end of the seventeenth century, the Canal District may have looked briefly like a new town, just completed, in which the many facades of brick, with their original crossbar windows and shutters, made an impression of uniformity. But soon this image was replaced by one of continuous transformation: new sash windows were introduced, replacing the original wooden crossbar frames with partly leaded glass and shutters. Many houses or facades were rebuilt in the eighteenth century, adding an extra floor and a raised cornice front or mezzanine, reverting the vertically oriented facades to horizontal, and adding extra features and special sculpted figures, coats of arms, or other sculpted references to the owners on top and plaques and sculpture around doorways and central bays. The degree to which the Canal District had evolved into an eighteenth-century cityscape by the 1770s is recorded in the spectacular engravings of the *Grachtenboek* (*Canal Book*), which show all the facades of the houses along the Herengracht and Keizersgracht between the Brouwersgracht and the Amstel River as they appeared then (Figure 6.4).

This evolution continued through the nineteenth century, when structural elements and heightened cornices became less ornate. Industrially produced glass in large panes facilitated the introduction of new window types, like Empire and T-windows. Due to changing modes of transportation, the appearance of the quays and their paving changed, and often the original single and double flight stoops and perrons were removed (and frequently reconstructed a century later). Surveying the present-day "streetscapes," we find that select parts of the Canal District are indeed still residential, as they were planned in the seventeenth century. But a change is also apparent, with other functions entering the area and introducing a more dynamic architectural development within the dictated framework. From a dominant residential area, especially along the Herengracht and Keizersgracht with houses that offered a home, office space, and some storage facilities, the later eighteenth and nineteenth centuries witnessed the introduction of office buildings and, along the Prinsengracht, warehouses and industrial buildings.

Continuous Transformation

Although it is customary to believe that failure to pursue architectural harmony within the Canal District is a modern phenomenon, it is in fact a returning one. In 400 years, there has not been one generation that did not leave behind new buildings in a variety of facades, ranging from traditional and harmonic interventions to utterly disharmonic innovations, while nondescript and mediocre works of architecture were also inserted. It is the natural way in which living urban landscapes tend to evolve, where exquisite interventions and experiments driven by individual architectural fancy and conspicuous behaviour alternate with less elaborate interventions, influenced by economy, sobriety, and sustainability. Among these, we see numerous structures being partially renovated, as well as houses being extended pragmatically rather than in an architecturally harmonious fashion. These deliberate breaks with tradition brought modernity to the Canal District. When the new quarters of the Felix Meritis cultural society was built around 1787 on the Keizersgracht 324 (Figure 6.5), the new building was anything but a harmonizing contribution to the Canal District in terms of form, scale, proportion, materials, and function (Schmidt, 2016: 241). Erected as a luxurious club of Amsterdam tradesmen and craftsmen for the advancement of trade, arts, and sciences that replaced four original houses, it was tailored to draw attention through contrast in a novel way. Even though this kind of classical architecture would eventually become the preferred style of distinction for the cultural and political elite, this intervention presents a deliberate and disharmonious break from the dominant architectural language of the Canal District. In fact, it can be considered a forerunner of later interventions that would also challenge the idea of the Canal District as a unified residential area with a common architectural language and grammar. Experimental interventions like Felix Meritis would subsequently be conducted within the Canal District at regular intervals. New compositions that did not harmonize in scale, form, proportion, ornamentation, materials, and function would continue, thus contributing to a dynamic

Figure 6.5 | Keizersgracht 324, the building for the cultural society Felix Meritis, built 1787–88 and designed by Jacob Otten Husly, prize winner of the international architectural competition for the new building. The building replaced four original houses. It forms a clear departure from the original character of buildings in the district, introducing a new kind of building with a different scale to the area. Notice the contrast with the probably slightly earlier facade of the house with the bell-shaped gable to the right.
Source: Collectie Rijksdienst voor het Cultureel Erfgoed, object number 321.980. Photograph by G.J. Dukker. Reprinted with permission.

Figure 6.6 | Herengracht 380–382, designed by architect A. Salm, 1888–90.
Source: Author.

process of architectural transformation within the original urban pattern of canals and blocks.

At regular intervals, contrasting interventions of new buildings, as well as small-scale makeovers of individual facades, would continue the transformation process throughout the nineteenth century. Later in the nineteenth century, the Canal District witnessed an increasing historical awareness and complexity in its approach to the existing fabric. Travellers were charmed by the picturesque aspects of the villages around the Zuiderzee, and in this artistic and often painterly vision of the later nineteenth century, Amsterdam became the Venice of the North, an almost forgotten but charming shadow of its glorious past. Architects and urban planners started noticing the Canal District as a unique piece of urban design around the same time that the dawning of a Second Golden Age seemed to revive the city's importance as a cosmopolite centre (Bakker, Kistemaker, van Neirop, Vroom, & Witteman, 2000). In new buildings, preferences for new modes of decoration, with exotic forms inspired by cultures that previously had not been integrated into Amsterdam's architecture, were increasingly applied to facades. Styles and ornaments associated with different nations, often afterwards labelled as neo-styles, were applied for their aesthetic appeal and the high quality of their craftsmanship and introduced a new sense of cosmopolite culture and consumerism, such as can be seen in the New York Life Insurance Company building (Keizersgracht 455, architect J. van Looy, 1891). The residence of the wealthy tobacco planter Jacob Nienhuys (Herengracht 380–382, architect A. Salm, 1888–90) was de-liberately planned to distinguish itself from the then popular Dutch Renaissance style and took inspiration from the French royal architecture of François I of the Loire Valley and William K. Vanderbilt's residence of 1879–81 on 5th Avenue in New York (van der Woud, 2001: 149; Figure 6.6).

In the early twentieth century, also as a result of Amsterdam's economic recovery and metropolitan ambitions, which in particular affected the city centre and traffic thoroughfares, the mostly residential Canal District witnessed an increasing interest for office and commercial space. Since then, varied and often conflicting ideas have shaped debates about its development and preservation. Companies arrived, building new structures, often in a scale that diverges from the general house type, with distinct facades boasting the success and cosmopolite ambitions of commercial business in tailor-made buildings. Along the canals, a variety of solutions were tried in which old elements were meant to harmonize with new ones, despite scale expansion and structural changes (Meurs, 2004: 81). Bank firms like Pierson & Co. (Herengracht 206–214, architects J.G. and A.D.N. van Gendt, 1917–18) built modern office buildings with facades that referred to the architecture of the seventeenth- and eighteenth-century patrician residences.

The Heritage Impulse

Parallel to these new buildings in both historically inspired and "modern" architectural styles, the unfolding of ideas about the heritage of the nineteenth century led to an awareness that rapid change was threatening the existing fabric of Amsterdam in its very essence. Artists, architects, intellectuals, and preservationists began to develop their aesthetics of contemporary urban design with reference to history. The image of the Canal District as we understand it today has been shaped particularly by nineteenth- and twentieth-century writers, cartographers, painters, architects, and urban planners, and it is their appreciation of the picturesque and monumental qualities that dominates our perception of heritage (Schmidt, 2012a: 221; 2012b: 59).

Many architects since the 1880s had the Canal District in mind when discussing the idea of a city designed according to a clearly conceived plan, or were inspired by Henry Havard's writings or Camilo Sitte's Der Städtebau nach seinen künstlerischen Grundsätzen (City Planning according to Architectural Principles; published in Vienna, 1889), for example, architect H.P. Berlage, who embraced a picturesque vision (van der Woud, 2001: 132). Alarmed by the speed and scale of attempts to change the historic inner city, groups of citizens united to form a countermovement, independent of the government's initiatives and policies of preservation. Thus, the heritage impulse entered a new phase in which a culture emerged of public debate and interest groups that focused on increasing aesthetic control over building activity in the historic inner city. Control went beyond simple building regulation. A number of architects held the opinion that the historical setting should inspire new interventions. This "conservative modernization," as formulated by C.B. Posthumus Meyjes, Jr. in 1916, meant applying the traditional ar-

chitectural rules of propriety, which at the time were quickly becoming ridiculed by anti-historical sentiments of the avant-garde. The Amsterdam government also undertook action by installing a Schoonheidscommissie (Aesthetics Committee) in 1922 and issuing the Monumentenverordening (Monument Ordinance) in 1927, along with other building regulations. In 1928, hundreds of buildings in the district were listed as special monuments of Dutch architecture simply on the basis of a general inventory of their outward appearance (Voorloopige lijst, 1928). Measures were taken to find ways to protect and "save" structures that were threatened with being sacrificed to commercial needs, infrastructural improvements, and a strong desire on the part of developers, planners, and architects to embrace modernity.

Partly as a reaction, and in close collaboration with both private and governmental, local, and national preservation societies and institutes, architectural practice also turned to reconstruction, which can be considered another kind of architectural activity that has greatly influenced the appearance of the Canal District as it is today. A high level of consensus existed among those involved, supporting the idea that the attraction of the Amsterdam cityscape could be largely attributed to the "lively silhouette" of its buildings (Meurs, 2000: 367). Adaptations should not ignore contemporary dynamics (372).

During those years, the architect Abel Antoon Kok was a prolific enthusiast, writing about the historic beauty of Amsterdam and its houses, and he led various reconstructive restorations (Beek, 1984). Kok's recipe to continue to build in the Canal District was basically a plea for craftsmanship and studying "the pure Amsterdam house, the 'volkskunst' [folk art] of between 1625 and 1675" (Kok, 1941: 194). Architects Albert Boeken, Jan de Meijer, and Willem Dudok expressed in 1940 how the individual houses and their continuing modernization reinforced the clear harmony of the urban plan (Meurs, 2000: 80, 373–5). Contemporary architecture could very well be integrated if the existing scale was observed, because the city manifested itself as the work of centuries, not of a particularly conserved era. More problematic interventions were those where mass, height, and width were threatening the subordination of building to block. Boeken (1940: 281) commented that "with large office buildings of the last half century the line has been crossed. The great office buildings ... with their large measurements crush the harmonic city image" ("Pas door de groote kantoorgebouwen van de laatste halve eeuw is de grens overschreden. De groote kantoorgebouwen ... verpletteren door hun grote afmetingen het harmonische stadsbeeld").

These architects opposed solutions where old fragments and gables were reused in new buildings, unless they were applied appropriately by qualified architects and authorized advisors (Boeken, 1940: 286). Some objected to the activities of a number of actors, including Eelke van Houten, chief inspector of the Amsterdam Municipal Building and Housing Department, active in the 1930s, who specialized in these kinds of buildings. But van Houten's approach was not really that new. Reuse of precious materials, such as carved stone, iron, and wooden (especially oak) beams, had been common practice in vernacular building since the beginning of Amsterdam. Objection to these practices may have also been caused by

a fear of losing architectural originality and artistic authorship, virtues on which the architectural profession founded its authority in the nineteenth century. In fact, van Houten was developing an existing practice in order to reinforce the anonymous and indigenous character of the Amsterdam house (Schoonenberg, 2012). It closely follows the "conservative modernization" impulse formulated in 1916, but practised long before the twentieth century, which would be continued after the Second World War by the Bureau of Monumentenzorg (Monument Care) and private parties like Stadsherstel (Urban Rehabilitation) and Hendrick de Keyser, the historic house association established as a private initiative in 1918. The bureau and different private initiatives for decades took an active part in the design of many reconstructions and new designs inspired by the historical setting of a certain period, mostly the long eighteenth century (Windig & van Eeghen, 1965). Many buildings received their eighteenth-century look in the 1950s or later, when reconstruction was a popular answer to reinforce the faded Canal District of the *Grachtenboek*. By deliberately refraining from conspicuous references to their recent completion, these structures give precedence to an image of the Canal District that refers to a more distant past and tends to suppress the legibility of the district's long history of continuous building activity.

Post-War Complexity

The discussion to find meaningful ways to integrate contemporary architecture into the historical city, in which architects and modern designers actively engaged, almost dried up after the war. Post-war reconstruction in the Netherlands demanded large-scale rebuilding of cities and development of the infrastructure (Bosma & Wagenaar, 1995). The Canal District, like most of pre-modern architectural history, was ignored in architectural debates and became the exclusive territory of the heritage industry, preservationists, and restoration architects, which may have stimulated further alienation of the supporters of harmonic intervention or architectural originality. Historical inquiries of the post-war period have focused almost exclusively on new architecture and urban planning, and much less on post-war associations with the historical architecture, at least in the Netherlands. But restoration of houses to their original state at the moment of completion increasingly became suspect in the eyes of many architects and heritage specialists. It was interpreted as style copying caused by lack of originality by advocates of modernity, who were looking for new architecture that seeks expression in contrast to the character of the existing urban fabric.

It is interesting that, in general, objections to reconstruction or building in eighteenth-century style is often expressed in ethical terms. In this line of argument, recapturing a style or complex of forms from a period in the past and turning it into a new form of contemporary architecture would be untruthful and therefore immoral. Behind this view lies the misconception that the creation of a new building in a form and style that approximate a precursor would be an admission of weakness in terms of originality and architectural expression, and that something ahistorical or "authentic and original" would be more appropri-

ate to building in any setting. Rather than perceiving reconstruction as a return to a previous situation or condition, it would be better to see it as a very deliberate act of architectural invention that involves intentions similar to those of designing in a contemporary way (or style) – to compose with the use of the past in historicist architecture or to preserve, restore, or destruct. It is a new creation made possible by a re-evaluation of a specific historical incident or era and by referring to old forms, which, by omitting the aspect of the passing of time, should persuade the viewer (to assume) that it is something else (from the past). The only difference with a new building created to express contrast is that it does not want to refer to a prior situation. In accordance with this notion, the much debated Singel 428 (architects A. Cahen, J.P. Girod, and J. Koning, 1964–65), as an example of a contrasting yet historically informed design, seems to have been rightly applauded by the architect Frans van Gool, despite "the less than precious material," concrete, when he stated that the charm of the city of Amsterdam was built upon "a coincidence of particular impulses and interplay of different building styles" (Edhoffer & van Dijk, 2010: 22).

Beautification and "Cleaning Up"

Regulations for the external appearance of new buildings in Amsterdam were first formulated in 1922. The first full-fledged official policy was drawn up in 1955, titled *Nota Binnenstad. De Schoonheid van Amsterdam* (*The Beauty of Amsterdam*) (Edhoffer, Jutte, Loof, & Mulder, 2013). The latest update appeared in

2016. This policy is the main instrument used by the Commissie Welstand en Monumenten (CWM; External Appearance and Historic Buildings Committee), which advises the municipality on the external appearance of buildings and monuments and related regulations and policy. The CWM supports article 21 of the Vienna Memorandum on "World Heritage and Contemporary Architecture – Managing the Historic Urban Landscape," which states that "urban planning, contemporary architecture and preservation of the historic urban landscape should avoid all forms of pseudo-historical design, as they constitute a denial of both the historical and the contemporary alike. One historical view should not supplant others, as history must remain readable, while continuity of culture through quality interventions is the ultimate goal" (UNESCO, 2005: 4). Designs that appear to be historical should thus be treated with caution; although reconstructions or buildings that use historical references are not forbidden, they should be assessed for their appropriateness to the context and logic of the direct environment (Edhoffer et al., 2013: 109). In practice, this assessment is dominated by architectural concepts rather than historical sensibilities. While the former tends to consider a structure as a design – a concept, as delivered on completion – the latter is also interested in the story of its appropriation and subsequent use, from the moment it was first occupied.

Within the CWM from time to time, heated discussions have taken place between architect members and representatives of historical societies. The architects sometimes put their faith in the reputation of a colleague instead of critically examining the design at hand, to the outrage of the preservationists (Edhoffer & van Dijk, 2010: 20–1). In the fifties, city architect Ben Merkelbach often tried to bridge the gap between the two opposites, suggesting that contemporary buildings should observe the existing scale. On the other hand, Cornelis van Eesteren, head of the city's Department of Urban Development until 1958, believed that carefully placed new buildings would not threaten the existing character. The CWM was often unanimous in its disapproval of breaks in scale, in which bigger complexes along the canals replaced multiple houses. With strong economic pressure from local politics, the CWM's advice could sometimes be ignored. In that case, only listed monuments or activist protest could put extra weight in the balance in favour of preserving the existing character. In 1966, this lack of authority led three aldermen to question the usefulness of the CWM, illustrating their case with a number of examples of what had gone wrong, including the office building at Keizersgracht 298–300 (architects C. de Gues and J.B. Ingwersen, 1955) with its "pretentious glass and concrete façade" (Edhoffer & van Dijk, 2010: 32; Figure 6.7). Eventually, discussion and accusations fuelled an uproar, which lead to a special public hearing with architects and artists, preservationists, activists, and entrepreneurs in August 1967. As a result, the city council decided to instate a committee to draw up a memorandum to reorganize the CWM and create a compendium of regulations (Verordening Welstandstoezicht), which was eventually issued years later.

Around the same time that architects and others in Amsterdam were discussing almost house by house the problem of how to deal with architectural

Figure 6.7 | Keizersgracht 298–300, designed by C. de Gues and J.B. Ingwersen, 1955.
Source: Author.

stated, can be as complex as studying the biography of a man (Rossi, 1982: 18, 162). This interesting comparison seems to have been ignored at the time, but the biographical reading of historical landscapes and urban environment would eventually, via detours in humanistic geography and cultural anthropology, be integrated into the field of heritage studies and discourse (Kolen & Renes, 2015). Rossi described the city as "fatto urbano," an urban artefact, divided into individual buildings and dwelling areas. Discussing the variety of monuments and permanent, vital, and pathological elements that together make up a city, Rossi posited "that the dynamic process of the city tends more to evolution than preservation, and that in evolution monuments are not only preserved but continuously presented as propelling elements of development" (Rossi, 1982: 60). To think that an urban artefact is "something tied to a single period of history constitutes one of the greatest fallacies of urban science" (61).

Rossi's reading of how the built environment can inspire new building, formulated over fifty years ago when Modernism cracked, helps to put in perspective the profusion of heritage literature that concentrates on mental appropriation and identification with existing material and immaterial culture (Bosma & Kolen, 2010; Halbertsma & Kuipers, 2014). The architect engages physically with the city through building. While rendering account of the existing historical fabric, he or she creatively participates in its further development. It may be that this approach, in which architectural history serves to read and understand the built environment before considering and designing new interventions, is more helpful in inspiring

interventions, the Italian architect Aldo Rossi was formulating ideas about similar problems. In his 1966 book *l'Architettura della Città* (*The Architecture of the City*), which appeared partly as an outcome of his investigations of Venice and Padua, Rossi tried to come to terms with the complexity of architecture in relation to time, acknowledging that precedent is crucial in understanding the built environment in order to intervene in it. Understanding the city, he

Figure 6.8 | Keizersgracht 271–303. The five office buildings built between 1955 and 1983, replacing seventeenth-century original houses, are new buildings that display efforts to create both post-war and quasi–eighteenth-century facades that attempt in scale, material, and rhythm to harmonize with the surrounding architecture of the district.
Source: Author.

future developments than the variety of good intentions that the heritage industry has on offer. This concept can have consequences for the future architectural development of the Canal District as well.

Some parties would like to see the Canal District become more historical than it ever was by selectively cleansing it of structures built during the last century or later and reconstructing the district to the way it looked before the twentieth century. Others prefer the term "reconstruction" to create an architecturally more agreeable appearance that erases markings and scars of different use and appropriation or neglect, preferring to restore or "clean up" a historical building as part of a renovation project for a new use, in the process removing any traces of prior use that relate to the prolonged life cycle or the "biography" of the building (Figure 6.8).

Implementing the perspective of architectural history means that reconstruction and beautification of heavily used and sometimes neglected buildings should respect the biography of the building, even if it means preserving bits that do not appeal to the eye of today's designers and restoration architects or that interfere with the original concept. Some buildings, hardly masterpieces and sometimes lamented soon after they were built, and often radically opposed by the preservationists and reconstruction lobby, have also contributed to this special character of the architecture of the Canal District, which is flexible and resilient enough to endure these kinds of interventions. Consequently, securing the vital permanence of the Canal District should not only allow interventions of "the highest possible quality" in order to maintain the "outstanding universal value," but also facilitate new interventions that render account of different pasts and refrain from erasing artefacts that do not please today's aesthetic and preservationist opinion.

Back to the Architectural Essence of the Canal District

Anybody with a general sense of architecture and an interest in the built environment can appreciate the usefulness of an instrument like the UNESCO listing to critically monitor the development of the architectural appearance of the Canal District, regardless of how pressing the underlying economic motives may

be for a city to intervene. For many preservationists, the Canal District can never be too historical. Some will applaud every attempt to reconstruct a previous situation and object to any "dissonant," that is, new contribution to the Canal District that could not be mistaken for an original pre-1850 building (Brinkgreve, 2004: 116). But this caesura in time to decide between what needs to be saved and what is considered unattractive, not worthy to take its place, is rather artificial and based on personal preferences, not on objective standards of architectural quality or singularity. Is this the way to preserve the Canal District's "outstanding universal value," or is it just the old picturesque interpretation of the built environment that shapes a pleasing, non-offensive version of the past and limits contrast to present a brushed up, idealized image that carefully deletes everything that interferes with it?

The Canal District is a seventeenth-century urban design, but its architectural fabric is the product of four centuries of building, living, and working (Kleijn & van Zoest, 2013). The canal houses we see, especially the older ones, show all the marking and sometimes the scars of their prolonged and frequently changed use. Often, it will take an expert's eyes to be able to see at a glance how old a building is, if it has been changed or to what degree it has been renovated, and how this transformation has been caused by changes of use, brought on by successive occupants and owners. The largest part of the Canal District consists of individual buildings with facades of an eclectic, almost vernacular architecture, standing shoulder to shoulder. To preserve this part of the architectural essence of the Canal

District, new building activity should take into account that not every new building or addition to the Canal District would need to be an architectural masterpiece claiming exclusivity. Experiments driven by personal architectural vanity may be better practised elsewhere, but neither should what is considered authentic always be repeated. The intention within the Canal District should be to differentiate and add to the district's basic formula. And this formula today is that of architecture with predominantly twentieth-century cosmetics presenting an early twenty-first-century appraisal of architecture, history, identity, and authenticity. It seems therefore essential, if one is interested in sustaining the idea of the Canal District as a resilient and dynamic part of a living city, to allow this transformation to continue.

It is of vital importance for any monument of a living culture that the outward appearance of its architecture be linked to the identity of the people who created, used, and maintained it and still inhabit it, in order to prevent it from becoming a memorial to a lost culture. The monument of a living culture is able to inspire new life, whereas a memorial to a lost culture only facilitates the creation of new stories. This chapter concentrated on the outward appearance of the Canal District without referring too much to its historical significance and meaning, which lies much less in its architecture than in the history of its inhabitants, their needs, desires, and behaviour. Although UNESCO, as so many other heritage institutions and initiatives, is interested in the history and memory of places, this interest means that it will be important to observe the intimate relation between the Canal District's architecture and the interior world behind its facades. It can be argued that the architectural essence of the Canal District can be safeguarded relatively well, in a material sense, by preserving the outward appearance of its canals, quays, and the facades of its houses. But attention is needed to maintain a relation between the architecture and the culture of the people who created, used, and maintained it. If they leave or lose interest, the Canal District will be detached from the internal world that created it. The original occupants, who created, crafted, and preserved their specific biotope in a manner that accommodated their needs, desires, and expectations, are essential to its survival. If this connection between the modern-day use of the buildings of the Canal District and everyday life in the city is lost, this artefact will lose its essential dynamics and become nothing more than a museum piece in a worldwide collection.

chapter seven

The Canal District:
A Continuing History of Modern Planning

LEN DE KLERK

Ever since the inception of the Amsterdam Canal District, its planning history has been a long search to balance a superb historic urban texture with the dynamics of changing economic needs and wants. The historic urban fabric of the district is admired for its beauty and atmosphere, but the area is also the "living room" of an important part of the urban economy.

For about two centuries (1670–1870), Amsterdam was a town of two tales, a medieval core surrounded by a magnificent seventeenth-century belt as a result of urban planning. Due to rapid growth at the time of the Industrial Revolution, within three decades the core and its belt changed position from the city as a whole to the inner city. In 1869, nearly all 282,500 inhabitants of Amsterdam still lived within the Singelgracht, a canal around the former city walls. A vast majority resided in the Canal District, including the Jordaan neighbourhood. In 1889, already 135,000 people found themselves in new districts outside the former city walls (van Hulten, 1968). In the year 2015, only 30,500 people remained in the Canal District, including 19,400 people in the Jordaan neighbourhood.

The Industrial Revolution turned society as a whole – the economy, transport systems, demography, politics, and social structure – upside down. Cities underwent a half century of unprecedented growth. Between 1880 and 1925, the population of Amsterdam increased from 317,000 to 714,000 inhabitants. Never before or after in Dutch history did cities grow so fast. Amsterdam was not even the fastest grower, and yet it became the largest industrial town of the Netherlands in 1900, whereas just over a century later Amsterdam has turned into a town with a modern service economy and only 4 per cent industrial jobs.

Amsterdam had been designed for water transport, but in the late nineteenth century the city had to adapt to new modes of transport over land. Economic and population growth brought major challenges, problems for a city that had to adapt from the barge age to the era of steam and fossil-fuel engines. The municipality borrowed millions of guilders to adapt streets, bridges, and places to accommodate the new modes of traffic like streetcars and automobiles.

Modern town planning itself is another of the Industrial Revolution's many inventions, but it is strongly rooted in seventeenth-century practices, as can be deduced from chapter 2 by Abrahamse on the original planning of the Canal District. New problems of the nineteenth century included transport infrastructure and the scale of everything, new living districts, industrial establishments, and socio-cultural facilities. It took almost a century before planning got some grip on the inner city. Two questions have dominated Amsterdam's ongoing history of inner city planning in the nineteenth and twentieth century: (1) how to balance dynamic economic activities with protection of the historic texture of the urban core and the Canal District; and (2) how to improve accessibility of the urban core in the motor age. After nearly a century of giving way to traffic and economic activities, the early 1980s turned to balancing economic and environmental values. Planning is very much about values.

New Problems in an Ancient Urban Fabric

In the second half of the nineteenth century, the inner city of Amsterdam was affected by four major problems: a bad hygienic condition; the rapid change from water to land traffic; (illegal) building of backyards by industries; and the decrepit condition of houses and public spaces after more than a century of neglect. Traditionally, canals had five functions in Dutch town planning in the seventeenth and eighteenth centuries: to act as transport systems; to function as regulatory systems to control ground water levels; to provide fresh water; to serve as sewage systems; and

to increase the amenities of the urban environment. In the last quarter of the nineteenth century, some of these functions became compromised.

Public hygiene suffered from the increasing population densities, which fostered the spread of epidemics. The problem had to be solved by the construction of improved fresh water supply systems and sewage systems. The latter was complicated and expensive. In fact, it was not until the second half of the twentieth century that most streets and canals in Amsterdam were connected to a proper sewage system. The obvious nineteenth-century solution, chosen for a number of reasons, was to fill in canals and ditches. The advantages of this solution were manifold: it was relatively cheap, it stopped the unbearable stench and helped to prevent epidemics, and it created more space for land traffic.

The Jordaan neighbourhood, the lower-class part of the Canal District, had a particularly bad reputation for its public health condition. Between 1850–70 and 1889–95, so many ditches and canals were filled in that the Jordaan lost 50 per cent of its water surface (van Rooijen, 1995). At the time, few people opined that filling in canals also meant the loss of amenity and historic urban landscape.

The Industrial Revolution was in particular a transport revolution, which affected cities as a whole and caused continuing planning challenges between the 1850s and 1980s. It was a cumulative effect of economic restructuring of the inner city and the emerging motor age. Before the Second World War, private cars were pretty rare in the Netherlands, but ownership across the country increased from half a million in 1960 to 2.4 million in 1970 and 5.1 million in 1990.

Nowadays, it is often forgotten that regional transit of goods, especially during industrial times, posed a challenge to many towns. Throughout the twentieth century, a large part of the increasing regional north-south (and vice versa) traffic in the province of North Holland had to cross the IJ and the North Sea Channel on the Amsterdam municipal ferries and then find its way through the city. Like other Dutch cities, Amsterdam was in no small part controlled by the traditionally powerful shipping lobby, which was able to prevent for a long time the construction of bridges. Add to this that the Department of Public Works in Amsterdam for nearly half a century refused to construct a tunnel, mainly because of technical problems with soil mechanics that would compel expensive solutions. The first fixed crossings were not constructed until 1957 (!): the Schellingwouderbrug across the IJ and the Velsertunnel across the North Sea Channel.

Central Business District Development

Between 1870 and 1940, the medieval core and the Canal District came into the grip of the central business district development process (CBD process), a spontaneous long-term process of turning the urban core into a business district of retail shops, department stores, and consumer and producer services. The CBD process was (and is) considered a self-evident economic phenomenon, a result of the new industrial economy of labour division and specialization of economic activities in a free market. Essentially, CBD development is a "shakeout process" of small-scale economic activities like sweatshops, handicrafts, small shops, and dwellings by more profitable (new) economic activities such as specialized shops, galleries, department stores (which became fashionable around 1900), and, not least, the fast-growing banking and insurance business in need of larger buildings.

The engine of this process of invasion and succession of economic activities was the land price mechanism, causing greater geographic differentiation of land prices between the urban cores and surrounding districts, consequently changing land use patterns. Many renters, small landowners, and shopkeepers could no longer afford the rising land prices and simply were priced out. The drawbacks of the CBD process were loss of dwellings, population loss, and damage to the historic urban texture by the invasion of out-of-scale office buildings and department stores. One must realize that the free market order was introduced in the Netherlands in the 1850s and 1860s, as the successor to a state-controlled mercantile order. CBD development was considered to do no harm to a city; on the contrary, it was seen as a positive sign of a dynamic economy and a road to more prosperity.

Three features characterized the new economy of the early 1900s: first, the foundation of new firms for new economic activities (banking on an industrial scale, insurance, accountancy, and consultancy), including the enormous expansion of the public sector; second, the emergence of big business by

Table 7.1 Population development of Amsterdam, 1869–2015

Location	1869	1899	1930	1970	2000	2015
Canal District[a]	33,800	33,700	38,200	17,300	11,400	11,500
Jordaan	64,000	77,800	44,200	7,200	18,700	19,400
Inner city[b]	255,400	292,800	145,400	71,600	73,700	58,200
Amsterdam	263,400	496,000	757,400	831,500	734,500	811,200

Sources: Statistische Jaarboeken Amsterdam 1900, 1930, 1970, and 2000; Amsterdam in Cijfers 2015 (OIS Amsterdam); CBS National Census Publications online; Wagenaar, 1990: 148, 365–7.

a The Canal District is defined as the statistical districts 02 (Grachtengordel-Noord) and 03 (Grachtengordel-Zuid). The entire Canal District also includes parts of the statistical districts 07 (Weteringschans) and 08 (Weesperbuurt-Plantage).
b Inner city includes the medieval section, the entire Canal District, and the Western and Eastern Islands.

autonomous growth and mergers; and, third, the geographic redistribution of economic activities over towns and between towns and urban regions through an endless process of relocation. Bigger firms needed bigger buildings, which most of the time were out of scale and architecturally out of touch with the existing urban environment. In the early twentieth century, growing industrial firms already relocated to new industrial parks at the urban fringe. For the urban fabric of the Canal District, the CBD process had three consequences: the redevelopment and re-use of most larger, residential houses for office activities and shops; the replacement of dwellings and warehouses by new office buildings; and traffic breakthroughs as a solution to gain better accessibility to the core district. The CBD process started in the 1860s as a piecemeal crowding of shops in the medieval core, but it accelerated around the turn of the century. In the longer run, the Canal District was affected in

two ways: first, many of its large houses were turned into prestigious office locations; and second, room had to be made for new radial access roads into the urban core.

In the last quarter of the nineteenth century, offices were still generally small, only occupying the ground floor of a mansion (Wagenaar, 1990). Table 7.1 shows that before 1900 the rather moderate CBD process hardly affected housing room, as it was a result of building in backyards. Change came with the start of big business around 1900. Due to its geographic position, its great mansions, and large inner yards, the inner city, including the Canal District, became attractive for business (re)location. Between 1899 and 1930, the number of dwellings in the inner city decreased by 35 per cent, from 69,600 to 45,100, and the number of inhabitants decreased from 292,800 to 145,400 (see Table 7.1).

The emerging banking industry concentrated at the Herengracht. In 1926, the Nederlandsche Handel-

Figure 7.1 | The Bazel Building (the Municipal Archives) was developed in the 1920s as the head office of the Nederlandsche Handel-Maatschappij, a bank, along the radial traffic breakthrough Vijzelstraat, crossing the Herengracht. Source: Author.

Maatschappij (Netherlands Trading Society), in those days one of the biggest Dutch banking companies, opened its new headquarters at the Vijzelstraat-Herengracht, a new radial access road. It is an example of a totally out-of-scale building in a fine-meshed urban texture. Because of its unique architectural design by architect Karel de Bazel, the building (now called "De Bazel") is a listed monument. It was refurbished in 2007 and has since been used by the city for storage of the Municipal Archives (Figure 7.1).

A rather small but interesting part of the process of change was the replacement and renovation of old houses. One of the most noticeable is the Nienhuys House at Herengracht 380–382, which was built in 1888 by the rich tobacco trader Jacobus Nienhuys (see Figure 6.6 in the previous chapter). Nienhuys started by renovating Husly House of 1775, which unfortunately burnt down after completion of the renovation works. A couple of months later, Nienhuys was able to buy the house next door, tore it down, and then built his grand new mansion on two lots in French Renaissance style, thus replacing two old monuments. In 1919, the Nienhuys family moved elsewhere and sold the house to Deutsche Bank. After 1945, the house again changed hands, going to De Nederlandsche Bank (Dutch National Bank), which, in turn, sold the house after two decades to the Ministry of Finance. Finally, in 1997, the house was completely refurbished to become the home of the National Institute of War, Holocaust and Genocide Studies (Bronkhorst, van den Eerenbeemt, & de Wilt, 2013: 164). The Nienhuys story illustrates the history of

other great houses in the Canal District: the invasion and succession of high standard office activities. In 1876, the Canal District numbered twenty-five banking premises (headquarters); in 1914, the number had more than doubled, to fifty-eight (Wagenaar, 1990).

Through the ages, the Canal District has always been a mixed living and business neighbourhood. In 1836, the new Palace of Justice at the Prinsengracht was opened in the renovated and partly reconstructed Aalmoezeniersweeshuis (Chaplain Orphan House) of 1666 (Figure 7.2). In 2015, the Palace of Justice was sold to a Chinese company, which aims to reshape the building into an international six-star hotel. Although the Orphan House illustrates that already the seventeenth century saw larger buildings in the Canal District, since the 1890s new office buildings, department stores, and hotels have become out of scale (volume and height) and, arguably, out of touch with the existing architecture. An example of such out-of-touch development was the Municipal Telephone Building of the 1920s at Herengracht 295, which after three decades had become technically obsolete and was replaced by a modernized out-of-touch building in 1955 (Figure 7.3).

Early Modern Planning

Modern planning had a false start in Amsterdam. In 1866, the municipal architect Jacob van Niftrik offered a plan for a new belt around the city

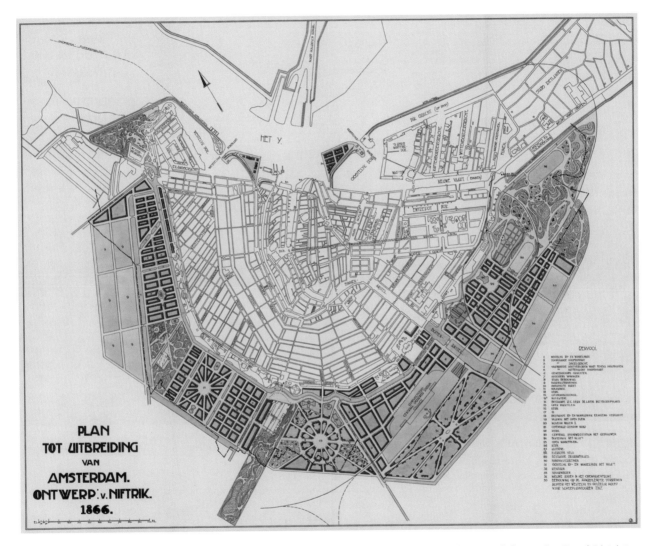

Map 7.1 | In 1866, Jacob van Niftrik presented the first city plan since 1664: a new belt around the entire Canal District.
Source: Municipal Housing Department of Amsterdam, printed with permission.

Figure 7.2 | The Palace of Justice in the 1830s was an early example of CBD redevelopment. In 2015, a Chinese developer bought the building for redevelopment into a hotel. Lithograph by A.J. van Lier.
Source: Collectie Stadsarchief Amsterdam, Beeldbank 010094005612. Public domain.

(Opposite) Figure 7.3 | Herengracht 295 is the (second) Municipal Telephone Building that replaced the houses shown in the Caspar Philips drawing (1768–71). Already in 1920, the houses had been torn down to construct the first Municipal Telephone Building, which was replaced in 1955 by the second building.
Sources: Detail of a drawing by Caspar Jacobsz. Philips (1732–89), Plate 12, from the Collectie Stadsarchief Amsterdam, Beeldbank 010097012567. Public domain. Photograph by author.

(Map 7.1), which showed his admiration for the plans by Eugene Haussmann for the reconstruction and beautification of Paris. The city council rejected his design because the conservative majority saw no way around the problems of large-scale land expropriation, which would be needed to realize the plan.

In 1876, Jan Kalff, director of Public Works, designed a new urban development plan. A civil engineer by training, Kalff had no feeling for urban design; his plan showed poor urban qualities, just converting the existing polder and ownership structures into a dull urban structure. Property and field boundaries and ditches appeared in the urban plan as roads, yards, and city blocks. The plan materialized in the "nineteenth-century belt" of rather poor residential blocks and a few small city parks. The Kalff plan was approved by a city council that was dominated by landowners, housing speculators, building contractors, and supporters of the free market economy. They predominantly considered urban development as an enterprise, in some cases their own private business (de Klerk, 2008).

After the turn of the century, everything changed. The political constellation of the city council had changed, adopting a more progressive direction, and the council now asked for more sophisticated town plans. Following the Housing Act of 1901, municipal authorities had a much greater grip on urban development, that is to say new residential development. Although renowned for its urban planning tradition, the Netherlands, in terms of planning law, was a pro-vincial backwater until 1900. Provided there was political will, larger cities could effectively apply private law (buying, selling, and exchanging land) to control new developments. For this purpose, the Amsterdam city council in the 1890s introduced a system of long-term land leases, a private law instrument. As a result, by 2015, the Municipality of Amsterdam still owned 80 per cent of the land within its municipal borders, a mighty instrument to control land use change.

For the existing urban fabric, the Housing Act did not provide specific instruments, so the application of private law instruments had to be continued, in some cases supplemented with expropriation, a slow and laborious means of planning. One of the few successful development projects of a traffic breakthrough with new shops, offices, and dwellings was the Raadhuisstraat project of 1894–97 (Figure 7.4). The project was designed by Dolf van Gendt, the architect of the famous Concertgebouw. Although the scale of the traffic breakthrough does not fit in the historical urban texture, today the Raadhuisstraat seems an almost natural historical development. The pretty 1900 architecture and character are attractive, and only a few visitors will realize that it was once a contested traffic break-through.

Radial Traffic Breakthroughs

The CBD process resulted in an increasing number of jobs in the city centre, causing steadily worsening traffic congestion, which in turn impeded the CBD process. That, in a nutshell, became the vicious circle of inner city planning in the twentieth century. The predominant planning question of how to solve traffic congestion to enable the CBD process received a rather simple and classical answer: create more room for traffic and car parking. In the postwar Rebuilding Age (1945–70), this solution got an extra stimulus from the general local economic policy. As a reaction to the Great Depression of the 1930s, city councils promoted diversification of the urban economy by literally shaping room for the tertiary sector (producer services) in inner cities. New office jobs were considered to replace the continuing loss of industrial jobs as part of the transition from an industrial to a service economy. In planning terms, inner city planning became a conscious and intensified continuation of the spontaneous CBD process (van der Cammen, de Klerk, Dekker, & Witsen, 2012) in order to accommodate this economic transition.

In the 1920s, the Amsterdam Department of Public Works started to produce reports on urban transportation problems, especially traffic congestion and accessibility in the urban core. The reports proposed traffic breakthroughs in the Canal District, among others in the Jordaan neighbourhood, where so many canals had been filled in. But the city council judged the plans too expensive. The 1926 Schemaplan voor Groot-Amsterdam was criticized because of its lack of vision for the future of the inner city. In the public debate, the city council was accused of pursuing a laissez-faire

policy, with participants pointing out an underlying problem: the absence of a plan for the development of new residential districts in combination with the CBD process. The council appeared insensitive to the fact that any new CBD development would attract more traffic as more jobs were created, and more inhabitants would have to move out.

The 1920s also witnessed the first voices articulating that view that the urban core of Amsterdam is too small and too beautiful to accommodate all possible effects and consequences of CBD development; in other words, choices had to be made. In 1927, a small group of councillors presented their own *Report on Urban Development and Traffic*, stipulating that the city council primarily ought to set the future path for employment in the inner city and that traffic plans should follow such a path (Hartman, Hellinga, Jonker, & de Ruijter, 1985). The discussion was continued in the *Municipal Report on Urban development and Traffic* of 1931, which proposed that the inner city fabric should be adapted to accommodate the economic core of the city as a whole (Map 7.2). The city council should abandon its laissez-faire policy and comply with the requirements of the economic core functions without damaging the urban core's historical beauty. The key question of "how to do this" was shifted to a future research report.

The municipal town planners considered the inner city traffic system to be the spine of inner city planning. No wonder the 1931 traffic scheme influenced inner city planning until the 1970s.

Figure 7.4a | The Warmoesgracht before the traffic breakthrough of 1894–97.
Source: Collectie Stadsarchief Amsterdam, Beeldbank 10019A000151. Photograph by Jacob Olie (1834–1905). Public domain.

Figure 7.4b │ After the traffic breakthrough, the Warmoes-gracht was renamed Raadhuisstraat, shown here in 2019. Source: Author.

Figure 7.4c │ The Raadhuisstraat in 2016, view to the west. Source: Author.

The report proposed the following:

- construction of an inner ring road around the urban core, defined as the medieval city;
- two outer ring roads just along the outside boundaries of the Canal District; and
- eight radial traffic breakthroughs between the core and the nineteenth- and twentieth-century districts.

The conceptual basis of the scheme was that the spatial allocation of the CBD process would be steered by traffic planning by making locations more or less attractive and more or less accessible. It was believed that new developments would be mainly located along the radials to the urban core. The 1931 scheme was integrated into the famous 1935 *Algemeen Uitbreidingsplan* (General Development Plan; Gemeente Amsterdam, 1935). The General Development Plan itself was limited to new developments and did not take make any proposals for the urban core and Canal District.

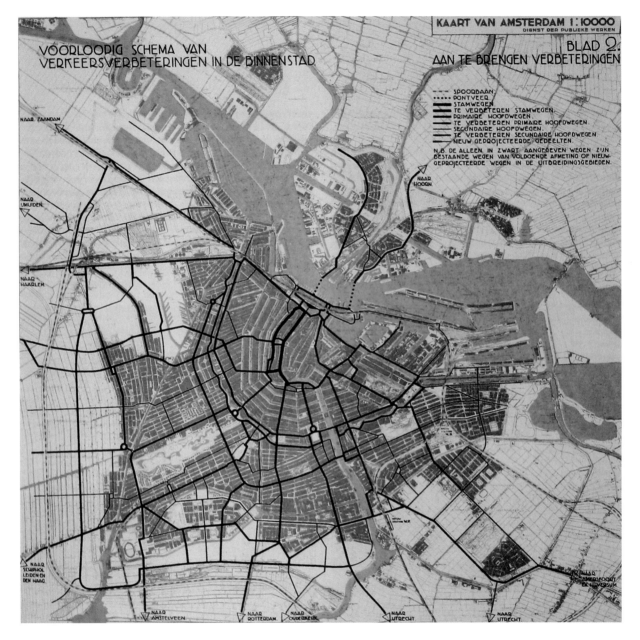

Map 7.2 | Inner City Road Scheme of the *Algemeen Uitbreidingsplan*, 1935. The main road pattern is directed towards improving the accessibility of the inner city.

Source: *Algemeen Uitbreidingsplan* 1935, Municipality of Amsterdam. Reprinted with permission.

Post-War Planning

In the 1950s, increasing prosperity and private car ownership forced the CBD process into a higher gear. How to solve congestion and parking problems? In 1955, Police Commissioner Kaasjager presented, out of the blue, his own provocative traffic plan. He proposed to fill in a number of main canals in and around the urban core, among others the Singel and canals in front of the Central Station (Figure 7.5). The resulting land would create enough room for inner and outer city ring roads and car parks. Perhaps Kaasjager had listened carefully to Henry Ford I, who, during his Amsterdam visit, declared that he could not understand why the authorities did not fill in the canals to create wide boulevards for the coming motor age. But even Kaasjager did not dare propose filling in the main canals of the Canal District, Herengracht, Keizersgracht, and Prinsengracht.

The Kaasjager plan was a wake-up call for public opinion, which could not quite believe that the police commissioner would "cut out the heart of the city." His plan encouraged a heated public debate on the future of the monumental fabric of the city, meticulous analysed by Rooijendijk (2005: 101–44). Kaasjager reacted in cold terms to all criticism, asserting that the next generation would not miss the historic town, because it would never have known it anyway. After the Kaasjager incident, the council executive (mayor and aldermen) presented the 1955 *Nota Binnenstad* (Report on the Inner City; Gemeente Amsterdam, 1955), which formulated the following inner city problems:

- aging and poorly maintained urban fabric;
- insufficient protection of the beauty and character of the inner city;
- a constrained CBD process; and
- traffic congestion and lack of car parking lots.

For the first time in modern planning history, filling in canals was categorically rejected, the only exception being the dilapidated Lijnbaansgracht, which was to make room for car parking. Still, in the 1960s, some isolated proposals to fill in canals were launched and then cancelled after protests by civic groups. Hidden reasons for these proposals included stopping expensive maintenance and repair of quaysides and bridges, as well as preventing exorbitant costs of alternatives such as expropriation of land for traffic breakthroughs. As to the historic urban fabric, the report's main concern was not so much the protection of individual buildings, but rather protecting the historical urban environment (urban landscape or cityscape) as a whole.

In the meantime, business and trade institutions like the Chamber of Commerce repeatedly, and with increasing urgency, begged the city council to solve the traffic chaos. But the council did not produce much more than hesitation and political spasm. This lame duck attitude was partly due to the lack of public law instruments. As for the Canal District, the council could not do much more than prevent the construction of new garages and stop the relocation and development of existing businesses in the inner city. In 1961, the Raad voor de Stedenbouw, a municipal advisory body of professionals, asked for a

Figure 7.5 | For more than half a century, the Singel canal has been the favourite proposed site for construction of an inner city ring road to improve the accessibility of the city centre by private car.
Source: Author.

general regeneration plan for the inner city. Four (!) years later, the Department of Public Works answered that such a plan would be impossible because of the endless variety of buildings and functions in the inner city (Grünhagen, 2007). So Public Works in fact condemned the administration to just muddling through management.

Decentralization of the CBD Process

In 1968, the white paper *Voorontwerp van de Tweede Nota over de Amsterdamse Binnenstad* (the Second Report on the Inner City; Gemeente Amsterdam, 1968) proposed the following policy goals:

- keep the main shopping centre in the urban core;
- relocate the humanity faculties of the University of Amsterdam to buildings that would become vacant by relocation of the Dutch National Bank and the Wilhelmina Gasthuis (University Hospital);
- renew the so-called Willekeuren (protective provisions of 1615 and 1663), which had worked well, but could not prevent building in back yards;
- reorganize car parking and the loading and unloading of goods; and
- create pedestrian areas in selected central shopping streets.

In order to prevent "too much damage to the historical urban texture," the report suggested relocating city functions to new hubs (sub-centres) of public transport in the nineteenth-century belt. The background of this report was a national population forecast of 21 million people in the year 2000 (the population reached 17 million in 2016). Six "radial city roads" should increase accessibility to the urban core, all connected by a "district distributor" on the inside and a "primary distributor" on the outside of the Singelgracht. This new urban traffic jargon was derived from *Traffic in Towns*, the well-known British report by Colin Buchanan (1964) on urban traffic and very influential in Dutch inner city planning. The central concept was to create a ring road "circumscribing the town centre with the object of distributing traffic round the centre and also acting as a town centre by-pass" (257). The historic town would be divided into sectors, which could only be accessed via the inner road.

In the same year, scholars from the University of Amsterdam published research on the inner city (Heinemeijer, van Hulten, & de Vries Reilingh, 1968). The geographers primarily analysed the dynamics of the spatial-functional organization and discovered that most shops were concentrated right in the city core and along only three radial roads through the Canal District: the Raadhuisstraat, Utrechtsestraat, and Vijzelstraat. Only 30 per cent of the urban core floor space was used for residential purposes (46 per cent in the Canal District) and 70 per cent for shops and offices (van Hulten, 1968). A new spatial-economic trend was discovered: the decentralization of urban core activities. Specialized shops (typical inner city shops) were relocating or starting branches in new shopping malls, while offices were relocating to new residential districts and office parks along new (planned) motorways around the city.

The city as a whole suffered from substantial population losses. Between 1960 and 1985, Amsterdam recorded a net population loss of 197,000 inhabitants, reaching its nadir in the 1970s with a net annual migration loss of 20,000 inhabitants. The inner city lost jobs, an ongoing process that continued during the 1970s and 1980s. Of 203,000 jobs in 1975, only 166,000 were left in 1982 (van der Cammen & de Klerk, 1993: 181–2) and 75,000 in 1995. The service sector shifted into a higher gear, and office business was scaling up. Lack of room for expansion in inner city locations and increasing traffic congestion were the main reasons for relocating out of the centre. Ignoring municipal planning, offices were not relocated to the proposed nearby hubs in the nineteenth-century belt, but hopped to new sub-centres further out, along the new ring road around Amsterdam. The planning authorities were locked up in the stalemate of car accessibility and needed more than a decade (1966–81) to acknowledge the decentralization trends.

Eventually, the answer came with a new planning model in the *Structuurplan 1981*, called "the compact city" (Gemeente Amsterdam, 1981). The central message of the plan was to improve the environmental qualities in order to attract people and firms, especially producer service activities. Planning was adapted to the new circumstances: small-scale residential projects on vacant yards and renovation of dilapidated housing. Car parking was divided into two types: short-term parking in the inner city parking garages and long-term parking in park and ride (P&R) facilities in the new sub-centres.

Citizens' Protests and the Reverse of Planning Values

At the end of the day, a century of CBD development resulted in three major traffic breakthroughs and the radials Raadhuisstraat-Rozengracht and Vijzelstraat en Utrechtsestraat as extensions of the urban core. The CBD process had not been stopped but was starkly mitigated. Overall, planning rationale was reversed, moving from the adaptation of the environment to new economic activities to the adaptation of activities to the existing urban environment. Tourism and socio-cultural activities and facilities gained recognition as important economic activities, in fact becoming the CBD activities. It can be said that the lack of proper planning law instruments had advantages as well as disadvantages. On the one hand, planning authorities were unable to halt the creeping CBD process of piecemeal functional change and small-scale replacement. On the other hand, the lack of instruments disallowed a full-fledged development plan that, most likely, would have destroyed the inner city as we know it.

Two external forces also helped to save the inner city: the decentralization of economic activities and the polarization of civic protests against the CBD policy. Increasing protest against the CBD policy and against the urban renewal policy of demolishing housing to construct a subway turned town planning from a technocratic approach into a political choice approach. The first protests against demolishing historical buildings had already been heard in the nineteenth century. In 1911, the Bond Heemschut, a private heritage foundation, was founded to prevent further damage to the inner city. In the 1950s, Geurt Brinkgreve, sculptor, councillor, and publicist, acted as a leading protester against demolishing the historic texture (Brinkgreve, 1956).

Two traffic plans served to increase controversy and discussion: the Kaasjager plan, discussed earlier, and the 1967 Jokinen plan. David Jokinen, an American traffic engineer, was hired by the Dutch national private car lobby to design solutions for the traffic and car parking chaos in inner cities. His plan worked as a catalyst on the anti-CBD protests. He proposed radical solutions such as construction of highways directly into the urban core and reconstruction of the Central Station by replacing the nineteenth-century canopies with a huge parking garage, arguing that canopies had become obsolete in the electrical age (Figure 7.6). Another of his proposals aimed to prevent the business flight from the inner city by developing a new city centre in the Pijp, a late nineteenth-century neighbourhood that had been heavily criticized for its ugliness and high densities. Jokinen presented his scheme as "the economy of renovation," arguing that it would allow the renovation of monuments (Jokinen, 1968). But, like Kaasjager, Jokinen too did not dare to propose filling in the main canals or to plan parking garages in the Canal District (Rooijendijk, 2005).

At the end of the 1960s, the social composition of the protesters changed from petty elite to a much broader post-war generation, who lived in the rather cheap private rental housing of the inner city. Some of these neighbourhoods were threatened by major traffic breakthroughs, the construction of an underground metro, and the more general planning concept calling for replacement of old housing stock by modern apartment housing. Protests against inner city policy became the pinnacle of a broader dissatisfaction with the rather paternalistic way decisions were made in Dutch political institutions like city councils. In Amsterdam, increasing protest against demolishing housing to construct the underground culminated in 1975 in the "Nieuwmarkt Riots."

These political clashes very much influenced the inner city planning concept in Amsterdam and other cities, to be summarized as the shift from the motto "form follows function" to "function follows form." In inner cities, no longer should the urban environment adapt to serve the changing spatial-functional organization; now, it was the other way around. From here on, economic activities in a historic urban fabric needed to be adapted to the existing small-scale urban texture in order to contribute to the protection of the historic environment. Referring to John Ruskin's 1851 book, *The Stones from Venice*, one may say that the stones of Amsterdam had won the redevelopment battle.

Protected by Law

Based on the Monuments and Historical Buildings Act of 1961, the city council in 1988 designated the entire inner city of 679 hectares (medieval core and Canal District) a conservation area (Map 7.3). In 1999, the designation was confirmed by the national government. The act defines these listings as "protection of village and cityscapes" containing all buildings, street patterns, canals, trees, and places

Figure 7.6 | Proposal by the American traffic engineer David Jokinen to prepare Amsterdam for the twenty-first century. The white oval marks the Rijksmuseum.

Source: Photocollage by Jokinen (1968), from the Collectie Stadsarchief Amsterdam, Beeldbank HVVA00181000023. Reprinted with permission and adapted by the author.

in the designated area. Since 1961, the act has provided the possibility to designate conservation areas, but municipalities have been hindered from taking such action by the lack of appropriate subsidies. Generally, the process of designation and confirmation of listed areas is simultaneously coordinated and decided by the city council and the provincial council and executive. After designation, a city council is obliged by law to adopt a land use plan as required by the Spatial Planning Act in order to implement protection of the conservation area. Such a plan "must determine whether and to what extent existing land use plans may be deemed to be protective plans" (Monumentenwet [Monument Act], 1988). In listed areas, the quality of the entire urban fabric must be mapped in an evaluation map of the listed urban area, which is used to judge building and renovation proposals. The combination of the evaluation map with a land use plan of the area, as a means to judge proposals to change building use, provides the municipality with strong instruments to control spatial-economic changes.

According to the law, the listed area of Amsterdam has been mapped into three categories. The first order contains all listed monuments according to the Monument Act. The second contains all buildings (built before 1940) of high architectural quality, which sustain the urban structure and are valued for the overall architectural quality of facades. The third order contains buildings of different qualities, which, in terms of scale and architectural details, fit to existing facades but have no extra architectural or urban environmental value. The evaluation maps conclude with a fourth and fifth order of buildings, those that

need to be replaced and those that were constructed after 1940.

The designation of the inner city as a conservation area marks the end of a long period of muddling through between CBD development and conservation, and signifies the turn to a more conscious policy of balancing between economic and environmental historical values. The designation does not make land use change impossible, but it does prevent serious damage to the intricate texture of the built environment. Since 1990, the nature of the CBD process has shifted towards adaptation to the condition of the historic environment and its content to medium- and small-scale functional change, which favours the tourism, consumer, and service industries. These days, the conversion of old buildings to new uses (mainly hotels) begins with the question of how to stand out from among many competitors. The answer is to use the specific historic identity of the environment and buildings as a trademark. Reconverting former office buildings into chic living apartments is also a niche in the present CBD trend, enhancing the residential function of the inner city. But it is also unmistakably a part of the ongoing displacement process.

With about 20 per cent of total employment, the inner city is today still a major economic location. The authorities want to keep it that way, while rejecting the "Venice option": an open-air museum is not wanted. At least, such is the rhetoric. Keeping up the existing historic structures and buildings has become a general interest, but balancing between historical and economic values is not an easy task. As the final chapter in this book illustrates, people are worried

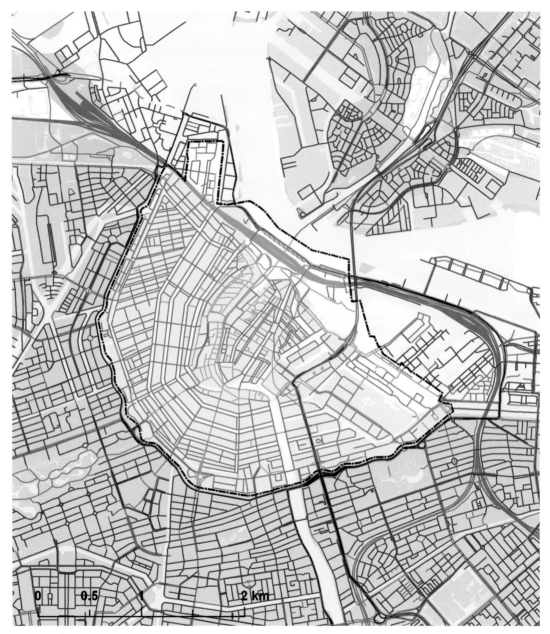

0   0.5   1   2 km

Map 7.3 | Listed conservation area, Municipality of Amsterdam, 1999.
Source: Municipality of Amsterdam.

about the rapid conversion of traditional neighbour-hood grocery stores into fashionable coffee houses and ice cream parlours. Old family shops are priced out by realty owners, who are eager to get their share of the fast-increasing tourist business.

Acknowledgments

The author is obliged to Jan Nijman and Peter Verdonk for their kindness in reading and suggesting improvements to the manuscript.

PART III

TWENTY-FIRST-CENTURY CHALLENGES

chapter eight

Preservation through Transformation:
Amsterdam through the Lens of Barcelona

MELISA PESOA, MARK WARREN, AND JOAQUÍN SABATÉ

The traditional pattern of development in established city centres is one of replacement and adaptation to meet contemporary needs. Obsolete or deteriorated structures are modified or replaced; infrastructure is modernized and expanded at the expense of the existing built environment. The preservation of select elements of the city is a relatively recent phenomenon, and one whose role in urban planning is still being defined. Cities today must decide what elements or structures of their built environment to preserve, and how to preserve them. These are difficult questions that lead to varied approaches to the preservation of historic urban centres, particularly as cities continue to adapt and modernize, and as they attempt to compete with each other. Renewal and preservation are often seen as incompatible forces that necessarily preclude each other, but Barcelona and Amsterdam have shown that these forces can, in fact, work together to positively transform cities' historic centres. It is desirable, though quite difficult, for a modern city to arrive at an appropriate balance between preservation and modernization: the interrelationship of the two should be considered a crucial element of planning in historic city centres (Figure 8.1).

The two cities, however, have taken different approaches to their historic centres' preservation in the past decades. In Barcelona, the process of replacement and modernization has continued in the city centre, with buildings of historic or cultural value either preserved or remodelled. In some renewal projects, the medieval street pattern is preserved or imitated; in others, it is ignored entirely. Amsterdam, on the other hand, has long appreciated its historic centre's architecture and canal structure, and has sought to preserve not just individual buildings but the whole historic urban environment. Certainly, new avenues have cut through Amsterdam's centre, and older structures continue to be replaced with modern ones, but these interventions are much more sporadic in Amsterdam than in Barcelona. New buildings often seek to blend in with the surrounding historic architecture and occasionally directly imitate earlier styles.

Though their approaches have differed, both cities have in the last half century seen their centres evolve

	Amsterdam	Barcelona
City total area (municipality)	219 km² (166 km² dry land)	102 km²
City total inhabitants	872,680 (2019)[a]	1,636,762 (2019)[b]
Study area	205 ha (Canal District core area)	305 ha (Old City)
Study area inhabitants	Canal District: 23,708 (2007)[c]	Old City: 100,714 (2018)[e]
	Amsterdam Centre: 86,862 (2019)[d]	El Raval: 46,948 (2018)[e]

Sources:

a Centraal Bureau voor de Statistiek (CBS). (2020). Bevolkingsontwikkeling; regio per maand. Retrieved from https://opendata.cbs.nl/statline/#/CBS/nl/dataset/37230ned/table?ts=1578685738191

b Instituto de Estadística de Cataluña. (2020). Barcelona. Retrieved from https://www.idescat.cat/emex/?id=080193&lang=es

c UNESCO. (2009). The seventeenth-century canal ring area of Amsterdam: Nomination document. Retrieved from https://whc.unesco.org/uploads/nominations/1349.pdf

d Gemeente Amsterdam. (2019). Kerncijfers Amsterdam 2019. Retrieved from https://data.amsterdam.nl/publicaties/publicatie/kerncijfers/14dfc30d-10dc-4613-9d14-bf43c1af8b63/

e Ajuntament de Barcelona. (2018). Estradística i Difusió de Dades. Cifras oficiales de población 1 de enero de 2018. Retrieved from https://www.bcn.cat/estadistica/castella/dades/barris/tpob/pad/ine/a2018/ine01.htm

Figure 8.1 | Amsterdam's Canal District and Barcelona's Old City, shown at the same scale and with key comparable statistics.

from stagnation or even decay into modern hubs that are desirable places to live and work and that have proven capable of attracting a remarkable level of tourism. In planning the transformation of historic city centres, however, it is no easy feat to make preservation and modernization work together. Excessive preservation of the built environment artificially interrupts the dynamic processes of urban development and adaptation to contemporary conditions. A failure to preserve enough, on the other hand, entails the loss of urban and architectural heritage (an economic asset in addition to a piece of socio-cultural identity) and of the city's historic form.

The question of preservation's role in historic cities' transformation is hardly new to Amsterdam, but today it seems more relevant than ever. The designation of the seventeenth-century Canal District to the UNESCO World Heritage List in 2010, with the rest of the historic centre considered as a "buffer zone," secures the role of preservation in the city's urbanism going forward. The need to constantly adapt the city to contemporary conditions to benefit residents and other users of the city, and to remain economically viable, will remain, however. The relationship between this transformation and the built environment's preservation is undoubtedly a vital issue of urbanism in Amsterdam's centre, without easy answers. Barcelona, too, has a historic centre that has been subject to the effects of the city's modernization. Over the past thirty-five years, it has undergone various renewal projects that have updated its built environment to meet modern standards, but preservation has been an important factor in this transformation. In this chapter, we discuss some of the successes and failures of preservation in Barcelona's recent urbanism in order to provide a comparison, and in some ways hold a mirror, to Amsterdam and other cities facing similar challenges.

Preservation of the Historic Centre

The history of preservation in Barcelona's Ciutat Vella (Old City) differs from that in Amsterdam's inner city and canal rings. Amsterdam's historic built environment was valued even during its construction, evident in its role as subject of numerous contemporary artworks – see, for example, Gerrit Adriaensz. Berckheyde's paintings of the Golden Bend in the Herengracht (1671–72). Appreciation for Amsterdam's aesthetic value was not limited to religious or political monuments, but extended to the private construction that lined the canals and would come to define the city's image. In Barcelona, certain monuments in Ciutat Vella were revered, but appreciation for the majority of the historic centre's construction did not shape the city's urban policies until after the city's transition to a democratically elected government in 1979.

Thus, Amsterdam's inner city developed for centuries with an awareness of its overall aesthetic value, allowing much of the historic city to survive and laying the foundations for its preservation. Certain projects to improve the city's traffic circulation and public transport caused the replacement of some portions of the historic centre with new construction, but an extraordinary proportion of Amsterdam's centre today consists of historic buildings that have been preserved or restored. In Barcelona's Ciutat Vella, historic buildings typically survived not because they were valued and protected, but because they were ignored. Ciutat Vella was considered a slum, largely left to deteriorate while other neighbourhoods of the city developed. In the 1980s, the process of replacement and modernization in Ciutat Vella began again, preserving certain historic elements but destroying others and building anew.

As a result, Barcelona's historic centre appears much more heterogeneous than Amsterdam's. Buildings from many eras stand side by side, interspersed with historic and recently created public spaces. Preserved buildings are typically rehabilitated and re-used, giving them a future as well as a past. The overall image is of a city centre that is historic but modern; one that preserves, but adapts.

Preservation in Barcelona's Ciutat Vella

Despite the early presence of Iberian tribes in Barcelona's area, the city started developing only during the Roman Empire. Its Roman splendour was in the second century, when it was known as Barcino. It was surrounded by a wall and had a forum, a temple, and important aqueducts. The Christians began to establish in the area during the third century, and after the barbarian occupation, agriculture in the area started to develop thanks to the utilization of canals and water streams. The feudal system, since the eleventh century, contributed to give importance to the city as the capital of the County of Barcelona. Since then, Barcelona began to establish itself as a capital of the Catalan region, one of the most important trading ports in the Mediterranean (Map 8.1).

Several "suburban" settlements appeared around the city in early modern times, mostly around churches or monasteries. Therefore, it became necessary to build a five kilometre (three mile) extension of the city walls with eighty towers. The economic activity in the city propelled it to greater prominence in the fifteenth century, when it was allowed by the Crown to construct a proper port. The walls were extended again, with several bastions and a citadel, including an area of orchards in the inner city. After a series of confrontations against the Kingdom of Spain, Barcelona in the eighteenth and nineteenth centuries experienced a fast and steady growth spurred by the Industrial Revolution. The demolition of the Ciutat Vella walls allowed for the building of the Eixample, the city extension proposed by Cerdà in 1859. The plan covered the whole plain of Barcelona, connecting suburban villages through a homogenous grid with spacious streets and green spaces in each block. It represented an answer to the unhealthy situation of the Old City at that moment: a dense and overcrowded district (180,000 inhabitants in 1850) with no infrastructures or public services.

The first calls to preserve Ciutat Vella accompanied the opening of Via Laietana (1908–13). This avenue was the only one executed among the three proposed by Cerdà, and its construction required the destruction of large portions of the area near the Cathedral in order to connect the Eixample to the port. Numerous buildings considered to be of historical and architectural value were razed, to criticism from local architects and intellectuals (Cócola, 2011). In response, they planned the monumentalization of the area around the Cathedral, highlighting its Gothic and Roman history. This plan involved the

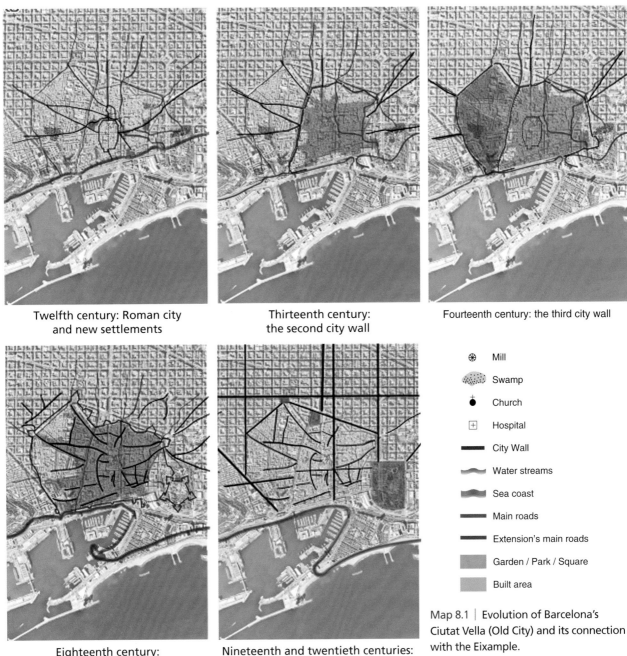

Twelfth century: Roman city
and new settlements

Thirteenth century:
the second city wall

Fourteenth century: the third city wall

Eighteenth century:
modern city wall and Citadel

Nineteenth and twentieth centuries:
Old City connected to Cerdà's Extension

⊛	Mill
▨	Swamp
●	Church
⊞	Hospital
▬	City Wall
∿	Water streams
∿	Sea coast
▬	Main roads
▬	Extension's main roads
▨	Garden / Park / Square
▨	Built area

Map 8.1 | Evolution of Barcelona's
Ciutat Vella (Old City) and its connection
with the Eixample.
Source: Authors.

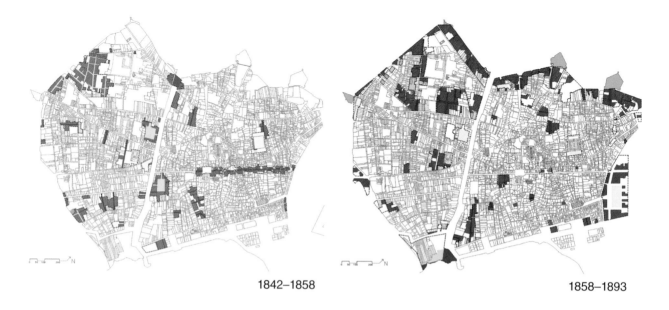

1842–1858   1858–1893

restoration of some buildings to their supposed original form à la Viollet-le-Duc and the destruction of others to allow for more picturesque views of the zone's monuments. This form of preservation did not extend to the entire Ciutat Vella, but was limited to specific monuments of the "Gothic Quarter" around the Cathedral and to some streets in the eastern portion of Ciutat Vella (Cócola, 2011). The rest of Ciutat Vella, meanwhile, continued as an overcrowded, unhealthy slum, while the city's activity and capital moved gradually to the Eixample (Map 8.2).

Apart from the Gothic Quarter, plans for Ciutat Vella in the first part of the twentieth century con-sisted mainly of cutting two more avenues like Via Laietana (one parallel, one perpendicular) through the fabric of the Old City. All three of these avenues had originally been included in Cerdà's 1859 extension plan for the city and remained a constant feature in plans for Ciutat Vella, appearing even in the 1976 Plan General Metropolitano (PGM; Metropolitan Master Plan). Their expected creation contributed to Ciutat Vella's blight, creating a disincentive for new construction and rehabilitation of existing buildings. In 1932, the modernist architects of GATCPAC[1] proposed an alternative that prefigured the city's urbanism of the democratic era, replacing

---

1. GATCPAC, acronym for Group of Catalan Architects and Technicians for Contemporary Architecture, was a group of architects as-sembled during the Second Spanish Republic (Sert, Bonet, Torres Clave). They designed a Master Plan for the City of Barcelona (1933–35), in which they proposed new squares to introduce air and light in a dense Old City.

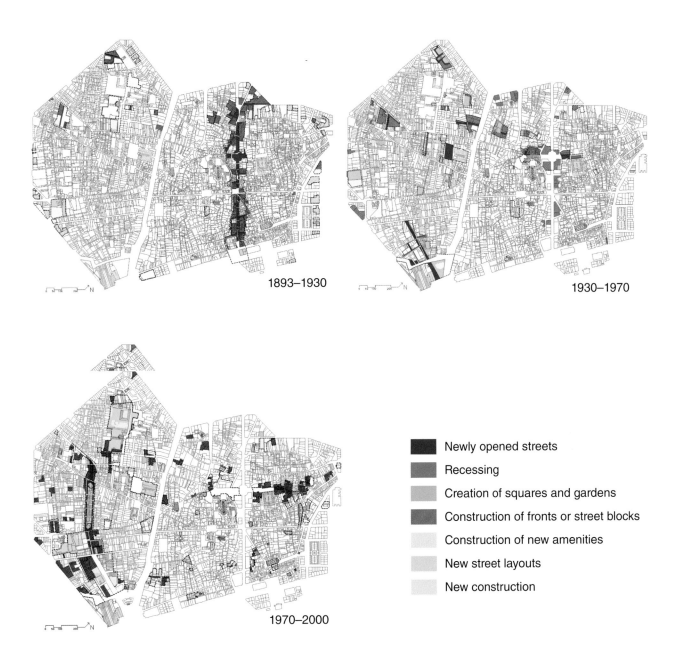

1893–1930

1930–1970

1970–2000

Newly opened streets

Recessing

Creation of squares and gardens

Construction of fronts or street blocks

Construction of new amenities

New street layouts

New construction

(Opposite and above) Map 8.2 | Sequence of transformations in the Old City between 1842 and 2000.
Source: Busquets et al., 2003.

deteriorated blocks with public spaces instead of "Haussmannising" the Old City. However, the Civil War between 1936 and 1939 halted all plans for Ciutat Vella's renewal. During Franco's dictatorship, the preservation and restoration of the Gothic Quarter continued, and the planned avenues returned through several plans until the 1976 PGM. All of them planned the destruction of large segments of the Old City, including many buildings of historic value, but only segments of the new avenues were built.

When the democratically elected government took over in 1979, Ciutat Vella was in quite poor condition. The built environment had a rich historical background, but after decades of neglect and decay the building stock was dilapidated and not up to modern standards; many zones suffered from a lack of maintenance due to the prospect of their planned destruction (Cabrera, 1998). Public services (schools, medical services, police, libraries, and so on) were greatly deficient in the neighbourhood, which also suffered from a lack of open public spaces and a shortage of social housing. Moreover, the narrow, crooked streets were still poorly suited to modern traffic needs. Streets were surrounded by buildings five and six stories tall, allowing little light to reach the ground. The need for Ciutat Vella's renewal was evident and urgent. The city government took the initiative to plan the historic centre's renovation; planners attempted to preserve the existing Ciutat Vella where possible, and to improve it where the current built environment could not be saved. For the first time in the city's plans for Ciutat Vella, an appreciation for the entire historic district was evi-

dent. Over the following decades, Ciutat Vella's preservation became a key concern in its transformation process.

Barcelona has tried to balance its need to modernize with its desire to preserve its historic centre. Some projects have adeptly harmonized these trends, while others have not been so elegant. The city's basic planning philosophy has been to preserve or rehabilitate buildings where possible, often entailing new uses, and to replace those that cannot be salvaged with public spaces, services, housing, or infrastructure. Through this methodology, in the 1980s Barcelona created a number of small plazas in Ciutat Vella where deteriorated blocks had once stood and provided an adequate level of new public services in the neighbourhood, as well as some new housing. These projects were typically well executed and were widely praised for improving quality of life for residents and other users of Ciutat Vella (Sabaté, 2006; Sabaté & Rondó, 2008).

Some larger renewal plans for Ciutat Vella were submitted by the city in 1982 and approved by the regional government in 1985. They dealt with the blighted areas where avenues had been previously planned, modifying the PGM to allow for the neighbourhoods' renewal instead of merely more traffic circulation. A broader rehabilitation area was designated in Ciutat Vella, allowing for the provision of government subsidies and assistance for historic buildings' maintenance. The renewal plans comprise the bulk of the city's recent urbanism in Ciutat Vella and demonstrate the complexity of the relationship between preservation and modernization. In some instances, they have led to the preservation of the historic city, while in others they have catalysed its renovation and modernization (Figure 8.2).

One of the first major renewal projects was implemented at the north end of El Raval neighbourhood in Ciutat Vella in the late 1980s and the first half of the 1990s. Much of the historic complex of a former convent was preserved and reused to house various cultural institutions, which have since been joined by new buildings belonging to two universities. Some of the original structure was destroyed to make room for the contemporary art museum (Museo de Arte Contemporáneo de Barcelona [MACBA]) in a new building designed by Richard Meier and for a large adjacent plaza. This project created large public spaces in an area that had none, and the cultural cluster around them in a combination of new and old buildings has proved an attractive asset for the neighbourhood's revitalization. The preservation of certain aspects of the zone shaped its renovated form and served as a vital part of its transformation from a physically and economically decaying area into a new centre of activity.

Just south of this new cultural hub, the Plan Especial de Reforma Interior (PERI) called for a much more controversial intervention. Five blocks in the centre of El Raval were razed to make room for a massive (317 by 58 metres [1,040 by 190 feet]), elongated plaza-promenade called the Rambla del Raval, inaugurated in 2000 (Figure 8.3). More blocks were destroyed at either end of this unusual new public space to build new housing, services, and traffic routes, and still more blocks along one of its sides were demolished to build a four-star high-rise hotel, offices,

housing, and a film centre. In this phase of the PERI, the preservation of the existing city has consisted of little more than restoring the facades of buildings along the Rambla del Raval, while many blocks in the centre of the city have been destroyed. Moreover, the renewal project introduced new urban forms (the enormous Rambla del Raval and the wide, straight streets at either end) thoroughly alien to the neighbourhood's pattern of narrow, crooked streets and smaller public spaces. The project of renewal around the Rambla del Raval ignored not only the preservation of individual buildings but also that of the historic city's urban form.

The execution of the PERI for the area around the Santa Caterina market in the eastern portion of Ciutat Vella involved much more attention to preservation, though it still required much of the zone's renovation. As in the construction of the Rambla del Raval, several blocks were destroyed, but the new construction that has replaced them attempts to cohere with the surrounding urban fabric. The new buildings and streets do not conform to the prior pattern, but rather imitate Ciutat Vella's morphology (winding streets, small public spaces, passageways beneath buildings) to fit in with the surrounding neighbourhood in a manner that meets modern urban standards. An effort has been made to preserve historical elements where possible, as with the facade of the renovated Santa Caterina market and its display of the archaeological ruins beneath it. In other instances, historic elements (facades, doorways, arches) have been preserved and face the new constructions. The preservation of certain physical elements, but even more significantly of

MACBA & CCCB: Cultural cluster

Rambla del Raval

Santa Caterina's Market

Pou de la Figuera

L'Allada Vermell Street

Figure 8.2 | Major interventions on Barcelona's Ciutat Vella (Old City) since the 1980s.
Source: Authors.

Figure 8.3 | Rambla del Raval, Barcelona.
Source: Authors.

the local pattern of urbanization, has shaped the recent physical transformation of the Santa Caterina neighbourhood.

From the 1980s onward, Barcelona leaned towards the modernization of Ciutat Vella rather than its preservation or restoration, which is not surprising given the neighbourhood's many deficiencies at the start of this period. At that time, the urgent needs of the resident population meant that projects for the renewal of the Old City were more appropriate than ones calling for its extensive preservation. However, the city's renewal policy for Ciutat Vella did include its preservation, which has played a key role in its transformation from a marginalized and degraded neighbourhood into a centre of activity once again.

The neighbourhood's renewal entailed not its destruction but rather its rebirth, with much of the original environment not only intact but in use.

Preservation in Amsterdam's City Centre

Amsterdam's historic centre, on the other hand, presents a much more unified and historic, nostalgic image. Amsterdam has its share of new traffic and transport routes (Raadhuisstraat, Vijzelstraat/Rokin, Weesperstraat, the north-south metro line, railways, as discussed in the previous chapter), which have cut axes of modern architecture and transportation through the historic centre, but vast stretches of canals and inner city streets remain unchanged since the seventeenth century. This longevity is due partly to their preservation over the centuries and partly to Amsterdam's continued deference to conservative and historicizing forms in the renovation and restoration of the city centre.

Since painter Jan Veth's protests in 1900 against the proposed filling-in of the Reguliersgracht, Amsterdam's citizens have proven quite sensitive to their city's preservation in the face of efforts to modernize it (Mak, 2004: 14). This appreciation for Amsterdam's historic construction was not limited to monuments, as in Barcelona, but encompassed the balance of the inner city. In the 1950s and 1960s, the status of Amsterdam's historic centre was similar to that of Barcelona in the 1970s: the physical environment was seriously deteriorated, and renewal was seen as necessary, with the city considering proposals for broad traffic routes and the complete renovation of the Jordaan and other run-down zones (Kupka, 2012: 81–98). Fierce citizen opposition led the city to alter its plans and instead pursue smaller-scale renewal projects that required less destruction of the extant city. At the same time, citizens started to form corporations to purchase, rehabilitate (or reconstruct), and manage historic properties (Eggenkamp, 2004). Over the second half of the twentieth century, buildings were restored or reconstructed to their presumed original state, contributing to the city's picturesque image. As in Barcelona, many of these preserved buildings were given new uses; the Waag in Nieuwmarkt, a fifteenth-century weigh house converted into a popular restaurant, is an excellent example.

Some recent buildings in Amsterdam's historic centre are patently modern, but a surprising number attempt to blend in with or even directly reproduce the city's historic structures. The city's new construction, when it is allowed to look new, is often striking, offering modern interpretations of earlier typologies or jarring juxtapositions. The development behind the Zuiderkerk above the new metro tunnel is an example of a new urbanistic project that preserves the feeling of the historic centre without adopting a historicizing aesthetic and creates small, attractive public spaces. Another experiment that preserves Amsterdam's historic urban typologies can be found not far from the old centre, on Java-eiland. Here, a slice of a canal district has been recreated in the former docklands, mixing nostalgia and postmodernity. The variety generated by the quirky canal house designs is somewhat negated by their ironic repetition on every quay, but they nevertheless show that new design can be accommodated in a preserved historic urban typology.

This expression of a modern and developing city, however, is at odds with the historic image the city has preserved. Instead, new buildings are often designed to be unassuming, and occasionally to mimic those of centuries past. Some have been remodelled to appear in their "original" form; others have been taken apart and reassembled to allow construction work to take place underneath (Schoonenberg, 2004: 143–5). This practice preserves the undeniably beautiful appearance of the historic centre, but at the cost of its authenticity. As a result, its built environment today appears much less diverse than Barcelona's, though perhaps more picturesque.

The Impact of Tourism in Barcelona and Amsterdam

Both Barcelona and Amsterdam have seen their historic centres transformed in the past half century from decaying and increasingly obsolescent zones into revitalized hubs of urban life. The preservation of elements of the existing built environment has helped shape the physical transformation, but forces beyond planners' control have led to important socio-economic changes as well. In Barcelona in the 1980s, Ciutat Vella's population was in decline (and it had lost a third of its residents in the previous decade) and consisted of a large proportion of senior citizens. The composition of the population has since changed drastically, thanks largely to the arrival of some 50,000 immigrants to Ciutat Vella between 1996 and 2006 and to the more recent incursion of students and young urban professionals, particularly around the neighbourhood's new cultural institutions. Scores of small businesses have opened, often operated by immigrants but aimed at markets ranging from local ethnic communities to international tourists. Tourism has boomed, injecting large quantities of foreign capital into the local economy. Young adults now make up the neighbourhood's largest demographic group.

Over the past years, Barcelona has become the third most visited city in Europe, after London and Paris, and this flow keeps growing. Barcelona has evolved and marketed itself, over time, in order to attract tourists and visitors. In 2019, over 21 million visitors spent at least one night in Barcelona, only about 10 per cent of them coming from the rest of Spain.[2] Barcelona has become a city brand, attracts more and more visits, and generates increasing expenditure per tourist. Several agents both public and private have been responsible for this "success." The city has been reinvented, transformed, adapted, and shaped in the last decades and keeps facing new challenges and adapting itself on a daily basis to the needs and expectations of this touristic flow (Porfido, Pérez, & Pesoa, 2019).

Experts and residents question this continuous remake and all the negative effects. Far beyond invading the city, tourism has become part of Barcelona itself. Touristic flows imply strong impacts on the city and its residents. Low-cost travelling exposes the city to high pressure, uncivil behaviour, and vandalism. A tendency for faster experiences is transforming traditional businesses; transformations also include price increases in restaurants, cafés, terraces, apartments, and products. Crowds on public spaces force residents to restrain their activities or to relocate them, losing valuable places, local identity, and interaction between neighbours. These impacts, clearly evident in the Old City, result in a tense interaction between residents and visitors, which quite often are expressed in daily life on the streets.

It is difficult to pinpoint the specific role of the Old City's renewal and preservation in these changes, but the urban interventions of the past thirty-five

---

2. Source: Ajuntament de Barcelona. (2018). Estradística i Difusió de Dades. Datos evolutivos de Barcelona y ámbitos. Retrieved from https://www.bcn.cat/estadistica/castella/dades/economia/teoh/evo/t23.htm.

years have been assimilated into the neighbourhood and embraced by the district's new population. The plazas around MACBA in the north of El Raval are constantly filled with local residents of all ages, visitors who come for the museums or the nearby cafés and shops that have opened around them, university students, tourists, and skateboarders from around the world. The Rambla del Raval, too, is intensely used: residents line the public space's benches, young people sit in circles on the pavement to talk and drink, visitors walk the promenade's length or enjoy bars' and restaurants' outdoor seating, and ambulatory beer vendors use the vegetation to hide their inventory. In Santa Caterina, the residents played a major role in shaping their own public spaces, protesting the installation of a parking lot and converting it themselves into a community garden and recreational spaces (Delgado, 2006).

The combination of a vibrant local community, appealing public spaces, popular cultural attractions, and the preservation of selected elements of the built environment have made Ciutat Vella an attractive place to live, work, and visit. The preservation of the historic centre is not merely an aesthetic or historical concern. As our post-industrial society's progress continues to obviate economic and social networks' dependence on physical location, a city's historic built environment becomes a terrific asset for remaining economically competitive. The preservation of historic elements also reinforces the city's social and cultural identity, which is a positive end in itself but also contributes to the city's overall appeal. Today, historic cities must compete with new urban areas that have more modern advantages for people

and capital; the growth of the area around Schiphol Airport is one example. Preservation can be a tool for distinguishing historic cities and for ensuring the continued inflow of business and tourism, provided this preservation allows for the accommodation of modern (and adaptation to future) economic activity.

Amsterdam's preservation has shaped the present state of the city as well. Since the city's approach has favoured the preservation, restoration, reconstruction, and reinterpretation of historic building types, rather than an approach more permissive of destruction and renewal, the outcome is different from that of the projects in Ciutat Vella. The overall image is more scenic, but the density of population is significantly lower, and the zone has become largely gentrified (Kupka, 2012: 86). It contains a mixture of economic activity, but the density of offices and commercial spaces is also lower than Ciutat Vella's. They tend to be concentrated along the main traffic thoroughfares marked by modern construction and are less common in the preserved zones. The historic city is a tourist attraction in its own right, a fact substantiated by the Canal District's UNESCO designation; Amsterdam received some 19 million visitors in 2018, making tourism an important part of the modern city's function. The same goes for Barcelona, which had roughly 21 million visitors in 2019.

Conclusions

Barcelona's and Amsterdam's historic centres have experienced dramatic transformations in recent decades, with preservation playing a key role. Preservation does not merely save aspects of the past; it also defines the present and future city. By including the preservation of valued historic elements in urban planning, cities are ensuring the future relevance (and thus the continued longevity) of these elements. Moreover, preservation does not need to stand in the way of modernization and renewal. Incorporating elements and structures that are to be preserved into plans for a city's transformation ensures they become an important part of its future development. In trying to reach an appropriate balance, however, Barcelona has tended more towards the at-times destructive modernization of the Ciutat Vella, while Amsterdam has made more of an effort to preserve its historic image. Each approach has advantages and disadvantages.

Thanks to its preservation, Amsterdam presents a picturesque historic environment capable of attracting residents, tourists, and businesses. This environment is not only aesthetically pleasing, but also a marketable quality in the present and for the future. However, the city has denied the natural process of its development in favour of preserving its historical image, sacrificing some of its authenticity – another rare and valuable asset in the postmodern age.

Barcelona's approach, on the other hand, has embraced the dynamism of urban development, preserving certain elements while destroying others to make room for new construction, infrastructure, and public spaces. This approach has helped the city's remarkable turnaround in the past three decades, and has made for a modern and adaptable centre that retains much of its heritage. However, new buildings are rarely as handsome as the historic ones they replace, and portions of the historic urban fabric have been obliterated. Some vestiges of the past have been sacrificed for the continued viability of the old centre in the present and future.

As the evolution of both cities testifies, reaching a balance between preservation and modernization is a formidable challenge, and the methodology is dependent on each city's unique historical conditions, development path, and future goals. The cities have also demonstrated that preservation does not necessarily require the calcification of the built environment, but rather can include the past in planning for the future.

chapter nine

The Canal District as a Site of Cognitive-Cultural Activities: "A Miracle of Spaciousness, Compactness, Intelligible Order"

ROBERT C. KLOOSTERMAN AND KARIN PFEFFER

The characteristic seventeenth-century facade of the Amsterdam Canal District seems to have changed little in four centuries. The fine-grained urban morphology with its intimate intertwining of land and water is still very much intact. The pre-industrial maritime technology implied that mercantile shipping was not just highly labour intensive but also that functions – loading and unloading, warehousing, coordination and control, as well as living and leisure – were bound to be in close proximity to each other as well as near the water. According to Mark D'Eramo (2015: 85), "the mansions of the great merchants were never far from the port; the quaysides functioned not only for the mooring, loading and unloading of ocean-going ships, but also as urban traffic routes and promenades." The merchants, then, combined living and working in their houses, presenting a function mix that was typical for the pre-industrial era (Mumford, 1961). At that time, Amsterdam was at the apex of the Western

world system, acting as a prime exchange of information on international trade and, related to this function, constituting a global financial centre *avant la lettre* (Braudel, 1979: 73; Israel, 1989; Lesger, 2001). One could even argue that the Amsterdam Canal District with its merchants and their globe-spanning trade networks was the very cradle and, for a while, the centre of a globe-spanning merchant capitalism that would link faraway parts in Europe, Asia, Africa, and the Americas through flows of goods, services, capital, people, and information (Braudel, 1979; Wallerstein, 1984; Prak, 2002).

Nowadays, functions directly related to the port have moved out of the Canal District. Behind the doors of what were once the mansions of great merchants, however, we can still, or perhaps even better, again find high-end economic activities mixed with residential and other functions. In this chapter, we offer an economic-geographic perspective on the Amsterdam Canal District today. We assess its

---

The quote in the title of this chapter is from Lewis Mumford (1961: 504): "The Plan of the Three Canals was a miracle of spaciousness, compactness, intelligible order."

importance as a milieu of production and consumption by providing a detailed mapping of its economic activities. We start with a brief depiction of the broader changes in the Amsterdam economy in recent decades to provide a backdrop for the development of the Canal District. We then turn to a discussion of the Canal District as an urban neighbourhood with very specific characteristics. Subsequently, we show how the more general trends of the Amsterdam economy are articulated in the Canal District.

The Resilience of Amsterdam's Twenty-First-Century Economy

The Amsterdam economy has been outperforming most other cities in the Netherlands for about three decades (Planbureau voor de Leefomgeving, 2016: 15, 53). Employment growth has been higher than the national average, especially with respect to highly paid jobs, and the overall wage level in Amsterdam has been higher as well, also when controlled for skill levels (16). Highly paid workers increasingly live in the city itself or in the greater Amsterdam metropolitan area, thereby further strengthening the urban economy (15). One might have expected that the Amsterdam economy would be hard hit after the credit crisis of 2008, given its relatively large financial sector. The city, however, displayed a strong resilience, and the growth of employment even accelerated after 2008, thereby diverging even more from national trends. It appears that Amsterdam has embarked on a new kind of economic growth path (Trip, Kloosterman, & Romein, 2016).

The strong performance of the Amsterdam economy can be attributed to several interrelated factors. The first explanation lies in the sectoral composition of the Amsterdam economy. As a historical financial centre *and* cultural capital and a second-tier global city (Kloosterman, 2004, 2014), Amsterdam was well positioned to benefit from what Allen Scott (2012) has labelled a shift towards a cognitive-cultural economy. According to Scott (2012: x), "capitalism itself has changed dramatically since the demise of high Fordism in the 1970s ... dependent more than it ever has been in the past on a labor force endowed with finely honed cognitive and cultural skills." A cognitive-cultural urban economy is dominated by an array of high-end producer services, cultural industries, and an extensive educational-healthcare complex, which includes vocational and academic institutions (Hutton, 2016). These cognitive-cultural activities are by definition dependent on the input and exchange of high levels of dedicated knowledge, and they can reap substantial agglomeration economies by clustering. Such spatial concentration, moreover, may set in motion a process of increasing returns whereby new layers of firms and workers (in related activities) and dedicated local institutions dealing with education, knowledge exchange, monitoring and certification of product quality, marketing, and distribution are added (Scott, 2012; Vermeulen, Teulings, Marlet, & de Groot, 2016). Sometime in the late 1980s, Amsterdam seems to have entered this path-dependent trajectory, giving a new kind of vibrancy to the urban economy (Kloosterman, 1994, 2014). Amsterdam has thus once more become a global city, with a concomitant cosmopolitan outlook and a strong presence in, for instance, consultancy and accountancy, advertising, design, and higher education (Röling, 2010; Fernandez, 2011; Kloosterman, 2013).

A second, related, explanation for the resurgence of the Amsterdam economy has been its ability to attract highly skilled workers from both the Netherlands and abroad (Pethe, Haffner, & Lawton, 2010; Sleutjes & Musterd, 2016). The share of highly educated workers in the Amsterdam workforce is one of the highest in the Netherlands. In absolute terms, the city has the largest highly educated workforce in the Netherlands (Kloosterman, 2014). These highly educated workers are attracted by the expansion of the local production system centred on cognitive-cultural activities. They are, however, also attracted by the amenity-rich environment of the city, its shops, cafés, restaurants, and museums (de Groot, Marlet, Teulings, & Vermeulen, 2010; Vermeulen et al., 2016). This pattern sets in motion a self-reinforcing process as more highly educated workers enable a further extension of these amenities, thereby attracting more of them. In addition, young highly educated workers especially come to Amsterdam to find and enjoy the company of other highly educated young people, as friends or partners (Latten & Deerenberg, 2013).

A third factor is the unique quality of the built environment, more specifically the legacy of the seventeenth century with the Canal District as its main focal point (de Groot et al., 2010). This highly diverse, rich, intricate, and aesthetically pleasing urban milieu has attracted dwellers, workers, entrepreneurs, visitors, and tourists ever since its construction. Housing prices (per square metre) in Amsterdam are the highest of all Dutch cities, especially in the city centre where prices far exceed those in the rest of the city (Vermeulen et al., 2016: 72). The numbers of visitors and tourists have also gone up. In the year 2000, about 4 million tourists (persons who stayed at least one night in Amsterdam) were registered. In 2015, the number had risen to nearly 7 million (Onderzoek, Informatie en Statistiek, n.d.), bringing vibrancy and monetary rewards, but also putting even more pressure on the city and the historic infrastructure of the centre.

Thus, Amsterdam has been able to exploit its historical legacy – both in terms of its deeply rooted global city profile and international orientation and by way of its seventeenth-century built environment. Indeed, it has done so quite well, judged by its economic performance after 1990. Without doubt, Amsterdam has become the most important city of production *and* consumption within the Netherlands (Figure 9.1).

The Quality of Place of the Canal District

The iconic Canal District forms an integral part of this buoyant Amsterdam economy. Before we present data on the economic profile of the Canal District, we will first briefly analyse its physical characteristics and then take a look at its demographic profile. Our definition of the Canal District is based on administrative boundaries, delineated according to physical and socio-economic characteristics and the presence of the canals. We have selected three neighbourhoods: Grachtengordel West (West Canal District), Grachtengordel South (South Canal District), and Nieuwmarkt/Lastage (East Canal District). The first two are very much part of the typical Canal District (and the designated UNESCO heritage) with their uniformly laid-out allotments stemming from the

(Opposite and above) Figure 9.1 | The south-central stretch of the Herengracht, built in the 1660s, soon became the most prestigious (and expensive) part of the entire Canal District and acquired the epithet "De Gouden Bocht" – the Golden Bend (on Map 9.1, it is located just above the "South" label).

The print (opposite) is from around 1694 by the artist Jan van Call. The photograph (above) shows the same area in 2019. This part of the Herengracht is still – or again – home to high-end services. The building in the photograph houses a number of internationally active firms such as Werkspot (a digital labour platform), Expedia (hotel booking site), Euroclear (ICT), Endesa (energy consultancy), and several financial services.

Source: Stadsarchief Amsterdam, Beeldbank010097000033, public domain (print); authors (photo)

original plan dating from the seventeenth century. The East Canal District was the last developed part of the "Fourth Extension" (see chapter 2 for a more detailed historical discussion of the successive "extensions" and the construction of the Canal District). Due to the economic downturn in the wake of the wars that broke out in 1672, there was not much development of the area in the sense of housing construction. Instead, much of the area was rented out as gardens from which it got its name, the "Plantage." It was only after 1850, when Amsterdam started growing again, that the area was built up (Abrahamse, 2013: 21). The East Canal District, then, is more mixed in terms of its layout, types of buildings, and their year of construction and, because of its rather different built environment, may serve as a contrast case with respect to the two other parts of the Canal District (see Map 9.1).

To assess the physical characteristics of the Canal District, we use the approach to "quality of place" as a determinant of economic activities developed by Sidika Bahar Durmaz (2015: 102) in her study on the clustering of a particular cognitive-cultural activity, namely the film industry in Soho, London, and Beyoğlu, Istanbul. Durmaz distinguishes four domains of physical characteristics relevant to cognitive-cultural economic activities: (1) location, (2) land use, (3) urban form, and (4) visual characteristics. What kind of quality of place, then, does the Canal District offer more specifically regarding cognitive-cultural activities, which are dependent on intensive knowledge exchange, when looking at these four characteristics?

Location is not so much a set of coordinates as a combination of centrality, proximity, and accessibility (Durmaz, 2015: 104). The centrality of the Canal District is evident. The horseshoe-shaped form of the Canal District encompasses the pre-seventeenth-century part of the city, and the Central Station, a major public transport hub, is located almost right in the middle of its two ends. Because of this highly central location, every single part of the Canal District is close to a wide array of urban amenities (for example cafés, restaurants, shops, theatres), many of them located within the district itself or just beyond the district boundaries. Even the southern tip of the Canal District is still within a distance of less than two kilometres (one mile) of the Central Station, which, in turn, is a fifteen-minute train ride away from Schiphol Airport. There is, in addition, a dense network of public transport (trams and buses). Given the relative narrow streets, the area is rather difficult to navigate by car, but its seventeenth-century compactness provides a very high level of walkability and, arguably, an even higher level of cyclability with its extensive bicycle infrastructure and deeply rooted bicycle culture (Jordan, 2013). The Canal District, then, offers a rare combination of a highly central location, proximity to a wide range of urban facilities, and good accessibility (though not so much for cars) on the level of the neighbourhood, the city, the country, and to other countries by train or by plane.

The second important physical characteristic of quality of place is the use of the urban land. Partly a legacy of the seventeenth century with its pre-industrial mix of functions, a dense, fine-grained mix of functions – residential, work, and urban amenities – can be found in the Canal District (Map 9.2). Living, working, shopping (daily, targeted, and fun-shopping), drinking a

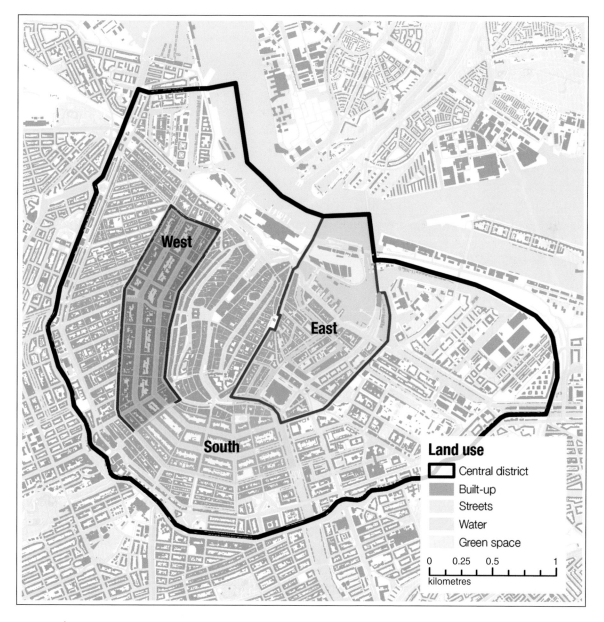

Map 9.1 | Boundaries of the Canal District neighbourhoods.
Source: Maps created by the authors; data from Cadastre Netherlands (http://maps.amsterdam.nl).

Function mix

Amenities
Work
Residential
Canal belt districts
Central district

0   0.25   0.5   1
kilometres

Map 9.2 | Function mix in the city centre.
Source: Map created by the authors; data from Cadastre Netherlands (http://maps.amsterdam.nl).

Table 9.1 Office and commercial spaces in the Canal District as shares of the city total, 2012

	West	South	East
Share of small-scale office space (%)	7.3	3.6	3.1
Share of commercial space (%)	1.6	1.0	2.9
Average office space (m^2)	110	114	114

Source: Gemeente Amsterdam, O+S Amsterdam, Stadsdelen in cijfers 2012, CBS statline.

craft beer or special coffee can all be done in less than a fifteen-minute walk or a ten-minute bike ride in the Canal District. This mix enables a 24/7 lifestyle and presence within the same neighbourhood, fostering the exchange of knowledge through frequent (chance) face-to-face meetings in professional places but also in a wide range of cafés, restaurants, and other social venues (Martins, 2015; Durmaz, 2015: 109; Rath & Gelmers, 2014). This quality is considered one of the essential drivers of agglomeration in cognitive-cultural activities, enabling a refined division of labour between firms in related economic activities (Kloosterman, 2010; Scott, 2012). Map 9.2 shows the concentration of amenities in the old centre and the emphatic mix of living and working in the Canal District itself.

Urban form is the third characteristic that determines the quality of place for businesses (Durmaz, 2015). Durmaz, following Jane Jacobs (1961), unpacks urban form into "permeability, traditional street pattern, porosity, micro-public places, legibility and compactness" (Durmaz, 2015: 112). A short walk through the Canal District or one brief look at its street plan (Maps 9.1, 9.2) makes it very clear that

this part of Amsterdam has a layout that displays Jane Jacobs's (1961: 51) "marvellous" complex order of an old city: no grid patterns, a hierarchy of streets, small blocks allowing for various routes, and safe and accessible streets for both cyclists and pedestrians (at least if they can stay out of the way of the former).

In addition, this part of the city – like the rest of the centre of Amsterdam – has not been transformed into a central business district with monofunctional high-rise towers. The Canal District instead offers a multifunctional, highly urban environment with predominantly relatively small office and commercial spaces averaging somewhat over 100 square metres (1,076 square feet; see Table 9.1). If one compares the shares of the population with those of the small office and commercial spaces, it becomes obvious that all three parts of the Canal District have much higher shares than could be expected on the basis of their population, and this fact holds especially for office spaces in the West Canal District.

The fourth characteristic comprises the visual characteristics. It refers to the built heritage, the

Table 9.2 Number of inhabitants, number of one-person households, and region of origin of inhabitants in the West, South, and East Canal Districts and Amsterdam as a whole, 2012

	West		South		East		Amsterdam	
	no.	**%**	**no.**	**%**	**no.**	**%**	**no.**	**%**
Inhabitants								
Men	3,730	53.1	2,310	53.9	4,725	52.4	389,035	49.2
Women	3,300	46.9	1,975	46.1	4,300	47.6	401,115	50.8
Total	7,030		4,285		9,025		790,150	
Households								
One-person households	2,888	62.9	1,720	63.0	4,124	68.0	237,944	55.0
Origin of inhabitants								
Dutch	4,286	61.0	2,692	63.0	5,644	62.6	390,813	49.5
Western migrants	2,135	30.0	1,184	28.7	2,274	25.2	122,839	15.5
Non-Western migrants	612	9.0	398	9.3	1,103	12.2	276,392	35.0

Source: Gemeente Amsterdam, O+S Amsterdam, Stadsdelen in cijfers 2012, CBS statline.

history, the architectural diversity, and the landmarks (Durmaz, 2015: 114). The Canal District evidently scores very high on these visual characteristics as testified by its inclusion on the UNESCO World Heritage List. According to UNESCO (n.d.), "the gabled facades are characteristic of this middle-class environment, and the dwellings bear witness both to the city's enrichment through maritime trade and the development of a humanist and tolerant culture linked to the Calvinist Reformation ... The Amsterdam Canal District represents an outstanding example of a built urban ensemble that required and illustrates expertise in hydraulics, civil engineering,

town planning, construction and architectural knowhow."

Demography is another important aspect of place, and the Canal District stands apart, in several respects, from the city at large. All three parts of the Canal District have higher shares of men than women – in marked contrast to the city as a whole – and also higher shares of one-person households than the city's average (Table 9.2). In addition, the Canal District can be qualified as an international urban neighbourhood with one-third of its inhabitants from other Western countries and one-tenth from non-Western countries. The relatively large presence of Western immigrants and low presence of non-Western foreigners is reversed in most of the rest of the city.

The quality of place and the attractiveness of the Canal District for native Dutch and foreigners are reflected in the housing prices as assessed by the local tax authorities. In all three parts of the Canal District, the average value of houses is higher than that of Amsterdam as a whole. In the western and southern part of the Canal District, both part of the UNESCO World Heritage List, the average real estate value in 2012 was about twice as high, slightly above 500,000 euros,[1] and by 2018 this disparity had grown even sharper.

The housing market in much of the Canal District differs from that of the city as a whole. Whereas social housing was still the largest type of housing in Amsterdam, in both the western and southern part of the Canal District, it is 5 per cent or less. Hence, these parts of the city are dominated by privately rented and owner-occupied housing. The distribution in the eastern part of the Canal District, with a rather different trajectory of development and housing construction, however, resembles more closely that of the entire city (Figure 9.2).

Considering the average real estate values and the ownership composition, the contrast between the West and the South Canal Districts, on the one hand, and the East on the other, shows that it is not just the central location that is important in relation to its functioning (and economic potential), because the East is as centrally located in the historic city as the other two. Also, the three other characteristics mentioned by Durmaz (2015: 114), notably those referring to the architectural qualities of the built environment on the level of individual buildings as well as on that of the streets and neighbourhood, are crucial.

The Canal District as a Locus of Economic Activities

The quality of place of the West and South Canal Districts is – as we just saw – outstanding when it comes to small-scale cognitive-cultural activities dependent on proximity with related activities and an amenity-rich urban environment. These kinds of activities were crucial in the turnaround of the Amsterdam economy after the grim 1980s. Being both the financial and the cultural capital of the Netherlands as well as its most cosmopolitan city, Amsterdam has benefitted from the structural shift to cognitive-cultural activities and showed strong employment growth, even after the outbreak of credit crisis. In this section, we will investigate how the Canal District fits within this larger picture.

In 2012, nearly 6 per cent of all employees in the city worked in the Canal District (Table 9.3), of which more than half were within the cognitive-cultural sector. Dominant sectors are the financial and law sector, computer firms and services, as well as the

---

1. Gemeente Amsterdam, O+S Amsterdam, Stadsdelen in cijfers 2012, CBS statline.

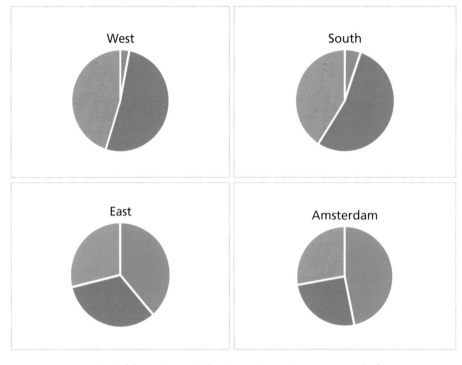

■ Social housing ■ Private rent ■ Owner-occupied

Figure 9.2 | Distribution of types of housing in the Canal District and in Amsterdam, 2012.
Source: Gemeente Amsterdam, O+S Amsterdam, Stadsdelen in cijfers 2012.

arts. Furthermore, there were 3,457 cafés and restaurants registered in Amsterdam in 2012, of which about 10 per cent were located in the Canal District and a considerable number in the neighbouring areas (Map 9.3).

We can also look at the shifts in employment that have taken place in the Canal District between 1996 and 2012. We first look at the overall trends in the eastern, southern, and western part of the Canal District and then zoom in on the employment trends in three key cognitive-cultural activities: financial services, law firms, and cultural industries (arts, advertising, and audio-visual entertainment). We also focus on trends in one-person firms in these sectors that are leading the cognitive-cultural urban economy.

Table 9.3 Presence of cognitive-cultural workers in the three Canal Districts and in Amsterdam, 2012

Sector	Number of employees									
	West		South		East		Canal District		Amsterdam	
	no.	%	no.	%	no.	%	no.	%	no.	%
Publishing	465	4.9	207	2.6	231	2.2	903	3.2	5,592	1.2
Architecture	364	3.8	187	2.4	193	1.8	744	2.7	8,805	1.9
Financial organizations	525	5.5	1,691	21.3	129	1.2	2,345	8.4	42,133	8.9
Higher education	40	0.4	0.0	0.0	518	4.9	558	2.0	12,599	2.7
Law	1,115	11.6	732	9.2	428	4.1	2,275	8.1	30,847	6.5
Computer firms	595	6.2	370	4.7	1,555	14.8	2,520	9.0	14,124	3.0
Computer services	595	6.2	370	4.7	15,554	14.8	2,519	9.0	13,969	2.9
Creative service sector[a]	911	9.5	425	5.4	399	3.8	1,735	6.2	19,326	4.1
Art	482	5.0	242	3.1	1,244	11.9	1,968	7.0	16,141	3.4
Media and entertainment[b]	652	6.8	429	5.4	393	3.7	1,474	5.3	12,990	2.7
Total cognitive-cultural employees	9,580		7,933		10,492		28,005		475,277	

Source: LISA 1996, 2000, 2004; ARRA 2008, 2012.

Note: there is some overlap in categories.
a This sector also contains categories of the architecture sector, specifically architects' offices.
b This sector also contains the publishing sector.

Figure 9.3 shows the trends in the number of workers in the three Canal District neighbourhoods. Employment rose in all three neighbourhoods between 1996 and 2000. After that, we can observe a marked decrease between 2000 and 2004. Between 2004 and 2008, we note an overall phase of stabilization. Interestingly, we see significant divergence after 2008, with a modest rise in the West Canal District, a strong increase in the East, and further drop in the South. The steady decline of employment in the South Canal District can be attributed to closures and relocations to the Zuidas of (larger) financial services. The West Canal District shows an almost continuous modest increase except for the period 2000–04. Employment in the East Canal District, the considerably cheaper part of the Canal District, increased uninterrupted with a very strong increase after 2008, surpassing the other two parts in importance as a site of employment.

The shift to cognitive-cultural activities is intimately intertwined with processes of vertical disintegration and flexibilization (Scott, 2012). Networks of partly co-located small firms are often better positioned to deal with volatile demand. Small firms

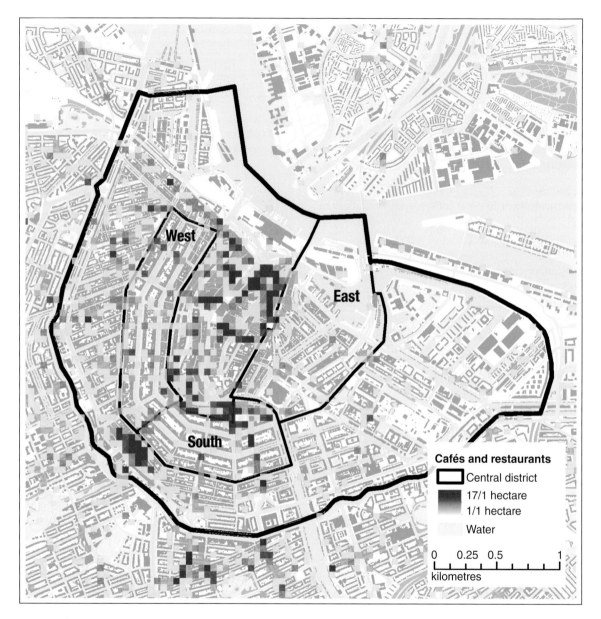

Map 9.3 | Density of cafés and restaurants.
Source: Map created by the authors; data from ARRA 2012 and Cadastre Netherlands (http://maps.amsterdam.nl).

have also been able to compete more successfully due to the steep decline in the cost of information and communication technology, thereby lowering the barriers to entry in many markets. Very small firms, one-person firms without personnel, are not just more nimble but they also may bypass all kinds of (tax and social benefit) regulations pertaining to employees, thus enabling them to undercut larger firms. Outsourcing to one-person firms has also become a strategy of larger firms to cut costs and become more flexible. This increase in small firms is expressed in the profile of many firms in the Canal District today (Figure 9.4).

Figure 9.5 shows the trends in one-person firms in the Canal District. All three parts of the district show a strong increase in this type of firm after 2004. We can even observe a rise of one-person firms in the South Canal District, notwithstanding its overall decline in employment. These findings chime with the quality of place characteristics of the Canal District with its small office spaces and its opportunities for face-to-face meetings and networking.

Our data also allow a breakdown into different types of leading cognitive-cultural sectors (Figure 9.6). We start with financial services. Employment in this sector has gone down, especially in the South Canal District. The downward trend during this period was in line with that of Amsterdam as a whole, which had been losing employment in financial services due to global processes of digitization and centralization of activities in first-tier global centres like London (Engelen, 2007). Since Brexit, there have been signs of a reverse pattern, with

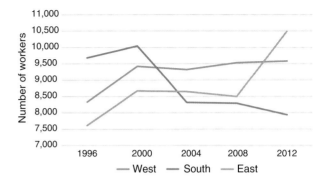

Figure 9.3 | Total number of workers in the West, South, and East parts of the Canal District, 1996–2012.
Data from LISA 1996, 2000, 2004; ARRA 2008, 2012.

Amsterdam drawing financial sector activity and employment from London; most of this new growth would have been concentrated in the Zuidas, the high-rise office location on the southern edge of the city, not in the Canal District.

A rather surprising pattern is displayed by employment in law firms. The South Canal District used to be the most important location for law firms within the Canal District, leaving both the West and the East Canal Districts behind. However, decline set in, and after 2000 the South was surpassed by the West, which has shown a continuous rise with a marked acceleration after 2004; the South trailed behind even when recovery set in. The "decline" of the South can be explained by the relocation of large law firms, similar to finance, to the Zuidas. The rise after 2004 is related to the overall shift to smaller firms, especially one-person firms. The East Canal

Figure 9.4 | Multinational co-working accommodations such as "Spaces" at the Herengracht offer flexible work spaces from 5 to 100 square metres (54 to 1,076 square feet). Co-working is often associated with self-employed workers and small firms – many users are highly educated and active in producer services (finance, consulting, ICT, and public relations). Source: Authors.

District showed an initial rise, 1996 to 2000, then a steep fall from 2000 to 2004, and an increase in employment from then on, surpassing in 2012 its previous peak of 2000, though still behind the two other posher parts of the Canal District.

Cultural industries constitute another mainstay of advanced urban economies. Figure 9.6 also shows the employment trends in key cultural industries (creative service sectors, arts, media, and entertainment). Creative services show a monotonic rise for both the East and the West Canal Districts and an almost monotonic, though very modest, rise in the South Canal District. Arts show a strong rise in the East and a much more modest one in the South, whereas the West displays a rise first and then a tapering off and even a slight decline. Media and entertainment are apparently quite volatile, with parallel rising trends in the three parts from 1996 to 2000 and after that a rather diverging picture, with a decline between 2000 and 2004 in the West and the South and a rise in the East. From 2004 onwards, employment in media and entertainment in the West increased again, but shrank in the two other districts.

The employment in the cultural industries is mainly to be found in the East Canal District. This less expensive part of the Canal District is clearly an most important site for cultural industries, with about 8,000 workers – slightly smaller than its population as a whole of about 9,000 (see Table 9.2) concentrated in a relatively small area – constituting a dense cluster of related and mutually supportive activities and significantly contributing to Amsterdam's status as national and international cultural capital.

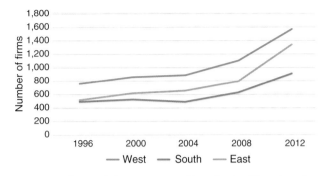

Figure 9.5 | Trends in one-person firms in the West, South, and East parts of the Canal District, 1996–2012.
Source: Data from LISA 1996, 2000, 2004; ARRA 2008, 2012.

Conclusions

The Amsterdam Canal District is anything but an open-air museum. It is still home to a diverse set of knowledge- and transaction-intensive activities, many of them related to Amsterdam's role as a (second-tier) global city. Although a serious decline of employment in financial services has taken place, other cognitive-cultural activities, notably law and cultural industries, have bucked this trend and more than compensated for this decline. With this shift in the composition of economic activities, we can also observe a clear trend towards very small firms (one-person firms) setting up shop in the Canal District. Just as in the seventeenth century, then, the Canal District is home to a dense mix of functions of home, work, and leisure.

This mix holds for the West and the South parts of the Canal District – both on the UNESCO World

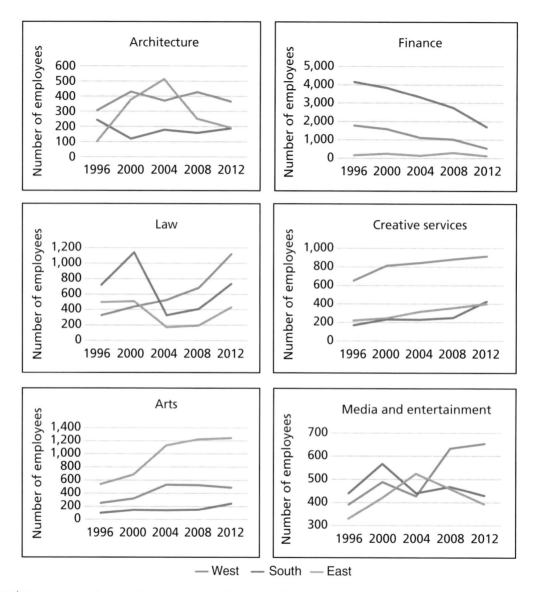

Figure 9.6 | Trends in employment in selected cognitive-cultural sectors in the West, South, and East parts of the Canal District, 1996–2012.

Source: Data from LISA 1996, 2000, 2004; ARRA 2008, 2012.

Heritage List – but also for the East (most of which is not on the UNESCO World Heritage List), which has a much more diverse built environment. Our comparison of the three parts brought to light significant differences between the planned seventeenth-century West and South Districts and the East District, which was developed much later in a more haphazard way when Amsterdam's "Golden Age" was already a distant memory. The luxurious canal houses of the West and South are on average still much more expensive than those in the East and the city as whole. In addition, the ownership structure is very different in the West and South Canal Districts, both dominated by private ownership with only a very small part social housing; the East, instead, resembles the city as a whole, with somewhat under 40 per cent social housing. These differences are reflected in the composition of the economic activities: law and creative services are strongly present in the West and to a lesser extent in the South, while the arts are particularly important in the East.

As during the seventeenth century, the economic activities taking place in the Canal District are very much part and parcel of the global economy. This time, however, the Canal District of Amsterdam is not so much an entrepôt of goods or a commanding global financial centre, but more an incubator of concepts in high-end producer services and cultural industries. As in the seventeenth century, the Amsterdam Canal District with its compactness and proximity offers a cosmopolitan urban milieu that fosters easy face-to-face exchanges and related networking – crucial for small firms – while digital technologies and a modern transport infrastructure enable intensive contacts with other parts of the world.

The Canal District is testimony to the endurance of a particular kind of urban planning that combines an overarching structure – in this case the canals, the hierarchy of the road system, and the plot size – with a freedom to come up with a bottom-up design of the actual houses. It also owes its longevity and long-term viability to a particular phase of rapid capital accumulation in the seventeenth century, which enabled the construction of sizeable, high-quality houses that have offered multifunctional spaces and attracted well-to-do residents over the ages.

Nowadays, the threats to the Canal District do not so much come from the wrecking ball as from the pressure due to its popularity as a unique historic urban environment. Housing prices are relatively very high and have been rising fast over the years. The high prices attract foreign investors and introduce absentee house owners on a large scale who do not have a stake or an interest in the wider neighbourhood (see chapter 11). In some ways, the Canal District is following the path of central London where certain areas are empty and dark at night, void of rooted residents. As elaborated elsewhere in this book, the increasing numbers of tourists in some ways pose an essential threat to the central city. Airbnbs, the conversion of neighbourhood-oriented amenities into souvenir shops, ice cream parlours, and cafés and restaurants catering primarily to tourists, as well as the sheer number of people pushing through the narrow streets and alleys, altogether are turning the Canal District into some kind of fair. A process of "self-destruction of diversity" – a term coined by Jane Jacobs (1961) – may be set in motion. A laissez-faire attitude towards these (partly global) forces may undermine the very socio-economic qualities of the Canal District. Flexible interventions and zoning policies are needed to make Lewis Mumford's (1961) qualification of the Canal District as a "miracle of spaciousness, compactness, intelligible order" still relevant in the future.

Acknowledgments

We thank Miranda Jonker, Rosa Koetsenruijter, and Irene Luque Marín for their help in data processing, editing, and fine-tuning of the maps. Special thanks to the Amsterdam Statistics Office for providing the employment data bases and to Klaas-Bindert de Haan from the Spatial Planning department for advice on the function mix map.

chapter ten

Cause Célèbre:
The Contested History of the Canal District

SUSAN LEGÊNE AND TESSA VERLOREN VAN THEMAAT

This chapter explores the opportunities and challenges for a policy to broaden the "Golden Age" focus of Amsterdam's historic Canal District by addressing its legacies of nineteenth- and twentieth-century imperialism – Amsterdam's "Second Golden Age" (Rouwendaal, 2015). An active engagement with the traces of the Dutch and European imperial past will not only strengthen the historical understanding and cultural awareness among the current diverse population of Amsterdam. It will also add more relief to the historical context of Amsterdam as a tourist destination, beyond its current focus on the Golden Age as a historical period "re-narrativized time and again" (de Waard, 2012b: 143). In a way, our approach reverses the perspective of de Waard's edited volume *Imagining Global Amsterdam*. We will focus not on the impact of globalization on Amsterdam's cultural geography (de Waard, 2012a: 14) but rather on how Amsterdam's cultural geography reaches out to a European imperial history, which even on today's World Heritage map is obscured by the dominance of local and national frames of reference for UNESCO's outstanding universal value of such sites.

Cultural tourism and urban self-marketing are interested in "a special performative situation in which a collective cultural identity is negotiated both as a selling point abroad and as a narrative of belonging 'at home.'" (de Waard, 2012b: 144). In the context of catering Golden Age experiences for tourists in Amsterdam, de Waard has expressed his concern that this historical frame might exhaust the variation for cultural tourists and cause an alienation from domestic residents. We agree and add here that we should not forget that these domestic residents, the Amsterdammers, do not form a homogeneous population; Amsterdam's Golden Age history as presented to tourists can also be a source for contestations *among* its residents. By highlighting the "European" imperial heritage profile of the Canal District, the city can develop a strategy to broaden its historical narrative both in time and geographical scope. We suggest that such an alignment of Amsterdam's self-presentation, as both a selling point for strangers and an inclusive strategy encompassing the diverse community of Amsterdammers, will contribute to the improvement of social cohesion within the city. It might be instrumental as well in diminishing the "tourist pressure" on Amsterdam's historic inner city as the sole location where the Golden Age can be "re-narrativized." Urban studies investigate how the form, use, and representation of modern European cities "have been shaped by the global history of imperialism in ways that continue to matter even in an apparently post-imperial age" (Driver & Gilbert, 1999: 3; see also de Waard, 2012a: 13). Amsterdam is such a European imperial city (Wintle, 2012); it was not just "shaped by," but took part in the shaping of imperialism. Explicitly addressing the imperial dimensions of Amsterdam's Second Golden Age, as an omnipresent layer of time merged with the Golden Age structures in the historic Canal District, will reposition Amsterdam in Europe (Slooff, 2011: 18). However, what is "imperial" and what does "European" mean in this context?

Understanding Europe

The Indian historian Dipesh Chakrabarty in his book *Provincializing Europe* famously referred to imperial Europe as an undefined entity that nevertheless is omnipresent in historical narratives in and about new nation-states after decolonisation. He describes this Europe as a hyper reality, which, in the nineteenth and early twentieth century, dominated large parts of the globe through imperial expansion, scientific development, and major migration movements (Chakrabarty, 2000: 43). The UNESCO World Heritage map, on which the historic Canal District of Amsterdam was inscribed in 2010, seems to confirm Europe as a hyper-real space. In many sites *outside* of Europe, like forts, castles, harbour fronts, or city centres, a European imperial history is being invoked through stories about conquest, competition, and control. However, UNESCO hardly seems to locate imperial Europe in Europe itself. Meanwhile, wherever World Heritage sites within Europe refer to the imperial past, they also do not frame this past in European or global historiographies; rather, they choose a fragmented *national* frame. Bilateral historical axes define colonial relationships: Amsterdam/New York, the Netherlands/Ghana, Belgium/Congo, and so on. Amsterdam's historic Canal District, inscribed on the list in 2010, is no exception.

In order to address this non-dialogical character of the sites on its World Heritage map, UNESCO has developed ancillary programs that apply a narrative template of roads, routes, trails, and dialogues.[1] These programs intend to establish active multilateral relationships between the sites. We suggest that, by explicitly linking the sites that express Europe's common involvement in imperialism, the same narrative template might help to move away from Europe as a hyper reality. It creates options for a more active engagement with Europe's history. Arguably, Amsterdam was essentially bourgeois when the Canal District was built. However, in its "Second Golden Age" 200 years later, it also came to reflect the European imperialism of the time. The capital cities of the European Union share an imperial past.

---

1. UNESCO. (2017). Routes of dialogue. Retrieved from http://www.unesco.org/new/en/culture/themes/dialogue/routes-of-dialogue/

Amsterdam is not the least among Europe's imperial cities, although it is hardly known as such (Wintle, 2012: 80). Acting as a node in a network, the city is already an intermediate station on various heritage routes, trails, roads, and ways "rooted" in continental history, such as the "European Mozart Ways" or the "European Routes of Jewish Heritage" (Walda, 2014). Likewise, the historic Canal District could become a pit stop on a route that engages both the diverse population of Amsterdam and the visitors with the colonial and imperial pasts of self and others in and outside of Europe. In line with the argument by Mary Louise Pratt (2008) in her seminal work *Imperial Eyes*, Amsterdam would profit from a change in (self) perception and visitor expectations, reaching outward to Europe beyond the Golden Age. As a historiographic intervention that addresses the European dimension of imperialism, this change might also be relevant for a sustainable development of the UNESCO program related to the World Heritage List (Westrik, 2012).

Performing in the Glow of the Golden Age

In "Quirks of Amsterdam, Revealed during Lunch," Russell Shorto explains to readers of the *New York Times International Edition* how Amsterdam makes him reflect on the concept of space: "For all the vastness of the world the Dutch once lorded over, they have restricted themselves to this small patch of it, a patch that remains cramped and ever-threatened by water." Telling for Amsterdam, he states, is the evidence all over the place that the city has always reached outward, and meanwhile has been maximizing the space in a constant process of "reinvention and repurposing this little corner of the earth" (Shorto, 2013). Of course, these dynamics refer first and foremost to the development of the historic Canal District of Amsterdam. When in 2010 the inscription of this site on the UNESCO World Heritage List was explicated in the Statement of Outstanding Universal Value (OUV), summarizing the attributes that, according to the nomination file, convey both its unique and its global values for humankind at large, many of these attributes referred to the constant reinvention and repurposing of the city.

The Statement of OUV and the nomination files define Amsterdam as a masterpiece of urban development, hydraulic engineering, and architecture. Trade turned Amsterdam into "the capital of the world-economy in its day."[2] The city was the seventeenth-century world's warehouse, the economic centre of a major maritime power trading within Europe as well as developing the overseas colonial trade of the Dutch East India Company (VOC), founded in 1602, and the Dutch West India Company (WIC), founded in 1621. Amsterdam maintained its regular traffic with the Baltic Sea and strategic forts along the shores of Africa, the East, and the

---

2. OUV Criterion (ii). World Heritage List. Seventeenth-century canal ring area of Amsterdam inside the Singelgracht – Outstanding universal value. Retrieved from http://whc.unesco.org/en/list/1349. See also Maas, Knol, & Weyermans, 2011; Slooff, 2011; Bureau of Monuments & Archaeology, 2009.

Figure 10.1 | Gable plaque commemorating the marriage of the original colonial owners of the canal house at Herengracht 518. Buisman and Verwey link their marriage to that of the seventeenth-century Geelvinck-Hinlopen couple, and add the name of their company, the Buisman groep, which provided the resources to acquire, restore, and exploit the canal house. The museum closed in 2015, and in 2019 the building housed the Embassy of the Seychelles.
Source: Authors, 2019.

New World. All around the world, one still can find a Fort Amsterdam and references to New Amsterdam. The OUV links this history of the Canal District to intangible features like navigation techniques, yards, and shipbuilding; to imported food crops and their industries like sugar, cacao, or tobacco factories; to slave trade; or to the 1883 International Colonial and Export Exhibition held at the very same location as today's Museum Square.

Despite the references in the nomination files to various other sites around the globe, Amsterdam's

Canal District barely mentions those other sites; nor does it answer the way in which those sites' nomination files link their histories to (the history of) Amsterdam. Although inscribed on a *World* Heritage map, Amsterdam's self-presentation is characterized by a one-way historical narrative of "place making" through references to a specific Dutch colonial past in which Europe is absent (Bureau of Monuments & Archaeology, 2009: 24–5). This Amsterdam-centred focus and the one-sided self-presentation is also seen in initiatives such as baptizing a new housing complex at a historic harbour location "VOC Cour" in 2009. An investment company is praised for its initiative to develop its canal house into a museum that also addresses the history of the slave trade, but it is evident that the owners actually branded the name "Geelvinck Hinlopen" and added the standing of history to their current commercial activities – in 2014 even putting their own names on a new gable plaque (Figure 10.1) – after which, in 2015, the museum closed (De Wilt, 2011; Meershoek, 2013; Hondius, Jouwe, Stam, & Tosch, 2014: 94). Another example at yet another location is the five-star Amstel Hotel, which in 2015 proudly advertised delicious "VOC cheese," and today recommends its tasteful use of "VOC spices."

These observations with respect to the nondialogical nature of a supposedly interconnected colonial world heritage discourse need some nuance. Not all Amsterdammers are simply uncritical consumers of the Golden Age's colonial past. Amsterdam's culturally diverse residential population, together with the tourists, is invited to identify with the inclusive city slogan "I amsterdam," and many interpret this slogan as not only an evocation of place but also a declaration of their presence (see Mac an Bhreithiún, 2012: 255, 260). With critical place-making initiatives, they address the historical standing of the Canal District and testify to an active engagement with the legacies of the seventeenth-century Golden Age. This involvement goes beyond a sheer enjoyment of "heritage." For instance, those Amsterdammers who actively engage with the slavery past have introduced the Bigi Spikri (Big Mirror) march to the former WIC headquarters at the West Indies House and to other canal houses like the mayor's official residence, once occupied by slave owners (Figure 10.2).

The annual commemorative walk precedes the Keti Koti (Break the Chains) festival on 30 June and 1 July to commemorate the abolition of the slave trade and slavery under Dutch colonial rule. When, in 2013, the Netherlands commemorated 150 years of the abolition of slavery, Theatre Embassy staged a performance in the Canal District's famous Golden Bend, re-baptized now as the Black Bend (Figure 10.3).

Various walks and boat tours also try to recreate examples of and promote discourse on the colonial past in Amsterdam's Canal District. The Amsterdam Museum, Maritime Museum, Tropenmuseum, and various canal house owners, along with the Office of the Mayor of Amsterdam, support this performative trend with exhibitions, commemorative plaques, and activities. The research project "Mapping Slavery" has developed a new narrative template that connects local histories of slave owners, abolitionists, and blacks to an international history of slavery (de Jong & Zondervan, 2002, 2003; Hondius, 2013; Hondius et al., 2014; Hondius, Jouwe, Stam, & Tosch, 2017; Beukers, 2015).

Figure 10.2 | The mayor of Amsterdam at the time, Eberhard van der Laan, receives at his Herengracht residence an African-Surinamese kamisa, the traditional dress of Surinamese maroons (descendants of enslaved Africans who escaped their plantation masters and established new communities in the rain forest). The mayor's residence was owned by a slave trader, which is acknowledged on a plaque near the front door. The mayor's button "1873" refers to the contested date 1863, when slavery was officially abolished; the slave owners were compensated for their "loss" on that date, but the emancipated plantation labourers were forced to stay on the plantation for another ten years.
Source: Annemarie de Wildt, Amsterdam Museum, 1 June 2013, reprinted with permission.

In this engagement with the colonial past, many forms of intangible heritage, like the mayor's Surinamese kamisa (see Figure 10.2), invoke a historical discourse on living under or escaping from conditions of slavery. These recreations of the shared but contested histories among the current people of Amsterdam

Figure 10.3 | *De Swarte Bocht* (*The Black Bend*), site-specific performance by Theatre Embassy, 2013. The portraits behind the windows of the Coymanshuis (Keizersgracht 117) were made in 1883, when Surinamese people were put on display at the International Colonial and Export Exhibition. The photographs were taken by F.C. Hisgen for Prince Roland Bonaparte, who in 1884 published *Les habitants de Suriname: Notes recueillies à l'exposition coloniale d'Amsterdam en 1883* (Paris: A. Quantin). The Coymanshuis was built by Jacob van Campen in 1625 for Balthasar and Johan Coymans. From 1669 until 1690, various family members of the Coymans' company traded thousands of enslaved Africans (Hondius et al., 2014: 61). Since 2003, the Dutch headquarters of Amnesty International has been located in this canal house.
Source: Photograph by Andrea Montenegro Vargas; stage design by Bartel Meyburg, Theatre Embassy Amsterdam, 2013, reprinted with permission.

are more than just spectacles. Former mayor of Amsterdam, Eberhard van der Laan, in his "Welcome to Amsterdam" introduction to the city's 2013 tourist guide, invited visitors to accept the Amsterdam Passport and join the residents in their engagement with the past. "Amsterdam's beauty lies in its subtleties," the mayor stated. "Once you make this connection, you will better understand the city's wonderful slogan: I amsterdam" (RAI Amsterdam, 2013: 3). The passport is a metaphor indicating that Amsterdam welcomes tourists as fellow citizens of a city whose subtle beauty refers to multilayered and contested histories.

The Canal District as Contact Zone

Shorto's analysis of reaching outwards while developing the inner city echoes a literary convention in travel writing described by Mary Louise Pratt as the dialectics of an "anti-conquest": a hegemonic but seemingly non-invasive and innocent observation of the essential characteristics of a foreign society, culture, and nature, published in order to inform readers back home (Pratt, 2008: 9). In *Imperial Eyes*, Pratt analyses how, from the seventeenth century onward, European travellers wrote travelogues about foreign regions outside of Europe. They were informed by their own observations, by information from indispensable local informants, and, not least, by earlier travelogues. Many such works were printed in Amsterdam (Schmidt, 2001; Bureau of Monuments & Archaeology, 2009). Pratt focuses in particular on the importance of "contact zones" for such travelogues, by which she means "social spaces," such as har-

bours and marketplaces, ships, plantation settlements, and factories, "where disparate cultures meet, clash, and grapple with each other, often in highly asymmetrical relations of domination and subordination" (Pratt, 2008: 7). The early travelogues revolved around the dynamics of these contact zones and contain numerous traces of "auto-ethnography": the voices of the informants – the guides and the hosts who informed and accommodated the traveller.

In a contact zone, everybody is affected in the process of exchange. Pratt points out the process of transculturation inherent in such exchange, both as a process of appropriation and one of resistance. Amsterdam in the Golden Age was at the receiving end of this "contact." Travelogues and the formation of private collections in places like the canal houses of Amsterdam played an important role in the emerging knowledge system of the "age of the catalogue" (Hooper-Greenhill, 1992; MacGregor, 2007: 27, 56 passim; van der Veen, 1992). The canal houses became powerful "windows on the world," with books and objects that familiarized readers in Europe with (the cultures of) supposedly subordinated others and helped shape Europe's "imperial" frames of reference and attitudes (Said, 1993: xii, xvi, xxiii). The information made travellers from Europe who arrived at foreign locations feel knowledgeable about what to expect. On arrival, they first recognized what they had read and seen before, and this knowledge confirmed their sense of control. Those "others," receiving the visitors, anticipated and answered the expectations of the newcomers.

Nowadays, we may well regard the Amsterdam Canal District as a contact zone – not at the "receiving end" anymore, but a contact zone negotiating our globalized time (see Clifford, 1997: 94, 204; Greenblatt et al., 2010), where active processes of transculturation happen and tourists arrive with expectations concerning the "easy going and tolerant atmosphere" (RAI Amsterdam, 2013: 11). Both the "I amsterdam" city branding (since 2004) and the World Heritage status of the historic Canal District under the glow of the Golden Age (since 2010) have become important features for framing tourist expectations in tourist guides such as the city's *Amsterdam Passport: I amsterdam* (RAI Amsterdam, 2013) or Lonely Planet's *Amsterdam* (Le Nevez & Blasi, 2018: 230–1). The historical contestations, as in the example of the performative initiatives to relocate the Dutch slavery past in the Canal District, are essential in the transcultural dynamics in this contact zone, but do not easily fit into that touristic frame. They show that transculturation is not a process of the past, a "first encounter" on unequal terms in faraway places between locals and foreigners a long time ago; rather, it is in itself a continuing history essential to Amsterdam. Consequently, the historic Canal District is not an authentic "small patch of the world" surrounded by a more hybrid larger urban conservation area. It is an essential part of that larger urban fabric that also redefines the Canal District time and again (Figure 10.4).

Vital contact zones do not condensate; they expand, providing room for cultural mobilization. In Amsterdam, the urban extensions surrounding the Canal District were entangled with the development of the modern European imperialism of the nineteenth and early twentieth century. Both in the Canal District and in new areas, offices, institutions, houses, harbours, stations, and factories were built or renovated to serve the expanding economy and social and cultural developments in Amsterdam's Second Golden Age. While after the turn of the century new housing projects for the working classes, like the "Indies neighbourhood" or "Transvaal," were constructed, with street names that taught Amsterdammers the names of the Netherlands East Indies' islands (such as Bali, Lombok, Soemba) and the names of the South African Republic's states and historical Afrikaner statesmen (such as Transvaal, Orange Free State, and Joubert, Krüger, Pretorius), the Canal District became part of a Dutch "imperial space" inside and outside of Europe (see Cooper, 2005: 22; Metz, 2012; Heijdra, 2019).

Transculturation therefore is not only an essential ingredient in Amsterdam's local history, it also *has* a global history in Amsterdam. Similarly, Pratt's notion of auto-ethnography translates in contemporary historical discourse not just as a local interaction: "the Amsterdammer" explaining the subtleties of the city to "the tourist." Auto-ethnography is also at stake as an aspect of globalization. The Black Heritage Amsterdam Tour, for example, is an initiative undertaken by Jennifer Tosch, a Surinamese-American born in the United States.[3] Such initiatives present Amsterdam's history to residents and tourists alike. Alternative narratives even have an impact on the Rijksmuseum, a contemporary contact zone par excellence. Through its emphasis on aesthetics and masterpieces, the museum represents a discourse reminiscent of Pratt's notion of anti-conquest: hegemonic, authoritative, and with a claim to art-historical universal value embedded in

---

3. For information about Black Heritage Tours, see http://www.blackheritagetours.com/herstory.html.

Figure 10.4 | In October 2018, the Amsterdam City Council decided to remove the "I amsterdam" logo from Museum Square, since it had become a tourist selfie hotspot, said to invoke rowdy behaviour and diminish the respectability of the square.
Source: Hollandse Hoogte, reprinted with permission.

Figure 10.5 | Page from the *Amsterdam Slavery Heritage Guide* (Hondius et al., 2014: 28), showing Margaretha van Raephorst's portrait with the black servant and Cornelis Tromp's gable stone with ship and black servant. The gable stone is still present at the Oudezijds Voorburgwal 136.
Source: © Photograph and book layout: Bert Brouwenstijn, Vrije Universiteit Amsterdam, reprinted with permission.

a national history of the Low Countries (Gosselink, 2014). In 2015, however, transculturation appeared, for instance, in new audio tours that added subaltern ethnographies to iconic masterpieces. Another example is the reconsideration of captions to paintings and objects replying to sensitivities with respect to stereotypical names and "othering" labels that are deeply embedded in the collection histories of the museum (Kammer, 2015a, 2015b; Modest & Lelijveld, 2018).

An illustration of this transcultural ethnographic change in the Rijksmuseum's story of the Golden Age concerns the description of a canonical painting, which shows a black servant helping Margaretha van Raephorst.[4] She is the wife of Cornelis Tromp, the captain of the Amsterdam Admiralty's flagship, the Golden Lion. This Rijksmuseum painting from 1668 has been integrated into the semi-permanent "Portrait Gallery of the Golden Age" exhibition at the Hermitage Amsterdam, which opened in 2014. Hermitage Amsterdam originally was a Deanery Home for Old Women, established in 1681 at the bequest of a wealthy merchant. Margaretha van Raephorst's portrait appears in the "Portrait Gallery" section on the sources of the riches, which also mentions the "Dirty Hands" made in the slave trade and slavery. In the first years, the exhibition explained the portrait in terms of visual contrast, suggesting that Margaretha van Raephorst's black servant was not a historic person but an artistic creation: his black skin had served the artist to make the lady's skin shine even whiter (see van der Meer, 2008: 263).

Today Hermitage Amsterdam has reversed the narrative of the painting with the caption "A Portrait of Injustice," following the Rijksmuseum, which now considers this visual tag no longer adequate and does not regard it as an essential feature of those being portrayed or of the artist's intentions. Meanwhile, as explained in Figure 10.5, the *Amsterdam*

---

4. Rijksmuseum Coll.nr SK-A-285. The painting has been widely published. See, for instance, van der Meer, 2008: 247, 263; the leaflet announcing the 2013 Geelvinck Hinlopen House exhibition "Swart op de Gracht – Slavernij en de Grachtengordel" (Black at the Canal – Slavery and the Canal District); the newspaper discussing the Rijksmuseum policy on object descriptions (Kammer, 2015b).

Slavery Heritage Guide, with the portrait of the same black servant as a page turner (in the margin of each page), has identified the young man as a historic person, locating him as a "real" historic inhabitant of Amsterdam, a fact also still visible in the Canal District house of the Tromp family. The authentic gable stone of that house shows a proud Tromp with his ship and black servant (Hondius et al., 2014: 28).

Amsterdam's Second Golden Age and the Heritage of Imperialism

It is a big leap in time from the Golden Bend and Cornelis Tromp's wife with their black servant to the imageries of "I amsterdam" today. Making that leap without acknowledging the epistemic turn of modernism, Darwinism, and imperialism brings only fragments of global history to the Amsterdam Canal District as we know it today (Hooper-Greenhill, 1992; MacGregor, 2007). The nomination file for the World Heritage status of the historic Canal District bridges the time gap by introducing "real" bridges, which were constructed in 1883: the Hogesluis Bridge and the Blauwbrug (Bureau of Monuments & Archaeology, 2009: 258). The bridges bear witness to the optimism of Amsterdam's Second Golden Age (Rouwendaal, 2015). They were constructed in 1883 in order to facilitate a specific imperial event: the first World Fair held in the Netherlands called the International Colonial and Export Exhibition.

The 1883 World Fair turned the city of Amsterdam as such into a window on the world in a period of economic growth. The organizing committee of wealthy and influential Amsterdammers intended to position the city as a contact zone in the imperial space of the Dutch Empire and further accommodate its role in international trade relations (Rouwendaal, 2015; Bloembergen, 2006; Cooper, 2005). The initiators were modern Amsterdammers, members of the Groote Club (see chapter 5 of this volume). Twenty years earlier, none of these families had owned slaves. That is to say, their names are not mentioned among the slave owners who were compensated by the state in 1863 when slavery was abolished.[5] With the 1883 World Fair, this entrepreneurial elite gave a boost to Amsterdam's urban development as well. The thousands of international visitors needed to be accommodated, and transport facilities needed improvement.

The relocation of Amsterdam in the epoch of modern imperialism resonates in the Canal District hotels, like the Krasnapolsky or the Doelen Hotel, and in many other buildings, as well as in the larger urban conservation area, which now protects the view of this World Heritage Site (see Vanvugt, 1998). The Amstel Hotel does not need VOC cheese or spices on their menu to tell in itself a full imperial history. Other examples are the Beurs van Berlage, headquarters of colonial companies like the Deli Tobacco Company, the Shipping House (Scheepvaarthuis), and the Netherlands Trading Society (Nederlandsche Handel-Maatschappij [NHM], predecessor of today's ABN AMRO bank). These and many other buildings link the history of the Canal District to the industrialization of the nineteenth century, to shipbuilding and transport companies, to Werkspoor

---

5.   We thank Jan Hein Furnée (see also chapter 5) and Dienke Hondius for checking the names in their databases.

Figure 10.6 | Statue of Multatuli (Eduard Douwes Dekker) by Hans Bayens at the Torensluis bridging the Singel. Multatuli was a prolific writer who had worked in the colonial administration in the Netherlands East Indies and wrote *Max Havelaar or the Coffee Auctions of the Dutch Trading Company* (1860), still regarded as a masterpiece of Dutch literature.
Source: Authors, August 2019.

and Stork in the Eastern Harbour District, to imported food crops and food-processing industries in the northwest and north, to the headquarters of banks and insurance companies, and to the premises of the major museums of Amsterdam, such as the Royal Tropical Institute (formerly Colonial Institute) in the East (Vanvugt, 1998; De Voogd, 2005; van Dijk & Legêne, 2011; Wintle, 2012).

The connections of these buildings and structures to Dutch imperialism are not merely reflected in their erstwhile functions. As in the case of the gable stones from the Golden Age, the history of the Dutch Empire is also evident in design and decorations like the two women East and West by Joseph Mendes da Costa, who guard the main entrance of the NHM headquarters that today houses the Amsterdam City Archives; in special features like the Winter Garden in Hotel Krasnapolsky; or in the collections kept in those premises and in museums. Form supported function. In the context of modern imperialism, economics and cultural imagery were closely wedded.

Contrary to the initiatives mentioned earlier, which firmly connect the slave-trade past to the canal houses of the slave owners, initiatives through which both Amsterdammers and tourists today encounter modern imperialism are rarely presented as another historical layer of the Canal District beyond the Golden Age. An example of a relatively new reference to the imperial past, centrally located in the Canal District, is the 1987 sculpture by Hans Bayens of Multatuli (Eduard Douwes Dekker), author of *Max Havelaar*, the famous 1860 novel that sharply critiqued colonial administrative practices in Java (Figure 10.6). The Multatuli House organizes tours

Figure 10.7 | Reconstruction of a wall advertisement at the intersection of Palmgracht/Palmdwarsstraat, near the Brouwersgracht, calling recruits for the Indies army, 1920s.
Source: Bert Brouwenstijn, Vrije Universiteit Amsterdam 2016, reprinted with permission.

through "Multatuli's Amsterdam," Canal District included, with imperialism as an implicit guiding context. Imperialism is implicit as well at the former premises of Stork and Werkspoor, where "heritage" refers to the VOC yards and to world trade, rather than to the machine industry as the engine of modern imperialism (Campo, 2002).

A clear example of explicitly addressing Amsterdam's imperial legacy was the performance in the 2013 Holland Festival, "Exhibit B" (the "human zoo") directed by Brett Bailey, outside of the Canal District adjacent to the Surinamekade. In breath-taking "tableaux vivants," actors re-enacted a series of people in various historic or more recent situations of exploitation, as had actually happened in Amsterdam with Surinamese people at the 1883 World Fair.[6] Another example was created in 2015 by Amsterdammer volunteers who reproduce historic wall advertisements all over the city at their original locations. In the Canal District, they painted two "colonial" advertisements. One sells tropical outfits for the Netherlands East Indies; the other, from the 1920s, calls unemployed Amsterdammers for overseas service in the colonial army (Figure 10.7).

Not all the neighbours were amused by a permanent view of the historic colonial army advertisement with its connotation of repression and violence (Wijland, 2015). Whether it will stay, therefore, remains to be seen; it still existed in 2019. What both advertisements underscore, however, is that by the end of the nineteenth century everyone in Amsterdam, not just the entrepreneurial elite in the canal houses, was implicated in imperial culture. Imperialism created jobs, changed consumption patterns, influenced thinking about self and others, and enhanced mobility (Gissibl, 2011). From the wage labourers at Werkspoor and Stork and the inhabitants of the neighbourhoods with their street names referencing the imperial space, to the readers of the novel *Max Havelaar* and the visitors to the 1883 World Fair, imperialism shaped their frame of reference with respect to understanding society. Because of this comprehensiveness and its entanglement with current global society, it is not easy to invoke imperialism as "just" another subtle historic layer of the Canal District.

I amsterdam: **Connecting the Historiographies of Imperialism's Heritage**

Jennifer Tee made two impressive "Tulip Palepai" at the new metro station at Amsterdam Central Station. In her explanation, she refers to her own family background (Figure 10.8). It is a subtle reference to the imperial past for the thousands of travellers who pass by every day. The realization of an explicit imperial self-presentation would strengthen the dialogical nature of Amsterdam's participation in the UNESCO World Heritage program. The European context is relevant here. Despite Amsterdam's weak perception of modern imperialism in its Statement of OUV and nomination files, so far Amsterdam has been rather exceptional among European World Heritage sites in explicitly making such a link to its colonial past at all.

Another example that makes this link is the industrial "Liverpool – Maritime Mercantile City," with explicit mention of values related to British imperialism in its Statement of OUV. Under Criterion (iii), the OUV brief synthesis on the UNESCO website states: "The city and the port of Liverpool are an exceptional testimony to the development of maritime mercantile culture in the 18th, 19th and early 20th centuries, contributing to the building up of the British Empire. It was a centre for the slave trade, until its abolition in 1807, and for emigration from northern Europe to America" (UNESCO, n.d.). The

---

6. See the description of the "human zoo" installation by South African director and playwright Brett Bailey at the Holland Festival held on 16–26 June 2013 in Amsterdam, http://www.hollandfestival.nl/nl/programma/2013/exhibit-b/.

Figure 10.8 | *Tulip Palepai – Navigating the Rivers of the World*, by Jennifer Tee. This mural is one of the two artworks at the new metro station at Amsterdam Central Station, inspired by the woven ancestor cloths, palepai (ship cloths), from South Sulawesi as well as the map of the Canal District. The tiny woven motives of a palepai are replaced by actual-sized tulip leaves.
Source: Authors, 2018

Liverpool City Council's (2003: 40) nomination of the site said: "Liverpool was a highly successful general-cargo port, for both import and export, and a major European port of trans-Atlantic emigration" (since 2012, the site has been on UNESCO's "List of World Heritage in Danger" because of urban development projects that threaten the OUV of the

historic site). Amsterdam, the seventeenth-century world's warehouse, and Liverpool, the major general-cargo port in the British Empire, suggest that "the colonial" happened elsewhere and entered Europe through global trade. Liverpool adds to this import/export history a history of emigration from Europe to the New World. Between 1830 and 1930, it accommodated the departure of over nine million Europeans to other continents (National Museums of Liverpool, n.d.).[7]

Within this European context, developing the narrative template of "routes" within Europe could become an explicit feature of Amsterdam's historic Canal District on the UNESCO World Heritage List. An imperial cities route would start with an exploration of the many options for imperial walks, tours, and trails that embed the Canal District within the city at large and link it to Europe's colonial past at other World Heritage sites, which up to now lack any such reference. Parallel to Amsterdam with the 1883 exhibition or Liverpool with its reference to the Industrial Revolution and emigration, the Eiffel Tower, for instance, might be reframed as an icon of Europe's imperial past through its reference to world exhibitions, to iron roads, or to the Palais de Chaillot with its museum history (Musée de l'Homme, Maritime Museum). Even closer to Amsterdam, the World Heritage Site of the art-nouveau Major Town Houses of the Architect Victor Horta in Brussels would be a case in point. One of these houses embodies a direct reference to Belgian colonialism in the Congo, as it was commissioned in 1895 by the diplomat and secretary general of the Congo, Edmond van Eetvelde. The Statement of OUV does not explore this link between form and function. Instead, it just declares: "The building was to provide a home for the family and a prestigious setting for the reception of international guests" (ICOMOS, 2000: 40). Such references remind one of the subtleties of Amsterdam.

Putting the wider frame of a European imperial city around the narrow image of the Golden Age will enable Amsterdam to link the nineteenth- and twentieth-century changes in the Canal District to World Heritage sites elsewhere in Europe. For instance, Amsterdam's World Heritage profile could bring the decorative program and function of the Horta van Eetvelde house as an imperial contact zone in Brussels in dialogue with the interior and outside decoration program of the Beurs van Berlage. Such connections will show both visitors and residents how transculturation processes at home were inspired by the development of a European imperial culture (Wintle, 2012). Addressing the imperial past in a wider European context will also enhance the inclusiveness of "I amsterdam," with its many residents whose biographies, in many different ways, link with colonialism and decolonisation, which is not restricted to the Netherlands and its former colonies alone.

Notwithstanding the beauty of ornaments and interesting site-specific histories, "imperial city" hardly seems an attractive collective cultural identity, constructive as both a selling point abroad and a narrative of belonging "at home" (see Schmidt, 2012). So far, the World Heritage sites in Europe, like the Canal District, turn a blind eye to imperialism as

---

7. In UNESCO's slave routes project, World Heritage ports in Europe are not explicitly connected to the history of the slave trade; their involvement in slavery or imperialism is not addressed at all. It is as if imperialism happened elsewhere, outside of Europe. See UNESCO. (2017). The Slave Route. Retrieved from http://www.unesco.org/new/en/culture/themes/dialogue/the-slave-route.

a place-making label. Imperialism is also absent among the existing thirty-five "Cultural Routes of the Council of Europe," organized under the aegis of the Institute of Cultural Routes (Walda, 2014: 212, 215–16, 225). With respect to the UNESCO World Heritage List, an explanation for this feature lies in the national frame, with nomination through state's parties. In the heritage policies of both UNESCO (established in 1945) and the Council of Europe (established in 1949), awareness of Europe's common imperial past and its associated heritage has been fragmented through the dominant national perspective of member states in their respective post-1945 historiographies. The entanglement of this heritage spread all over Europe has disappeared from view (Aldrich & Wards, 2010; Legêne & Eickhoff, 2014; Wintle, 2012). Imperial heritage features were nationalized and localized, the effects of imperialism on the composition and histories of its population homogenized. This practice is another aspect of "provincializing," implied in Chakrabarty's (2000) analysis *Provincializing Europe*.

Europe would benefit if sites like Amsterdam were to take initiatives to create another narrative concerning its location in European history. It would place the larger Amsterdam in a contact zone where residents are encouraged to reposition their histories in a European frame that encompasses sameness and differences between people beyond the frame of national belonging. It would strengthen the dialogue with the sites (forts, historic inner cities) outside of Europe where reference to *European* colonialism, rather than to separate colonial powers in Europe, is made. And it would redirect tourists' expectations from a single focus on the glow of the Golden Age to the whole range of global history to be discovered in Amsterdam as one of the imperial cities of Europe. "I amsterdam" then will invite residents and tourists alike to use the *Amsterdam Passport: I amsterdam* as an activation code to be at home in the world.

chapter eleven

The Present-Day Canal District as Home: Living in a Commodified Space

WILLEM R. BOTERMAN AND FENNE M. PINKSTER

In the past decade, Amsterdam has experienced unprecedented growth in tourism. Like other historic city centres in Europe, the Canal District has become an object of cultural consumption in an ever-expanding global consumer market, fuelled by the emergence of the experience economy and enabled by increased availability of mass transportation, communication, and information technologies (Nijman, 1999; Urry, 1990). For cities, there are clear economic benefits. The tourist industry forms an important source of revenue for the city and for residents, and many local governments therefore take an active role in marketing their cities as a place to visit (Judd & Fainstein, 1999). Yet, it is becoming increasingly clear that there are also drawbacks. The fast expansion of tourism is transforming the urban landscape in unanticipated ways and taking its toll on local social and cultural life. In cities like Amsterdam, Venice, and Barcelona, visitors far outnumber residents on an average summer day, and the transformation of urban space geared to the experience of visitors – often referred to as a process of commodification or "disney-fication" (Gotham, 2005; Zukin, 2008) – is beginning to undermine the role of city centres as everyday places for residents to live, meet, and interact (Colomb & Novy, 2016; Pinkster & Boterman, 2017).

This chapter explores the tension between the historic Canal District as an object of leisure and consumption on the one hand and as an ordinary everyday place for residents on the other. The Canal District is a particularly interesting case because of the unique combination of a living city *and* an attractive site in the business of tourist promotion and place marketing. In recent years, however, this combination is increasingly contested by local residents, and the World Heritage designation is often viewed as a mixed blessing.

Setting the Scene: Amsterdam as a Tourist Destination

Amsterdam has seen unprecedented growth in tourism in the last decades. International visitors as well as Dutch day trippers are attracted by the intriguing mix of its unique historic architecture and high arts, and its reputation of permissiveness and liberal

---

This chapter is adapted and extended from a previous article: Pinkster & Boterman, 2017.

attitudes rooted in the youth (hippie) cultures of the sixties and seventies that centred around individual expression (and drugs) (Nijman, 1999; Terhorst, van de Ven, & Deben, 2003). In a single day, visitors can combine a canal cruise and the Van Gogh museum with a walk through the Red Light District or a visit to one of the city's "coffee shops."

It is now hard to believe that, in the immediate aftermath of the Second World War, the world-famous Canal District was run down and considered, by some at least, obsolete (see chapter 7, this volume). In the post-war years, the area was increasingly abandoned by both residents and businesses for more modern and accessible spaces in the suburban periphery, and the municipality developed plans to fill in the canals and demolish the now famous canal gables to create room for a "proper" central business district (Terhorst & van de Ven, 2003). However, these plans for the comprehensive restructuring of the old city centre received strong opposition, specifically by a group of young, highly educated baby boomers and social activists – often working in the cultural sector and academia – who had started to move into the area in the late sixties. This new group of upper-middle-class residents contributed substantially to the revitalization of the Canal District, not only by successfully lobbying for historic preservation but also through their own financial investment, triggering a steady process of upgrading (Figure 11.1).

In 1999, the municipality designated the area as a protected urban landscape, effectively freezing the built environment. Around the same time, the city also developed its first place-marketing policies. Promoting the city as a place of culture and historic architecture was central to the city's strategy to boost the local economy (Kavaratzis & Ashworth, 2007). Tourism formed the cornerstone of these city marketing initiatives, which aimed to attract not only more visitors but more *affluent* visitors, in place of low-budget tourists who only flocked to the city for its liberal attitudes towards sex and drugs. These efforts to rebrand the city culminated in the successful lobby of a broad coalition of stakeholders – including not only local government but also residents and corporate partners – for UNESCO World Heritage status in 2010.

Since the mid-1990s, the number of visitors to the city has indeed grown exponentially. In 1994, with 2 million guests spending on average two nights in the city, inhabitants still clearly outnumbered visitors. Within a decade, however, this situation changed (see Figures 11.2 and 11.3). The number of visitors and hotel nights spent in the city doubled, and this trend has accelerated in recent years. By 2015, the total number of visitors staying overnight was estimated at 7 million. Including day trip tourists, the number of visitors went up to 17 million, peaking at large events such as King's Day or the annual Gay Canal Parade, when between 500,000 and a million people come to Amsterdam on a single day. Considering that most visitors concentrate in the historical inner city, which is home to approximately 85,000 locals, on many days visitors now outnumber residents.

The Canal District as Home

The focus of this chapter is on the sense of home felt by long-term residents in the western section of the

Canal District and how residents are affected by the rapid changes in their neighbourhood. Interviews[1] were conducted with residents who have lived in the district from eighteen to sixty-four years. Many moved into the area at the start of their housing and working careers and therefore embody the incumbent upgrading of the area during the seventies and eighties. In addition, a number of key informants from different stakeholder groups were interviewed, such as political, resident, and local shopping street representatives, to gain insight into the changes in the Canal District in recent years.

What stands out in the conversations with long-term residents about their neighbourhood is a declared strong emotional attachment to the area. Respondents spoke about themselves as "having long ago struck roots here" and compared the neighbourhood to a "comfortable, warm winter coat." In their appreciation of the Canal District as home, two main themes can be identified: on the one hand, the highly personal, embodied experience of the area's unique material landscape and, on the other, the way in which living in the dynamic city centre reflects their cosmopolitan, middle-class lifestyles.

Dwelling in Beauty

Above all, residents' sense of home is rooted in their sensory experience of place, of being able to consume this unique urban landscape on a daily basis.

Respondents expressed how they appreciate being surrounded by beauty, pointing out details in the scenery around them. The sensation of dwelling in beauty is reinforced through daily walks along the canals and the experience of coming home after a trip abroad, each time rediscovering how special the area really is. This appreciation of the area clearly goes beyond the architectural ensemble of the Canal District and is rooted in a broad sensory experience of place. Respondents also described the subtle, seasonal changes in their surroundings and how the neighbourhood feels during different types of weather (Figure 11.4). Some likened the Canal District as it is now to the winter images of the Canal District in paintings of Dutch masters of the Golden Age, clearly valuing the long history and the heritage of the area. Marc (twenty-four years in the neighbourhood) observed:

> I am very attached to the neighbourhood. I just think it is really very beautiful. I enjoy the aesthetics of the winter, of the summer, of spring, and of autumn. When the leaves turn brown, it's fantastic; when it's getting all white, it's even better. Look at how beautiful it all is: the length of the canals, the panorama, the sense of space, the gables. I just think it's an aesthetical pleasure to live here.

Many residents were familiar with the particular history of their own house, recounting who

---

1. Interviews were carried out in Dutch for a research project on the Amsterdam Canal Belt. For details, see Pinkster & Boterman, 2017. Translations are by the authors.

(Above and opposite) Figure 11.1 | Upgrading of the canal gables: before and after restoration at Herengracht 300 (above) and Leliegracht 36 (opposite).

Source: Stadsherstel, reprinted with permission.

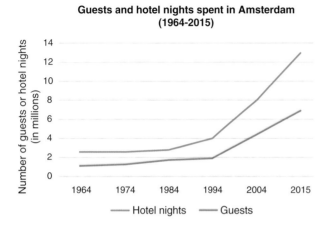

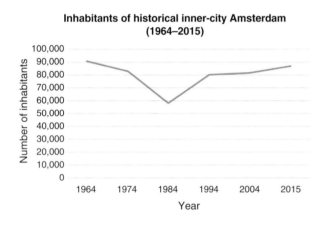

originally built it, how the building was used over time, and what elements in the house still point back to that time. Moreover, home owners displayed a strong sense of pride, seeing the preservation of this unique architectural ensemble as their own achievement. They were the ones to first recognize the value of the neighbourhood when others did not. Several respondents described at length the restorations done to their house, and many also noted the costs associated with the maintenance of 350-year-old buildings. In this respect, the respondents demonstrated a sense of home that seems closely related to the humanist notion of "dwelling," showing an embodied knowledge of and familiarity with their neighbourhood, which comes from having lived in the area and experienced place over a long period of time. Ivan (forty-four years in the neighbourhood) expressed himself this way:

> This is a beautiful neighbourhood. I am privileged to be able to have so much space, so comfortable. Among these beautiful canals ... these seventeenth-century houses that people from all over the world come to see, that are so familiar to me. It is an extraordinary place to call home.

Enacting Cosmopolitan Lifestyles

As many respondents emphasized, however, the Canal District is more than just beautiful scenery. Part of the unique character of the Canal District appears to reside in its rhythm and spectacle: its combination of beauty and stillness at some parts of the day with liveliness at other times. The particular

Figure 11.2 | Tourism in Amsterdam (measured by guests/hotel nights) and the local population, 1964–2015.
Source: Data from Onderzoek, Informatie en Statistiek (OIS) Amsterdam, 1965, 1975, 1985, 1995, 2005, 2016.

mix of residences, businesses, and consumption spaces, and the dynamic flows of people that this mix generates, creates an urban atmosphere that matches residents' own urban lifestyles. Residents enjoy observing the business and urban spectacle of the city centre, as Frank (age seventy-six) illustrated in his comments:

> It's not just that it's beautiful. It's the whole atmosphere. The shabby chic. The majestic houses on the one hand ... but also the liveliness. The bustle. I still have that ... after all those years, I still love to sit out here [on the bench in front of the house] whenever possible, and look at the people go by. On bikes, on the water, people going about their business. It's so nice.

In fact, several respondents explained that they consciously chose to move to this area rather than buy a house in the more "boring" established middle-class areas in the city or the suburbs. For example, when Robert started looking for houses in the late eighties, his realtor at first did not want to include the Canal District in his search, because he considered the area entirely inappropriate for someone with a law degree and a respected career. For Robert, moving into this area was a way to show his public engagement and an act of rebellion against "those conservative people" in his field.

Reflecting their urban lifestyles and cosmopolitan habitus, several respondents indicated explicitly that they prefer being called Amsterdammers over "residents of the Canal District." They described the area as "not really a neighbourhood" and represented

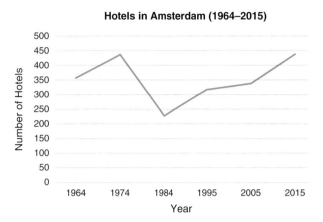

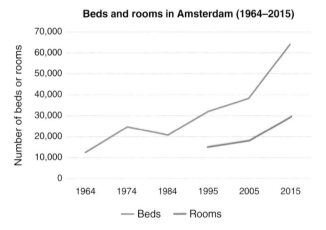

Figure 11.3 | Number of hotels, rooms, and beds, 1964–2015.
Source: Data from OIS Amsterdam, 1965, 1975, 1985, 1995, 2005, 2016.

Figure 11.4 | The beauty of the canals in the winter, Keizersgracht (the western part of the Canal District).
Source: Matthias v.d. Elbe, "Amsterdam, Netherlands, Keizersgracht." Wikimedia, printed under CC BY-SA 4.0 licence.

themselves as "not neighbourhood-minded people." Mostly, this attitude seems to be a rejection of the notion of "community," which is very different from respondents' own neighbourly relations. These were described as incidental and mostly functional concerning shared home issues. Otherwise, residents make few claims on each other's time, and several respondents noted that they appreciate living among like-minded people who have similar attitudes about preserving each other's privacy. Nevertheless, respondents do appreciate familiar faces in local shops or along the streets.

Still, in the everyday routines of these long-term residents, the Canal District forms only a marginal space. While respondents appreciate the availability of local specialty food shops and cafés, their time-space routines are much wider in scope. The neighbourhood serves as a "hub," providing access to the city as a whole. For example, many respondents elaborately discussed Amsterdam's cultural amenities in terms of museums, classical music concerts, and high-quality restaurants. Moreover, the district's proximity to Central Station and the airport also provides access to the rest of the country and places abroad, enabling respondents to travel conveniently to other cities.

Living in a Theme Park

Although these long-term residents have developed a strong sense of belonging to the neighbourhood, their experiences of home are threatened by the growing pressures of tourism. The respondents expressed ambivalence about their own responses to visitors. On the one hand, they feel that tourism contributes to the dynamic sense of place, which characterizes city centres. To some extent, it seems that the popularity and fame of the Canal District provides residents with symbolic capital, especially when the district is experienced and discussed by tourists, guide books, and international newspapers in ways that fit with residents' views. Tourists obviously come to enjoy the beauty of the canals that respondents themselves appreciate. In a way, residents themselves also look at the landscape of the neighbourhood with a "tourist gaze" (Urry, 1990) and understand and appreciate its appeal. On the other hand, the reality of sharing the neighbourhood with visitors is experienced quite negatively.

First, residents employed a theme park metaphor to describe the change that tourism is generating in their neighbourhood. They pointed out how growing crowds of visitors affect the "natural" or "ordinary" rhythm of everyday life. Many respondents referred to the mass character and increasing frequency of festivals, such as King's Day, the Gay Pride Canal Parade, and the Canal Concert Night, which were described as bursting out of their seams (Figure 11.5). Some enjoy these events, feeling they belong in the centre of the city and contribute to the urban atmosphere. However, the crowds seem to have become a more permanent feature on regular summer days. Respondents also described how the changing flows of people lead to new traffic bottlenecks, particularly in certain "hotspots" along the canals such as in front of the Anne Frank House or some of the smaller shopping streets. Residents

Figure 11.5 | Queen's Day celebration, Prinsengracht (the western part of the Canal District), 2012.
Source: Jan Nijman.

observed how wandering tourists get in the way of their own pace of walking. Typical to Amsterdam, visitors do not only walk but also ride (rental) bikes, described as dangerously zigzagging along the road, oblivious to other traffic, distracted by the views and spectacle around them. This situation was considered particularly problematic by some of the older respondents, who were becoming more aware of their growing physical vulnerability.

The theme park metaphor refers to more than just the crowds. It also refers to the activities visitors engage in. Tourists want to experience not just the museums or architectural heritage of cities, but also the distinctive ambience of the city, its broader sense of place. In this respect, urban tourism lies at the intersection of globalization processes on the one hand and expressions of local identity on the other. Being a tourist has been likened to a performance in which visitors strive to play the part of being a local and engage in local customs (Fuller & Michel, 2014; Bock, 2015). In the case of Amsterdam, tourists are attracted as much by pictures of the Canal District as by the image of the city as a tolerant place, which has become "packaged" as permissiveness and liberal attitudes. Nijman (1999: 156) noted some twenty years ago: "The theme of the 'park' is ... drugs and sex under a pretence of normalcy." This representation of tolerance is only loosely related to the original, historical meaning of tolerance and has little to do with ordinary everyday life in the city. Nevertheless, the growing numbers of tourists hoping to experience this facet of Amsterdam have in some ways made it a reality (Terhorst et al., 2003).

While in the past these tourist activities – drinking, smoking up, and partying – were more concentrated in the Red Light District and other nightlife areas, the theme park can now be encountered throughout the city centre. Ivan, who has lived in the area since 1972, explained that the reputation of Amsterdam as a city where "anything goes" triggers all sorts of behaviour that, he would argue, do not belong in a public space:

> Yes, the beer bike, that's a good example. Just the idea in itself! That these things are allowed in public space, I find that completely unacceptable. That people don't understand that is a serious issue ... I consider people who produce that kind of noise as brainless. You are not alone in the world!

Some of these forms of entertainment – such as the beer bike – seek to somehow allude to supposedly Dutch traditions, but they are, at best, extrapolations of it. They were often described by respondents as examples of staged authenticity, derived from local customs but never really a local custom. Residents increasingly encounter forms of entertainment for visitors that have little to do local customs. Gerald (thirty-three years in the neighbourhood) explained:

> I see tourism changing the city. Amsterdam used to be a more gritty place. But now it is in danger of becoming Disneyland. We saw it coming: the double-decker buses. They belong in London ... It is a tourist thing. It is not Amsterdam. The beer bike, the rickshaw taxi, it's just getting ... The Segways. And everyone has to wear a helmet. It just doesn't

fit here ... And then the huge groups of Chinese. Sixty Chinese following an umbrella. Amsterdam has always been an individualistic city!

Residents find that the centre is being used in ways that do not belong in a residential neighbourhood. They experience a growing sense of frustration with the continuous flow of visitors who do not know how to behave appropriately. Jan, who has lived in the area since 1973, remarked:

> The crowds are not just walking along the canals. They are on the water as well. You know, rental boats with loud customers. It's escalating. Even during the day, groups of guys who are plastered, just drunk ... what do you call them ... stag parties? With their striptease acts and the loud dance music. The bass that drums through your house ... until late at night. And these boat people dump their trash bags on the banks along the way. And the worst? The sauna boat. Almost naked in a boat with twenty people.

Some respondents attributed such "vulgar" theme park behaviour to generational differences. Younger tourists are perceived to disrupt the Canal District's unique sense of place in various ways: through the trash they leave behind, their engagement in "tasteless" activities, and their "inappropriate" outfits.

Moreover, these activities often create a lot of noise, which cannot be ignored by closing the curtains. Residents are bothered by the loud behaviour of groups of tourists on beer bikes or stag parties on their way to the next bar – noise that invades respondents' homes. Worse even is the loud dance music from leisure boats, reverberating between the facades along the canal. Rudi, who has lived in the neighbourhood since 1984, commented on the noise:

> Well, now I have double-layered windows so it is not as bad. But I came back on King's Day, and it was hell. You just have to get out. I hate it. Normally, I try to get away. Of course, just getting back from vacation it is even worse ... You know, the crowds themselves are not so bad. It's the noise.

While these festivals may be extreme events, many other respondents commented on how the sounds of tourists invade their homes, ranging from the noise of beer-drinking tourists sitting in outdoor cafés to the sound of travel trolleys full of anonymous others on the cobbled streets, disturbing the silence of the early mornings and late evenings. These disturbances were particularly emphasized by respondents who were retired or worked from home, but others also commented on these sensory disruptions in their homes. At the same time, as noted earlier, respondents feel torn about the negative undertone in their own stories. Concerned about coming across as intolerant, several respondents reflected on how their sensitivity to visitor behaviour is to some degree related to their own age.

In addition to these day-to-day disruptions, respondents were concerned about a more permanent loss of place, whereby the everyday ordinary function of the area for residents disappears and the neighbourhood becomes an empty shell for visitors. Venice and Barcelona were often referred to as negative examples. Jeanette (twenty-six years in the neighbourhood) observed:

> I have travelled my whole life, also often to Barcelona. That city has changed beyond recognition. As a tourist it used to be nice to see the Ramblas, but now I avoid it. There's nothing there anymore. As my husband says, it's an adverse effect. I now avoid cities that are swarmed by tourists. I just don't enjoy it. And Amsterdam is increasingly moving in that direction.

One indicator of this process is the replacement of ordinary shops such as butcher shops, bakeries, and green grocers by consumption spaces that cater to tourists, such as lunch rooms, hotels, and boutiques (Figure 11.6). The bakery where residents used to buy bread is now a ciabatta sandwich shop, while the regular pharmacy has become an upscale make-up boutique. Although this transformation of the commercial landscape goes together with increasing rents and the influx of high-end commercial stores, it is experienced by long-term residents as a process of downgrading. Diana, who has lived in the neighbourhood most of her adult life, commented:

> In this street, there used to be regular shops, but they are all gone. Now it is restaurants. It's just sad. Around the corner here, there's at least ten of them, expensive too. And those fancy clothing boutiques. 189 euros for a pair of jeans with holes in them ... Ridiculously expensive. And for whom? Tourists.

Figure 11.6 | Commercial transformations catering to tourists: emerging monocultures.
Source: Donald Trung Quoc Don, "A small local souvenir shop in the city of Amsterdam," Wikimedia. Printed under CC BY-SA 4.0 licence.

Residents also observed a process of mainstreaming, whereby the city centre is increasingly dominated by ice cream stores that are the same in every other tourist city. In this respect, touristification is also associated with a loss of authenticity. Indeed, several respondents reflected on how some areas that used to smell of weed now smell like Belgian waffles. The growing tension between the commercial value of the Canal District as a tourist destination and the residential value of the Canal District also becomes clear in the increasing numbers of hotels and the growing number of private homes offered as short-stay rentals. Respondents were worried that "normal people," who are necessary to keep the area "alive," are being pushed out to accommodate the ever-growing number of visitors. Simultaneously, new business models and technologies such as Airbnb also increase the encounters between residents and tourists (Maitland, 2008; Chapuis, Gravari-Barbas, Jacquot, & Mermet, 2012). The municipality estimates that in 2015 approximately 16,000 residences were offered for rent through Airbnb (Municipality of Amsterdam, 2015).

Residents observed that, in particular, short-stay rentals in the Canal District change the nature of ordinary interactions in everyday life, creating a sense of estrangement and alienation. Theo, who has lived in the neighbourhood since 1984, pointed out:

> These days a lot of apartments are rented out. You know, short stay. Not just the houses, also the house boats. It's a shame ... well, the neighbourhood disappears. Where you used to know people, now it's just ... just tourists. We used to know each other, or recognize each other. And now there is a continuous flow of new people who don't know the rules. They dump garbage everywhere.

Airbnb thus brings in anonymous others who cannot easily be approached or admonished when they behave inappropriately or disturb the careful balance between privacy and proximity, which residents themselves preserve so carefully.

Individual Coping Strategies and Public Contestations

The encounters with tourists and the more permanent changes in the economic structure and housing market are experienced quite negatively by long-term residents. They described the tourist spectacle as being "out of control," going far beyond a healthy and appreciated form of liveliness and threatening the public function of the area as the centre of the city. Tourism is perceived to undermine the area's unique sensory experience of place. Jakob, who

moved to the district in 1971, cynically concluded: "The nicest time of the year is when it is raining, because there are few people around and you can see how beautiful the city is. Mornings like this ... then it is really a blessed place." Although not all respondents experienced the same levels of nuisance – due in part to different locations in relation to identified "hotspots" and differences in the amount of daytime spent at home – many described a sensation of being "invaded" and feel that the neighbourhood has been "taken over." In response, respondents have developed various coping strategies to deal with the disruptions of their neighbourhood.

At home, everyday nuisances are dealt with by closing windows, closing the shades, or relocating within the home to the rooms at the back. Strategies of retreating behind closed doors take on extreme forms during festival days, when some respondents avoid going out altogether, avoiding the public sphere completely. Alternatively, "invasions" of the neighbourhood also trigger avoidance strategies. Many respondents leave the city during large-scale events. They arrange to go on holiday or find other temporary escapes from the city, such as going cycling to the countryside for a day or visiting family and friends. These strategies were described as a "flight" away from the city. For example, Barbara (twenty-nine years in the neighbourhood) stated: "If it is really bad, my sister's partner lives in Haarlem in a house with an enormous garden and then we go there. It is really ... we can still flee there."

While occasional events are more easily dealt with, overcrowding and disneyfication of the city are increasingly permanent features of the Canal District.

Patrick (thirty-six years in the neighbourhood) sighed: "There used to be a tourist season. Now it lasts all year long." A number of residents respond by spending more and more time away from the neighbourhood. One common strategy is the acquisition of a second home, abroad or in the more rural parts of the Netherlands, which allows people to temporarily escape the busiest times of the year while maintaining their home in the Canal District. While many residents respond to the temporary and/or partial loss of place with occasional trips away from home, some opt for more radical solutions. Several respondents had considered moving away from the Canal District altogether. The desire to get away was primarily informed by the described nuisance and not because they were attracted by a better alternative elsewhere. For example, Iris (forty-three years in the neighbourhood) felt that "enough is enough":

We live close to the water, and the noise ... the pleasure boats used to be there only on Friday and Saturday afternoon. Now it is all day, every day. The shouting, the noise ... I am sick of it. The loud engines. Even at night. To some degree it is part of the city, the noise. But I don't want to be part of that any more.

Other respondents had thought about moving at some time or another, but were hesitant because any move seemed a deterioration of their housing situation. On the one hand, this reticence is related to the concerns about increases in housing costs, which for many long-term residents are relatively low due to having either paid off their mortgages or accumulated the benefits of rent protection. On the other hand, they simply do not want to leave the Canal District because, despite the negative developments, to them it is still the most beautiful place to live. As Nick (thirty-six years in the neighbourhood) reflected:

I guess I am like an old tree. Not so easily uprooted anymore. If I move ... I am thinking of a place a few streets over. Just a small section of the neighbourhood which is still peaceful. Quiet. I sometimes go there when the crowds get to me. Just to sit. Not even a few hundred metres away. And then as soon as you step back out onto the main street, you are right back in the mess.

For many residents, the choice to stay is therefore deliberate and made more bearable through specific forms of mobility over very short distances as well as much longer ones. These are made possible by respondents' financial means, their social capital, and – specifically for those who have retired – the availability of time. While these coping strategies reflect the relatively affluent social position of this group of highly educated residents, they go hand in hand with a growing sense of powerlessness. Residents feel little control over the processes that are taking place. Gerald (age sixty-seven) reflected: "I mean, what can I do alone? I mean, I will just be someone fighting windmills. That's pointless. No, one should tackle this at a higher level."

Many residents expressed the feeling that the municipality should "do something about it." While they recognized that some aspects of tourism are difficult to regulate, they advocated a more comprehensive policy approach to tourism that should explicitly include the interests of residents and create a "balance" between different stakeholders. This stance was eloquently formulated by the chairman of a local residents' organization:

> The feeling among residents is that the neighbourhood is off balance and leans towards tourism. One should not forget that people live here ... They feel like ... it's getting out of control. People say things like "the Canal District belongs to everyone." But that does not feel right. There are people here who moved in all those years ago when nobody wanted to live here. Do they get pushed aside? No! Those people made this place what it is. So beautiful, and so liveable. That deserves respect and support ... We live here, listen to us!

Many residents feel that the local government has for too long taken the side of business to generate economic benefits rather than supporting the residents. Indeed, local councillors and urban professionals are beginning to realize that tourism is indeed taking its toll, but they are often ambivalent in their stance towards tourism and do not want to jeopardize the considerable revenues of tourism for the city (Milikowski, 2016). For example, in 2015 Alderman Ollongren, who represented the Department of Economic Affairs, publicly voiced her doubts whether the municipality could actually do anything about the overcrowding:

> The municipality can't just say we want more or fewer tourists. The global trend is that it is increasing, because it has become much easier to travel. We can't put a fence up around the city. Yet, we can think about what kind of tourism is good for the city: tourists that stay longer are economically more interesting.[2]

As a consequence, residents have started to make use of their social and political connections and communication skills to bring their perspective across to politicians, policy makers, and the media. Many respondents showed an active interest in the regulation of tourism, and some indicated that they themselves have communicated their concerns to local politicians. Through a continuous stream of letters in local and national newspapers, they bring the issues of overcrowding, disruptive behaviour, and Airbnb-related problems to the public's attention. In addition, residents have started public initiatives to demand the regulation of what they see as the most ostentatious aspects of tourism. An example is the recent residents' petition demanding that the despised beer bike be banned from public space, which was signed by thousands of residents, including many of the respondents in this study.

---

2. Kajsa Ollongren during a Room for Discussion meeting at the University of Amsterdam in 2015, as quoted in Kooijman, M. (2015, 23 November). Toerism-expert Hodes: "Het is vechten tegen de bierkaai." Folia. Retrieved from http://www.folia.nl/actueel/97769/toerisme-expert-hodes-het-is-vechten-tegen-de-bierkaai.

In addition, local interest groups, such as the foundation Friends of the Amsterdam Historic Centre, are lobbying for more strict enforcement of the prohibition against inappropriate behaviour in public spaces and short-stay rentals. While members of this foundation originally focused their activities on the preservation of the historic district, they have recently shifted their attention to "putting a halt to disneyfication" and "restoring balance." In this respect, the chairman refers to their early efforts of historic preservation as a pyrrhic victory: thanks to its UNESCO status, Amsterdam as a tourist destination has become too successful for its own good. Efforts to create public and political awareness about residents' concerns now include a wide range of activities, ranging from the showing of documentaries on the destructive effects of tourism in Venice to speaking up at public debates of the municipal council to advocate the prohibition of temporary holiday rentals of privately owned homes.

Up to 2018, the most explicit response to these forms of protest and collective action from part of the municipality has been the "dispersion policy," aimed at distributing the number of tourists more equally across the city and also to other parts of the region, even going as far as rebranding the beach of the seaside town IJmuiden (more than fifteen miles [twenty-four kilometres] away) as "Amsterdam Beach," which most people would call a stretch. At the same time, permits were handed out for thousands of hotel rooms to be built in the coming years, and little was done about mitigating the effects of growing tourism in the hotspots of the city, including the Canal District. So far, tourism is not directly targeted as a single policy issue but addressed in the broader context of "The Balanced City" (Municipality of Amsterdam, 2015). The city has not integrated concerns about tourism in policies aimed at the housing market or commercial real estate. Regulation of tourist-related activities occurs permit by permit, building by building, and terrace by terrace.

Since the 2018 elections, however, the political discourse has changed. Tourism inevitably became a central topic in the election campaign of several political parties. Left-wing parties like the Labour Party (PvdA), Socialist Party (SP), and Green Left (Groen Links) connected the emergence of Airbnb to rising housing prices and expressed concerns about the growing economic "monoculture" of tourist shops and ice cream cafés. The new coalition formed by these parties formulated strong ambitions about "damming in" the negative effects of tourism, promising to crack down on holiday rentals and everyday nuisances and promote locally oriented small business. Whether they will actually succeed in realizing these ambitions remains to be seen; in the meantime, overcrowding and over-tourism remain highly contentious issues among Amsterdammers.

Conclusion

The transformation of the Canal District into a place for tourism, leisure, and consumption is experienced by long-term, middle-class respondents as a form of downgrading and a loss of place. On the one hand, residents experience a strong attachment to place: they feel privileged to live in such a beautiful place.

On the other hand, their sensory experience of place is increasingly undermined by urban tourism. The tourist spectacle disrupts the fine balance between stillness and liveliness, which first attracted these residents to the area. This disruption is not only related to the sheer numbers of visitors, but also to the ways in which tourists use the neighbourhood.

Having been actively involved in the resurrection of the area from the early 1970s onward as a place of residence, these long-term, middle-class residents are used to being "in control" of processes of place making. Now, they are beginning to experience a sense of powerlessness in the face of the global flows of visitors and capital that are reconfiguring the real estate market, the structure of the local economy, and the dynamics of public space. Respondents individually cope with the challenges of living in a commodified space by combining a strategy of mobility – using their money, time, and social connections – with retreating into their own homes. The obvious question is how durable this balancing act is, as the number of tourists keeps growing and interactions between residents and visitors through short-stay arrangements such as Airbnb become even more frequent.

Typical to the Dutch context, residents are looking to local government to find solutions, increasingly expressing their frustrations publicly in order to put their concerns on the political agenda. However, the municipality is partly responsible for creating the current situation. Years of city marketing and pro-growth policies have facilitated the enormous growth in tourism. For many years, the policy response to tourism has been ambiguous, and policy initiatives have been more focused on short-term annoyances than the long-term effects of tourism. What is more, urban professionals and politicians themselves seem to experience a sense of powerlessness in the face of the sheer scale of growth. Conservative estimates indicate that in the next ten years millions of additional visitors will come to the city from emerging economies like China and India. These tourists cannot be stopped by "putting a fence around the city." Without a doubt, the function of the city centre as a place to live will increasingly come under pressure. For example, the municipality currently has limited tools to regulate commercial real estate. If the local bar is bought and converted into a pancake house, there is little the local government can do.

Finally, this study highlights the temporality of urban transformations. While in previous years gentrification has been the major driving force of urban change in Amsterdam, current changes have little to do with local class dynamics. Rather than transforming into an elite domain, as has been observed in some gentrification areas, Amsterdam's Canal District is on an entirely different track, as the local economy and housing market are becoming disconnected from the everyday life of the city. This situation raises fundamental questions about the future of the centre of the city as a place for the city.

References

1 Introduction: Amsterdam's Canal District in Global Perspective

Attoh, K.A. (2011). What *kind* of right is the right to the city? *Progress in Human Geography*, *35*(5), 669–85. https://doi.org/10.1177/0309132510394706

Benevolo, L. (1980). The free city in Greece. In L. Benevolo (Ed.), *The history of the city* (pp. 55–134). Cambridge, MA: MIT Press.

Eichholtz, P.M.A. (1997). A long run house price index: The *Herengracht Index*, 1628–1973. *Real Estate Economics*, *25*(2), 175–92. https://doi.org/10.1111/1540 -6229.00711

Girouard, M. (1985). *Cities and people: A social and architectural history*. New Haven: Yale University Press.

Lefebvre, H. (1968). *Le droit à la ville*. Paris: Anthropos.

Nijman, J. (1994). The VOC [Dutch East India Company] and the expansion of the world-system, 1602–1799. *Political Geography*, *13*(3), 211–27. https://doi.org /10.1016/0962-6298(94)90027-2

Nijman, J. (1999). Cultural globalization and the identity of place: The reconstruction of Amsterdam. *Cultural Geographies*, *6*(2), 146–64. https://doi.org/10.1177 /096746089900600202

Rossi. A. (1982). *The architecture of the city*. D. Ghirardo & J. Ockman (Trans.). Cambridge, MA: MIT Press. (Original work published as *L'architettura della città*. Padua: Marsilio Editori, 1966)

Sennett, R. (2018). *Building and dwelling: Ethics for the city*. London: Penguin Books.

Taylor, P.J. (1995). World cities and territorial states: The rise and fall of their mutuality. In P.L. Knox & P.J. Taylor (Eds.), *World cities in a world system* (pp. 48–62). Cambridge: Cambridge University Press.

Tilly, C. (1992). *Coercion, capital, and European states, AD 990–1992*. Cambridge, MA: Blackwell.

Trouw. (2019, 7 June). In heel Nederland blijven huizen maar duurder worden. *Trouw*.

2 Between Art and Expediency: Origins of the Canal District

Abrahamse, J.E. (2011). A Roman road in the Dutch Republic. Jacob van Campen's "Via Appia" in the Utrecht countryside. *Journal of the Society of Architectural Historians*, *70*(4), 442–65. https://doi.org/10.1525 /jsah.2011.70.4.442

Abrahamse, J.E. (2019). *Metropolis in the making: A planning history of Amsterdam in the Dutch Golden Age*. Turnhout: Brepols.

Abrahamse, J.E., Kosian, M.C., & Schmitz, E. (2010). *Tussen Haarlemmerpoort en Halfweg. Historische atlas van de Brettenzone in Amsterdam*. Bussum: Thoth.

Abrahamse, J.E., Kosian, M.C., & Schmitz, E. (Eds.). (2012). *Atlas of Amstelland: The biography of a landscape.* Bussum: Thoth.

Abrahamse, J.E., & Rutte, R.J. (2016). 1500–1800 – Changes in urbanization. Differentiation, expansion and contraction. In R.J. Rutte & J.E. Abrahamse (Eds.), *Atlas of the Dutch urban landscape: A millennium of spatial development* (pp. 188–211). Bussum: Thoth.

Asaert, G. (2004). *1585: De val van Antwerpen en de uittocht van Vlamingen en Brabanders.* Tielt: Lannoo.

Borger, G., Horsten, F., Engel, H., Rutte, R., Diesfeldt, O., Pane, I., & de Waaijer, A. (2011). Twelve centuries of spatial transformation in the western Netherlands, in six maps. Landscape, habitation and infrastructure in 800, 1200, 1500, 1700, 1900 and 2000. *OverHolland,* 10/11, 4–124. https://doi.org/10.7480/overholland .2011.10-11.1653

Brand, A.D. (2012). *De wortels van de Randstad. Overheids-invloed en stedelijke hiërarchie in het westen van Nederland tussen de 13de en de 20ste eeuw.* Delft: Faculty of Architecture and the Built Environment.

Burger Jr., C.P. (1918). Amsterdam in het einde der zestiende eeuw. Studie bij de uitgaaf van den grooten plattegrond van 1597. *Jaarboek Amstelodamum, 16,* 1–103.

De Graauw, J. (2011). De middeleeuwse bouwgeschiedenis van de Amsterdamse Sint-Anthonispoort. De Waag op de Nieuwmarkt nader onderzocht. *Bulletin KNOB, 110,* 117–28. https://doi.org/10.7480/knob.110.2011.3/4.109

De Roever, N. (1969). *De kroniek van Staets. Een bladzijde uit de geschiedenis van het fabriek-ambt der stad Amsterdam.* Amsterdam: Ten Brink & De Vries.

Keuning, H.J. (1979). *Kaleidoscoop der Nederlandse Land-schappen: De regionale verscheidenheid van Nederland in historisch-geografisch perspectief.* The Hague: Martinus Nijhoff.

Kuijpers, E. (2005). *Migrantenstad. Immigratie en sociale verhoudingen in 17e-eeuws Amsterdam.* Hilversum: Verloren.

Lourens, P., & Lucassen, J. (1997). *Inwonertallen van Nederlandse steden ca. 1300–1800.* Amsterdam: NEHA.

Noordkerk, H. (1748–78). *Handvesten ofte Priviligien ende octroyen, mitsgaders willekeuren, costuimen, ordonnantien en handelingen der stad Amstelredam* (Vols. I–V). Amsterdam: Hendrik van Waesberge, Salomon and Petrus Schouten.

Nusteling, H. (1985). *Welvaart en werkgelegenheid in Amsterdam 1540-1860. Een relaas over demografie, economie en sociale politiek van een wereldstad.* Amsterdam/Dieren: De Bataafsche Leeuw.

Rutte, R.J., & IJsselstijn, M. (2016). 1000–1500 – Town formation and waterways. The big urban boom. In R.J. Rutte & J.E. Abrahamse (Eds.), *Atlas of the Dutch urban landscape: A millennium of spatial development* (pp. 172–87). Bussum: Thoth.

Smit, C. (2001). *Leiden met een luchtje. Straten, water, groen en afval in een Hollandse stad, 1200-2000.* Leiden: Primavera Pers.

Van Bavel, B.J.P., & Van Zanden, J.L. (2004). The jump-start of the Holland economy during the late-medieval crisis, c.1350–c.1500. *Economic History Review, 57*(3), 503–32. https://doi.org/10.1111/j.1468-0289.2004.00286.x

Van Deursen, A.T. (2006). *De last van veel geluk. De geschiedenis van Nederland 1555–1702.* Amsterdam: Bert Bakker.

Van Gelder, H.A.E. (1925). *Memoriën en adviezen van Corne-lis Pietersz.* Hooft II, Utrecht: Kemink.

Van Leeuwen, M.H.D., & Oeppen, J.E. (1993). Recon-structing the demographic regime of Amsterdam 1681–1920. *Economic and Social History of the Nether-lands, 5,* 61–102.

Van Maanen, R.C.J. (Ed.). (2003). *Leiden. De geschiedenis van een Hollandse stad* (4 Vols.). Leiden: Stichting Geschiedschrijving Leiden.

Von Zesen, F. (1664). *Beschreibung der Stadt Amsterdam.* Amsterdam: Joachim Noschen.

3 Designing the World's Most Liberal City

Abrahamse, J. (2019). *Metropolis in the Making: A Planning History of Amsterdam in the Dutch Golden Age.* Turnhout: Brepols.

Bastin, J. (1996). The changing balance of the Southeast Asian pepper trade. In M.N. Pearson (Ed.), *Spices in the Indian Ocean world* (pp. 283–316). Aldershot: Variorum.

Brugmans, H. (1973). *Geschiedenis van Amsterdam*. Utrecht: Het Spectrum.

Carasso-Kok, M. (Ed.). (2004). *Geschiedenis van Amsterdam* (Vol. 1). Amsterdam: Sun.

De Vries, J. (1974). *The Dutch rural economy in the Golden Age, 1500–1700*. New Haven: Yale University Press.

Elias, J. (1963). *De vroedschap van Amsterdam, 1578–1795*. Haarlem: N. Israel.

Israel, J. (1995). *The Dutch Republic: Its rise, greatness, and fall*. Oxford: Clarendon.

Killiam, T., & van der Zeijden, M. (1978). *Amsterdam canal guide*. Utrecht: Het Spectrum.

Lesger, C. (2006). *The rise of the Amsterdam market and information exchange*. Hants: Ashgate.

Sprunger, K. (1994). *Trumpets from the tower: English Puritan printing in the Netherlands, 1600–1640*. New York: Brill.

Sutton, P. (2006). *Jan van der Heyden (1637–1712)*. New Haven: Yale University Press.

UNESCO (United Nations Educational, Scientific and Cultural Organization). (2010). Seventeenth-century canal ring area of Amsterdam inside the Singelgracht. Retrieved from http://whc.unesco.org/en/list/1349

Unger, R. (1978). *Dutch shipbuilding before 1800*. Assen: Van Gorcum.

Unger, R. (1980). Dutch herring, technology, and international trade in the seventeenth century. *Journal of Economic History*, 40(2), 253–79. https://doi.org/10.1017/S0022050700108204

4 A Privileged Site in the City, the Republic, and the World Economy

Abrahamse, J.E. (2019). *Metropolis in the Making: A Planning History of Amsterdam in the Dutch Golden Age*. Turnhout: Brepols.

Bakker, B. (2004). De zichtbare stad 1578–1813. In W. Vrijhoff & M. Prak (Eds.), *Geschiedenis van Amsterdam. II-1 Centrum van de wereld 1578–1650* (pp. 17–101). Amsterdam: SUN.

Bakker, B., & Schmitz, E. (2007). *Het aanzien van Amsterdam. Panorama's, plattegronden en profielen uit de Gouden Eeuw*. Amsterdam: Stadsarchief Amsterdam.

Blaeu, J. (1649–52). *Toonneel der steden van de Verenighde Nederlanden met haare beschrijvingen* (Vols. 1–2). Amsterdam: Blaeu.

Braudel, F. (1984). *The perspective of the world*. London: Collins.

Burke, P. (1974). *Venice and Amsterdam: Study of seventeenth-century elites*. London: Temple Smith.

Burke, P. (1998). *The European Renaissance: Centres and peripheries*. Oxford: Blackwell.

Diederiks, H. (1987). Arm en rijk in Amsterdam. Wonen naar welstand in de 16e–18e eeuw. In W.F. Heinemeijer & M.F. Wagenaar (Eds.), *Amsterdam in kaarten. Verandering van de stad in vier eeuwen cartografie* (pp. 48–9). Ede: Zomer en Keuning.

Faber, S., Huisken, J., & Lammertse, F. (1987). *Of Lords, who seat nor cushion do ashame. The government of Amsterdam in the 17th and 18th centuries*. Amsterdam: Stichting Koninklijk Paleis.

Girouard, M. (1985). *Cities and people: A social and architectural history*. New Haven: Yale University Press.

Howell, M. (2016). The amazing career of a pioneer capitalist. *New York Review of Books*, 63(6), 55–6.

Israel, J.I. (1989). *Dutch primacy in world trade, 1585–1740*. Oxford: Clarendon Press.

Israel, J.I. (1995a). *The Dutch Republic: Its rise, greatness, and fall, 1477–1806*. Oxford: Oxford University Press.

Israel, J. (1995b). A golden age: Innovation in Dutch cities, 1648–1720. *History Today*, 45(3), 14–20.

Kriegel, B. (2011). *La république et le prince moderne*. Paris: PUF.

Modelski, G., & Thompson, W.R. (1988). *Seapower in global politics, 1494–1993*. London: Palgrave Macmillan.

Nijman, J. (1994). The VOC and the expansion of the world-system, 1602–1799. *Political Geography*, 13(3), 211–27. https://doi.org/10.1016/0962-6298(94)90027-2

Prak, M. (2002). *Gouden Eeuw. Het raadsel van de Republiek.* Nijmegen: SUN.

Schmidt, F. (2008). Een stad aan de muur. In J.E. Abrahamse, M. Carasso-Kok, & E. Schmitz (Eds.), *De verbeelde wereld* (pp. 30–5). Bussum: Thoth.

Smith, W.D. (1984). The function of commercial centers in the modernization of capitalism: Amsterdam as an information exchange in the seventeenth century. *Journal of Economic History*, 44(4), 985–1005. https://doi.org/10.1017/S0022050700033052

Taylor, P.J. (1996). *The way the modern world works: World hegemony to world impasse.* Chichester: Wiley.

Taylor, P.J. (2013). *Extraordinary cities: Millennia of moral syndromes, world-systems and city/state relations.* Cheltenham: Edward Elgar.

Tilly, C. (1992). *Coercion, capital, and European states, AD 990–1992.* Cambridge, MA: Blackwell.

van Lakerveld, C. (Ed.). (1977). *The Dutch cityscape in the 17th century and its sources.* Amsterdam/Toronto: Amsterdams Historisch Museum/Art Gallery of Ontario

Vis, P.C. (2010). *Andries de Graeff 1611–1678. 't Gezag is heerelyk: doch vol bekommeringen.* (Master's thesis, University of Amsterdam). Retrieved from http://www.triomfdervrede.nl/images/andries_de_graeff_20100113.pdf

Vroom, W. (2008). "Eine der wunderbarsten Städte Europas." Amsterdam in vroege reisgidsen (1838–circa 1865). In J.E. Abrahamse, M. Carasso-Kok, & E. Schmitz (Eds.), *De verbeelde wereld* (pp. 18–23). Bussum: Thoth.

5 Bourgeois Homes: The Elite Spaces of the Canal District, 1600–1910

Abrahamse, J.E. (2019). *Metropolis in the Making: A Planning History of Amsterdam in the Dutch Golden Age.* Turnhout: Brepols.

Algemeen Adresboek der Stad Amsterdam 1853. (1853). Amsterdam: Stemvers.

Bruin, K., & Schijf, H. (1984). De eerste bewoners in een deftige straat. In M. Jonker, L. Noordegraaf, & M. Wagenaar (Eds.), *Van stadskern tot stadsgewest. Stedebouwkundige geschiedenis van Amsterdam* (pp. 133–56). Amsterdam: Verloren.

Calisch, N.S. (1851). *Liefdadigheid te Amsterdam.* Amsterdam: Schooneveld.

de Vries, B. (1986). *Electoraat en elite. Sociale structuur en sociale mobiliteit in Amsterdam, 1850–1895.* Zutphen: Walburg Pers.

de Vries, B. (2006a). Van deftigheid en volksopvoeding naar massacultuur. Het Amsterdamse verenigingsleven in de negentiende eeuw. *Jaarboek Amstelodamum, 98,* 83–105.

de Vries, B. (2006b). Voluntary societies in the Netherlands, 1750–1900. In B. Morris, G. Morton, & B. de Vries (Eds.), *Civil society, associations and urban places: Class, nation and culture in nineteenth-century Europe* (pp. 103–16). Aldershot: Ashgate.

Dudok van Heel, S.A.C. (1997). Regent families and urban development in Amsterdam. In P. van Kessel & E. Schulte (Eds), *Rome – Amsterdam: Two growing cities in seventeenth-century Europe* (pp. 124–45). Amsterdam: Amsterdam University Press.

Frederiks, J.G., & Frederiks, P.J. (Eds.). (1890). *Kohier van den tweehonderdsten penning voor Amsterdam en onderhoorige plaatsen over 1631.* Amsterdam: Ten Brink en De Vries.

Johnston, R.J. (1984). *City and society: An outline for urban geography.* London: Penguin.

Lesger, C. (2005). Stagnatie en stabiliteit. De economie tussen 1730 en 1795. In W. Frijhoff & M. Prak (Eds.), *Geschiedenis van Amsterdam. Zelfbewuste stadstaat 1650–1813* (pp. 219–65). Amsterdam: SUN.

Lesger, C. (2006). *The rise of the Amsterdam market and information exchange: Merchants, commercial expansion and change in the spatial economy of the low countries, c.1550–1630.* Aldershot: Asghate.

Lesger, C., van Leeuwen, M.H.D., & Vissers, B. (2013). Residentiële segregatie in vroegmoderne steden. Amsterdam in de eerste helft van de negentiende eeuw. *Tijdschrift voor Sociale en Economische Geschiedenis, 10*(1), 71–101. https://doi.org/10.18352/tseg.186

Nusteling, H. (1985). *Welvaart en werkgelegenheid in Amsterdam 1540–1860. Een relaas over demografie, economie en sociale politiek van een wereldstad.* Amsterdam: Bataafsche Leeuw.

Sjoberg, G. (1960). *The pre-industrial city, past and present.* New York: Free Press.

Soltow, L., & van Zanden, J.L. (1998). *Income and wealth inequality in the Netherlands, 16th–20th century.* Amsterdam: Het Spinhuis.

Taverne, E. (1978). *In 't land van belofte: In de nieue stadt: Ideaal en werkelijkheid van de stadsuitleg in de Republiek 1580-1680.* Maarssen: Schwartz.

Thorold, P. (1999). *The London rich: The creation of a great city, from 1666 to the present.* London: Viking.

van der Leeuw-Kistemaker, R.E. (1974). *Wonen en werken in de Warmoesstraat van de 14de tot het midden van de 16de eeuw.* Amsterdam: Werkschriften Historisch Seminarium van de Universiteit van Amsterdam.

van Dillen, J.G. (1970). *Van rijkdom en regenten. Handboek tot de economische en sociale geschiedenis van Nederland tijdens de Republiek.* Den Haag: Nijhoff.

van Leeuwen, M.H.D., & Oeppen, J.E. (1993). Reconstructing the demographic regime of Amsterdam 1681–1920. *Economic and Social History in the Netherlands, 5,* 61–102.

Wagenaar, M. (1990). *Amsterdam 1876–1914. Economisch herstel, ruimtelijke expansie en de veranderende ordening van het stedelijk grondgebruik.* Amsterdam: Universiteit van Amsterdam.

Zandvliet, K. (2006). *De 250 rijksten van de Gouden Eeuw. Kapitaal, macht, familie en levensstijl.* Amsterdam: Rijksmuseum.

6 The Architectural Essence of the Canal District: Past and Present

Bakker, M., Kistemaker, R., van Nierop, H., Vroom, W., & Witteman, P. (Eds.). (2000). *Amsterdam in de tweede Gouden Eeuw.* Bussum: Thoth.

Beek, M. (1984). Abel Antoon Kok: Architect, activist en verzamelaar. *Ons Amsterdam, 36,* 61–8.

Boeken, A. (1940, 7 September). Bouwen en restaureeren in oud-Amsterdam. *Bouwkundig Weekblad Architectura, 36,* 279–87.

Bosma, K., & Kolen, J. (Eds.). (2010). *Geschiedenis en ontwerp. Handboek voor de omgang met cultureel erfgoed.* Nijmegen: Vantilt.

Bosma, K., & Wagenaar, C. (Eds.). (1995). *Een geruisloze doorbraak. De geschiedenis van architectuur en stedebouw tijdens de bezetting en de wederopbouw van Nederland.* Rotterdam: NAi.

Brinkgreve, G. (2004). The preservation of historic buildings in Amsterdam. In L. Deben, W. Salet, & M.-T. van Thoor (Eds.), *Cultural heritage and the future of the historic inner city of Amsterdam* (pp. 101–20). Amsterdam: Aksant.

Edhoffer, L., Jutte, T., Loof, M., & Mulder, W. (2013). *De schoonheid van Amsterdam.* Amsterdam: Gemeente Amsterdam.

Edhoffer, L., & van Dijk, A. (Eds.). (2010). *De schoonheid van Amsterdam. 111 jaar welstandsadvisering: Vol 2. 1940–1978.* Amsterdam: Commissie voor Welstand en Monumenten.

Halbertsma. M., & Kuipers, M. (Eds.). (2014). *Het erfgoeduniversum. Een inleiding in de theorie en praktijk van cultureel erfgoed.* Bussum: Coutinho

Kleijn, K., & van Zoest, R. (Eds.). (2013). *The canals of Amsterdam: 400 years of building, living and working.* Bussum: THOTH.

Kok, A.A. (1941). *Amsterdamsche woonhuizen.* Amsterdam: Allert de Lange

Kolen, J., & Renes, J. (2015). Landscape biographies: Key Issues. In J. Kolen, H. Renes, & R. Hermans (Eds.), *Landscape biographies: Geographical, historical and archaeological perspectives on the production and transmission of landscapes* (pp. 21–47). Amsterdam: Amsterdam University Press.

Meurs, P. (2000). *De moderne historische stad. Ontwerpen voor vernieuwing en behoud, 1883–1940.* Rotterdam: NAi.

Meurs, P. (2004). Amsterdam: A modern historical city. In: L. Deben, W. Salet, & M.-T. van Thoor (Eds.), *Cultural heritage and the future of the historic inner city of Amsterdam* (pp. 73–83). Amsterdam: Aksant.

Rossi. A. (1982). *The architecture of the city*. D. Ghirardo & J. Ockman (Trans.). Cambridge, MA: MIT Press. (Original work published as *L'architettura della città*. Padua: Marsilio Editori, 1966)

Schmidt, F. (2009). Building artists: History, modernity and the architect around 1630. In H.P. Chapman & Joanna Woodall (Eds.), *Nederlandsch kunsthistorisch jaarboek/ Netherlands yearbook for history of art: Vol. 59. Envisioning the artist in the early modern Netherlands* (pp. 314–44). Leiden: Brill.

Schmidt, F. (2012a). Amsterdam's architectural image from early-modern print series to global heritage discourse. In M. de Waard (Ed.), *Imagining global Amsterdam: History, culture and geography in a world city* (pp. 219–38). Amsterdam: Amsterdam University Press.

Schmidt, F. (2012b). De ontdekking van de grachtengordel. In M. Slooff & J.E. Abrahamse (Eds.), *Amsterdams werelderfgoed. De grachtengordel na 400 jaar* (pp. 48–61). Amsterdam: Bureau Monumenten & Archeologie.

Schmidt, F. (2016). *Passion and control: Dutch architectural culture of the eighteenth century*. Farnham: Ashgate.

Schoonenberg, W. (2012). De Van Houtenmonumenten. Een reconstructie van de werkwijze van Eelke van Houten (1872–1970). *Bulletin KNOB, 111*(4), 221–31. https://doi.org/10.7480/knob.111.2012.4.356

UNESCO (United Nations Educational, Scientific and Cultural Organization). (2005). Vienna Memorandum on "World Heritage and Contemporary Architecture – Managing the Historic Urban Landscape." Retrieved from http://whc.unesco.org/archive/2005/whc05 -15ga-inf7e.pdf

UNESCO (United Nations Educational, Scientific and Cultural Organization). (2009). *The seventeenth-century canal ring area of Amsterdam within the Singelgracht:* *Nomination document*. Retrieved from https://whc .unesco.org/uploads/nominations/1349.pdf

van der Woud, A. (2001). *The art of building. From classicism to modernity: The Dutch architectural debate 1840–1900*. Aldershot: Ashgate.

Vlaardingerbroek, P. (Ed.). (2013). *De wereld aan de Amsterdamse grachten*. Amsterdam: Bureau Monumenten & Archeologie / Bas Lubberhuizen.

Voorloopige lijst der Nederlandsche monumenten van geschiedenis en kunst. (1928). Vol. 5, 2: *De Gemeente Amsterdam*. Den Haag: Algemeene Landsdrukkerij. Retrieved from https://www.dbnl.org/tekst/_voo016voor04_01/

Windig A., & van Eeghen, I.H. (Eds.). (1965). *Bewaard in het hart. Een selectie van 63 Amsterdamse woon-en pakhuizen uit de periode van 1450 tot 1825 gekozen uit een totaal van 650 percelen, die tijdens de eerste tien jaar van het bestaan van het gemeentelijk Bureau Monumentenzorg zijn gerestaureerd (1953–1963)*. Amsterdam: Stadsdrukkerij.

7 The Canal District: A Continuing History of Modern Planning

Brinkgreve, G. (Ed.). (1956). *Alarm in Amsterdam, of het lot der oude binnensteden*. Amsterdam: Elsevier.

Bronkhorst, A., van den Eerenbeemt, M., & de Wilt, K. (2013). *Grachtenhuizen – Amsterdam canal houses*. Amsterdam: Lectura Cultura Books.

Buchanan, C. (1964). *Traffic in towns: The specially shortened edition of the Buchanan Report*. Hammondsworth: Penguin Books.

de Klerk, L.A. (2008). *De modernisering van de stad 1850-1914. De opkomst van de planmatige stadsontwikkeling in Nederland*. Rotterdam: NAi Uitgevers.

Gemeente Amsterdam. (1935). *Algemeen Uitbreidingsplan (Nota van Toelichting; Bijlagen)*. Amsterdam: Gemeente Amsterdam.

Gemeente Amsterdam. (1955). *Nota Binnenstad.* Gemeenteblad 1955. Afd. 1 Nr. 255.

Gemeente Amsterdam. (1968). *Voorontwerp van de Tweede nota over de Amsterdamse binnenstad.* Amsterdam: Gemeenteblad, bijlage C.

Gemeente Amsterdam. (1981). *Structuurplan 1981.* Amsterdam.

Grünhagen, H. (Ed.). (2007). *Uitgebreid Amsterdam. 50 jaar Amsterdamse Raad voor de Stadsontwikkeling.* Bussum: Uitgeverij Thoth.

Hartman, W., Hellinga, W.J., Jonker, M., & de Ruijter, P. (1985). *Algemeen Uitbreidingsplan Amsterdam 50 Jaar.* Amsterdam: Amsterdamse Raad voor de Stedebouw.

Heinemeijer, W.F., van Hulten, M., & de Vries Reilingh, H.D. (1968). *Het centrum van Amsterdam. Een sociografische studie.* Amsterdam: Polak and Van Gennep.

Jokinen, D. (1968). *Geef de stad een kans.* Roosendaal: Stichting Weg.

Monumentenwet [Monument Act]. (1988). Section 36-2. Den Haag: Ministerie van Volkshuisvesting en Ruimtelijke Ordening.

Rooijendijk, C. (2005). *That city is mine! Urban ideal images in public debates and city plans, Amsterdam and Rotterdam 1945–1995.* (Doctoral dissertation, University of Amsterdam). Amsterdam: Vossiuspers UvA.

van der Cammen, H., & de Klerk, L.A. (1993). *Ruimtelijke ordening. De ontwikkelingsgang van de ruimtelijke ordening in Nederland.* Utrecht/Antwerpen: Het Spectrum.

van der Cammen, H., de Klerk, L.A., Dekker, G., & Witsen, P.P. (2012). *The selfmade land: Culture and evolution of urban and regional planning in the Netherlands.* Houten: Het Spectrum.

van Hulten, M. (1968). Minder én meer bevolking in de binnenstad. In W.F. Heinemeijer, M. van Hulten, & H.D. de Vries Reilingh. *Het centrum van Amsterdam. Een sociografische studie* (pp. 69–128). Amsterdam: Polak and Van Gennep

van Rooijen, J. (1995). *De drooglegging van Amsterdam. Een onderzoek naar gedempt grachtwater.* Amsterdam: Gemeentelijk Bureau Monumentenzorg Amsterdam (stageverslag).

Wagenaar, M. (1990). *Amsterdam 1876–1914. Economisch herstel, ruimtelijke expansie en de veranderende ordening van het stedelijk grondgebruik.* (Amsterdamse Historische Reeks, no. 16). Amsterdam: Universiteit van Amsterdam.

8 Preservation through Transformation: Amsterdam through the Lens of Barcelona

Busquets, J., et al. (2003). *The old town of Barcelona: A past with future.* Barcelona: Ajuntament de Barcelona.

Cabrera, P. (1998). La transformació urbana de la Ciutat Vella. *Barcelona Societat, 9,* 14–30.

Cócola, A. (2011). *El Barrio Gótico de Barcelona. Planificación del pasado e imagen de marca.* Barcelona: Madroño.

Delgado, M. (2006, 10 October). El " forat de la vergonya." *El País.* Retrieved from http://elpais.com/diario/2006/10/10/catalunya/1160442449_850215.html

Eggenkamp, W. (2004). Stadsherstel Amsterdam. In L. Deben, W. Salet, & M.-T. van Thoor (Eds.), *Cultural heritage and the future of the historic inner city of Amsterdam* (pp. 197–210). Amsterdam: Aksant.

Kupka, K. (2012). *Redevelopment by tradition: Urban renewal in world heritage cities.* Venice: Cluva.

Mak, G. (2004). Nostalgia and modernity. In L. Deben, W. Salet, & M.-T. van Thoor (Eds.), *Cultural heritage and the future of the historic inner city of Amsterdam* (pp. 13–22). Amsterdam: Aksant.

Porfido, E., Pérez, C., & Pesoa, M. (2019). Cuando el planeamiento atrae el turismo. El caso del barrio del Raval. *Revista Papers, 62,* 78–92. Retrieved from https://iermb.uab.cat/es/revistapapers/n-62-turismo-i-metropolis-reflexiones-para-una-agenda-integrada/#close

Sabaté, J. (2006). Luces y sombras en el proyecto urbanístico reciente de Barcelona. In M. Carmona & A. Arrese (Eds.), *Globalización y grandes proyectos urbanos* (pp. 57–68). Buenos Aires: Infinito.

Sabaté, J., & Tironi Rodó, M. (2008). Globalización y estrategias urbanísticas. Un balance del desarrollo reciente de Barcelona. *Cuaderno Urbano, 7*(7), 233–60. https://doi.org/10.30972/crn.77996

Schoonenberg, W. (2004). Without reconstruction, no inner city. In L. Deben, W. Salet, & M.-T. van Thoor (Eds.), *Cultural heritage and the future of the historic inner city of Amsterdam* (pp. 133–48). Amsterdam: Aksant.

9 The Canal District as a Site of Cognitive-Cultural Activities: "A Miracle of Spaciousness, Compactness, Intelligible Order"

Abrahamse, J.E. (2013). De derde en vierde uitleg. In K. Kleijn, E. Kurpershoek, & S. Otani (Eds.), *De grachten van Amsterdam. 400 jaar bouwen, wonen, werken en leven* (pp. 44–51). Bussum: Uitgeverij Thoth.

Braudel, F. (1979). *Civilisation matérielle, economie et capitalisme: Les jeux de l'echange*. Paris: Armand Collin.

de Groot, H., Marlet, G., Teulings, C., & Vermeulen, W. (2010). *Stad en land*. Centraal Planbureau: Den Haag.

D'Eramo, M. (2015). Dock life. *New Left Review, 96*, 85–99. Retrieved from https://newleftreview.org/issues/II96/articles/marco-d-eramo-dock-life

Durmaz, S.B. (2015). Analyzing the quality of place: Creative clusters in Soho and Beyoğlu. *Journal of Urban Design, 20*(1), 93–124. https://doi.org/10.1080/13574809.2014.972348

Engelen, E. (2007). "Amsterdamned"? The uncertain future of a financial centre. *Environment and Planning A, 39*(6), 1306–24. https://doi.org/10.1068/a38208

Fernandez, R. (2011). *Explaining the decline of the Amsterdam financial centre: Globalizing finance and the rise of a hierarchical inter-city network*. (Doctoral dissertation, Universiteit van Amsterdam).

Hutton, T.A. (2016). *Cities and the cultural economy*. London/New York: Routledge.

Israel, J. (1989). *Dutch primacy in world trade, 1585–1740*. Oxford: Clarendon Press.

Jacobs, J. (1961). *The death and life of great American cities*. New York: Vintage Books

Jordan, P. (2013). *In the city of bikes: The story of the Amsterdam cyclist*. New York: Harper Perennial.

Kloosterman, R.C. (1994). Amsterdamned: The rise of unemployment in Amsterdam in the 1980s. *Urban Studies, 31*(8), 1325–44. https://doi.org/10.1080/00420989420081181

Kloosterman, R.C. (2004). Recent employment trends in the cultural industries in Amsterdam, Rotterdam, The Hague and Utrecht: A first exploration. *Tijdschrift voor Economische en Sociale Geografie, 95*(2), 243–52. https://doi.org/10.1111/j.0040-747X.2004.00304.x

Kloosterman, R.C. (2010). Building a career: Labour practices and cluster reproduction in Dutch architectural design. *Regional Studies, 44*(7), 859–71. https://doi.org/10.1080/00343400903236873

Kloosterman, R.C. (2013). The Amsterdam economy and its impact on the labor market position of migrants, 1980–2010. In N. Foner, J. Rath, J.W. Duyvendak, & R. van Reekum (Eds.), *Immigration and the new urban landscape, New York and Amsterdam* (pp. 107–21). New York: NYU Press.

Kloosterman, R.C. (2014). Faces of migration: Migrants and the transformation of Amsterdam. In B. Kochan (Ed.), *Migration and London's growth* (pp. 127–43). London: London School of Economics.

Latten, J., & Deerenberg, I. (2013). Nieuwkomers grote steden per saldo economisch sterker. *Bevolkingstrends 2013*. Centraal Bureau voor de Statistiek, Retrieved from https://www.cbs.nl/nl-nl/achtergrond/2013/43/nieuwkomers-grote-steden-per-saldo-economisch-sterker

Lesger, C. (2001). *Handel in Amsterdam ten tijde van de Opstand; Kooplieden, commerciële expansie en verandering in de ruimtelijke economie van de Nederlanden ca. 1550–1630.* Hilversum: Uitgeverij Verloren

Martins, J. (2015). The extended workplace in a creative cluster: Exploring space(s) of digital work in Silicon Roundabout. *Journal of Urban Design*, 20(1), 125–45. https://doi.org/10.1080/13574809.2014.972349

Mumford, L. (1961). *The city in history: Its origins, its transformations, and its prospects.* Penguin Books: London.

Onderzoek, Informatie en Statistiek. (n.d.). *Dashboard toerisme.* Gemeente Amsterdam [Online]. Retrieved from http://www.ois.amsterdam.nl/visualisatie /dashboard_toerisme.html

Pethe, H., Haffner, S., & Lawton, P. (2010). Transnational migrants in the creative knowledge industries: Amsterdam, Barcelona, Dublin and Munich. In S. Musterd & A. Murie (Eds.), *Making competitive cities* (pp. 163–91). Chichester: Wiley-Blackwell.

Planbureau voor de Leefomgeving. (2016). *De verdeelde triomf. Verkenning van stedelijk-economische ongelijkheid en opties voor beleid. Ruimtelijke verkenningen 2016.* Den Haag: Planbureau voor de Leefomgeving.

Prak, M. (2002). *Gouden Eeuw. Het raadsel van de Republiek.* Nijmegen: SUN.

Rath, J., & Gelmers, W. (2014). Coffee in the city *The Proto City.* Retrieved from http://theprotocity.com /coffee-city

Röling, R.W. (2010). Small town, big campaigns: The rise and growth of an international advertising industry in Amsterdam. *Regional Studies*, 44(7) 829–43. https:// doi.org/10.1080/00343400903427928

Scott, A.J. (2012). *A world in emergence: Cities and regions in the 21st century.* Cheltenham: Edward Elgar.

Sleutjes, B., & Musterd, S. (2016). Revealed residential preferences of international migrants working in creative and knowledge intensive industries. In S. Musterd, M. Bontje, & J. Rouwendal (Eds.), *Skills and cities* (pp. 237–56). London: Routledge.

Trip, J.J., Kloosterman, R.C., & Romein, A. (2016). Divergent resilience: The employment growth paths of Amsterdam and Rotterdam, 2000–2014. Paper presented at the Regional Studies Association (RSA) Winter Conference 2016, 24–25 November, London, UK. Retrieved from https://www.regionalstudies.org/wp-content/uploads /2018/07/Trip__Kloosterman__Romein_-_Divergent _resilience.pdf

UNESCO (United Nations Educational, Scientific and Cultural Organization). (n.d.). *Seventeenth-century canal ring area of Amsterdam inside the Singelgracht.* UNESCO World Heritage List [Online]. Retrieved from http:// whc.unesco.org/en/list/1349

Vermeulen, W., Teulings, C., Marlet, G., & de Groot, H. (2016). *Groei & Krimp Waar moeten we bouwen – en waar vooral niet?* Nijmegen: VOC Uitgevers

Wallerstein, E. (1984). *Politics of the world-economy.* Cambridge: Cambridge University Press.

10 Cause Célèbre: The Contested History of the Canal District

Aldrich, R., & Wards, S. (2010). Ends of empire: Decolonizing the nation in British and French historiography. In S. Berger & Ch. Lorenz (Eds.), *Nationalizing the past: Historians as nation builders in modern Europe* (pp. 259–81). Basingstoke: Palgrave Macmillan.

Beukers, E. (Ed.). (2015). *De Bosatlas van Amsterdam.* Groningen: Noordhoff Atlasproducties.

Bloembergen, M. (2006). *Colonial spectacles: The Netherlands and the Dutch East Indies at the world exhibitions, 1880–1931.* B. Jackson (Trans.). Singapore: Singapore University Press.

Bureau of Monuments & Archaeology. (2009). *The seventeenth-century canal ring area of Amsterdam within the Singelgracht. Nomination document.* Amsterdam: City of Amsterdam. Retrieved from https://whc.unesco.org /uploads/nominations/1349.pdf

Campo, J.N.F.M. (2002). *Engines of empire: Steam shipping and state formation in colonial Indonesia.* Hilversum: Verloren.

Chakrabarty, D. (2000). *Provincializing Europe: Postcolonial thought and historical difference.* Princeton, NJ: Princeton University Press.

Clifford, J. (1997). *Routes: Travel and translation in the late twentieth century*. Cambridge, MA: Harvard University Press.

Cooper, F. (2005). *Colonialism in question: Theory, knowledge, history*. Berkeley, CA: University of California Press.

de Jong, R., & Zondervan A. (2002). *De kleine geschiedenis van de slavernij. Sporen in Amsterdam*. Amsterdam: KIT Publishers.

de Jong, R., & Zondervan A. (2003). *De kleine geschiedenis van de slavernij. Sporen in Amsterdam II*. Amsterdam: Artoteek Zuidoost/het Nieuwe Podium.

De Voogd, C. (2005). *"A safe deposit"? Het cultureel erfgoed van Amsterdam / Le patrimoine d'Amsterdam / The cultural heritage of Amsterdam*. Amsterdam: Stadsdrukkerij Amsterdam N.V.

de Waard, M. (2012a). Amsterdam and the global imaginary. In M. de Waard (Ed.), *Imagining global Amsterdam: History, culture, and geography in a world city* (pp. 9–24). Amsterdam: Amsterdam University Press.

de Waard, M. (2012b). Rembrandt on screen: Art cinema, cultural heritage, and the museumization of urban space. In M. de Waard (Ed.), *Imagining global Amsterdam: History, culture, and geography in a world city* (pp. 143–67). Amsterdam: Amsterdam University Press.

De Wilt, K. (2011, 25 June). Herengracht 518. Het verhaal achter het Geelvinck Hinlopen Huis. Eigenaar: Jurriaan Buisman (1960) econoom. *Het Financieel Dagblad*.

Driver, F., & Gilbert, D. (Eds.). (1999). *Imperial cities: Landscape, display and identity*. Manchester: Manchester University Press.

Gissibl, B. (2011). Imagination and beyond: Cultures and geographies of imperialism in Germany, 1848–1918. In J. M. MacKenzie (Ed.), *European empires and the people: Popular responses to imperialism in France, Britain, the Netherlands, Belgium, Germany and Italy* (pp. 158–94). Manchester/New York: Manchester University Press.

Gosselink, M. (2014). Repliek van het Rijksmuseum. *BMGN-LCHR, 129*(1), 170–80. https://doi.org/10.18352/bmgn-lchr.9445

Greenblatt, S., Županov, I., Meyer-Kalkus, R., Paul, H., Nyiri, P., & Pannewick, F. (2010). *Cultural mobility: A manifesto*. Cambridge: Cambridge University Press.

Heijdra, T. (2019). Amsterdam – thuishaven. Onze Indische buurten. Retrieved from https://indischebuurten.nl/buurten/amsterdam

Hondius, D. (Ed.). (2013). *Atlasje van het slavernijverleden / Concise atlas of Dutch slavery. Kaarten en plattegronden / Maps and floorplans* (preliminary ed.). Amsterdam: Vrije Universiteit Amsterdam.

Hondius, D., Jouwe, N., Stam, D., & Tosch, J. (2014). *Amsterdam Gids slavernijverleden. Slavery Heritage Guide*. Arnhem: LM Publishers

Hondius, D., Jouwe, N., Stam, D., & Tosch, J. (2017). *Dutch New York histories: Connecting African, Native American and slavery heritage / Geschiedenissen van Nederlands New York. Verbonden met Afrikaans, inheems en slavernij-erfgoed*. Volendam: LM Publishers.

Hooper-Greenhill, E. (1992). *Museums and the shaping of knowledge*. London: Routledge.

ICOMOS (International Council on Monuments and Sites). (2000). Horta houses (Belgium), No 1005. In World Heritage Convention (WHC) nomination documentation: Major town houses of the architect Victor Horta (Brussels) (pp. 189–93). Retrieved from https://whc.unesco.org/en/list/1005/documents/

Kammer, C. (2015a, 10 December). Eskimo's en bosnegers verdwijnen. *NRC-Handelsblad*. Retrieved from https://www.nrc.nl/nieuws

Kammer, C. (2015b, 12 December). Een negerbediende heet voortaan een jonge zwarte bediende. *NRC-Handelsblad*. Retrieved from https://www.nrc.nl/nieuws

Legêne, S., & Eickhoff M. (2014). Postwar Europe and the colonial past in photographs. The NIOD-archive in Amsterdam as a site of memory-construction. In A. Rigney & C. de Cesari (Eds.), *Transnational memory: Circulation, articulation, scales* (pp. 287–311). Berlin/Boston: De Gruyter.

Le Nevez, C., & Blasi, A., (2018). *Amsterdam*. [City travel guide]. 11th ed. London: Lonely Planet.

Liverpool City Council. (2003). *Maritime mercantile city – Liverpool: Nomination of Liverpool – Maritime mercantile city for inscription on the World Heritage List*. Liverpool: Author. Retrieved from https://whc.unesco.org /uploads/nominations/1150.pdf

Maas, L., Knol, N., & Weyermans I. (2011). *Grachtengordel Amsterdam Werelderfgoed*. Amsterdam: Bureau Werelderfgoed.

Mac an Bhreithiún, B. (2012). Graphic design, globalization, and placemaking in the neighbourhoods of Amsterdam. In M. de Waard (Ed.), *Imagining global Amsterdam: History, culture, and geography in a world city* (pp. 255–71). Amsterdam: Amsterdam University Press.

MacGregor, A. (2007). *Curiosity and enlightenment: Collectors and collections from the sixteenth to the nineteenth century*. New Haven, NJ: Yale University Press.

Meershoek, P. (2013, 14 April). West-Indisch Huis wil niet geassocieerd worden met slavernijverleden. *Het Parool*. Retrieved from https://www.parool.nl/nieuws/west -indisch-huis-wil-niet-geassocieerd-worden-met -slavernijverleden~b5892afc/

Metz, D. (2012, 28 April). Transvaalbuurt, tussen Boerenoorlog en anti-apartheid. *Ons Amsterdam*. Retrieved from https://onsamsterdam.nl/transvaalbuurt -tussen-boerenoorlog-en-anti-apartheid

Modest, W., & Lelijveld, R. (Eds.). (2018). *Words matter: An unfinished guide to word choices in the cultural sector* [Work in Progress]. Amsterdam: Tropenmuseum, Africa Museum, Museum of World Cultures, World Museum. Retrieved from https://www.materialculture .nl/en/publications/words-matter

National Museums of Liverpool. (n.d.). Liverpool and emigrations in the 19th and 20th centuries. [Maritime Archives and Library Information Sheet 64]. Retrieved from http://www.liverpoolmuseums.org.uk/ maritime/archive/sheet/64

Pratt, M.L. (2008). *Imperial eyes: Travel writing and transculturation* (2nd ed.). London: Routledge.

RAI Amsterdam. (2013). *Amsterdam passport: I amsterdam, 2013/2014*. Retrieved from https://issuu.com /amsterdamrai/docs/acp2013_def_290813_web

Rouwendaal, R. (2015). Het verlangen naar grootsheid. De Wereldtentoonstelling van 1883 in Amsterdam als symbool van de bloeiperiode van de Tweede Gouden Eeuw. (Master's thesis, Vrije Universiteit Amsterdam). Retrieved from http://www.ubvu.vu.nl/pub/fulltext /scripties/13_2541525_0.pdf

Said, E.W. (1993). *Culture and imperialism*. New York: Afred Knopf.

Schmidt, B. (2001). *Innocence abroad: The Dutch imagination and the New World, 1570–1670*. Cambridge: Cambridge University Press.

Schmidt, F.H. (2012). De ontdekking van de grachtengordel. In M. Slood & J.E. Abrahamse (Eds.), *Amsterdams werelderfgoed. De grachtengordel na 400 jaar* (pp. 48–61). Amsterdam: Bureau Monumenten en Archeologie.

Shorto, R. (2013, 19 April). Quirks of Amsterdam, revealed during lunch. *New York Times International Edition*. Retrieved from https://www.nytimes.com /2013/04/21/travel/quirks-of-amsterdam-revealed-during-lunch.html

Slooff, M. (2011). Een monument van wereldformaat. De grachtengordel op de Unesco Werelderfgoedlijst. In V. van Rossem, G. van Tussenbroek, & J. Veerkamp (Eds.), *Amsterdam: Monumenten & archeologie. Jaarboek 10* (pp. 10–21). Amsterdam: Bureau Monumenten & Archeologie/Bas Lubberhuizen.

UNESCO (United Nations Educational, Scientific and Cultural Organization). (n.d.) Liverpool – Maritime mercantile city. Retrieved from https://whc.unesco .org/en/list/1150/

van der Meer, T. (2008). Jan Mijtens 1613/14–1670. Portrait of Margaretha van Raephorst, wife of Cornelis Tromp, 1668. In E. Schreuder & E. Kolfin (Eds.), *Black is beautiful: Rubens to Dumas* (p. 263). Amsterdam /Zwolle: De Nieuwe Kerk/Waanders.

van der Veen, J. (1992). Dit klain Vertrek bevat een Weereld van gewoel. Negentig Amsterdammers en hun kabinetten. In E. Bergvelt & R. Kistemaker (Eds.), *De wereld binnen handbereik. Nederlandse kunst- en rariteitenverzamelingen, 1585–1735* (pp. 232–58). Zwolle/Amsterdam: Waanders/Amsterdams Historisch Museum.

van Dijk, J., & Legêne, S. (Eds.). (2011). *The Netherlands East-Indies at the Tropenmuseum: A colonial history*. Amsterdam: KIT Publishers.

Vanvugt, E. (1998). *De maagd en de soldaat. Koloniale monumenten in Amsterdam en elders*. Amsterdam: Jan Mets.

Walda, M. (2014). "Europe is a Journey." The European cultural route as an instrument for heritage revival. In L. Egberts & K. Bosma (Eds.), *Companion to European heritage revivals* (pp. 207–68). Heidelberg/New York: Springer Open.

Westrik, C. (2012). *The future of world heritage: The Netherlands and the UNESCO World Heritage Convention*. Amsterdam: Vrije Universiteit.

Wijland, R. (2015, 15 September). Gevelreclame uit 1920 wekt wrevel bij buurtbewoners Palmgracht. *Het Parool*. Retrieved from https://www.parool.nl/nieuws/gevelreclame-uit-1920-wekt-wrevel-bij-buurtbewoners-palmgracht~bd0e65e2/

Wintle, M. (2012). Visualizing commerce and empire: Decorating the built environment of Amsterdam. In M. de Waard (Ed.), *Imagining global Amsterdam: History, culture, and geography in a world city* (pp. 67–82). Amsterdam: Amsterdam University Press.

11 The Present-Day Canal District as Home: Living in a Commodified Space

Bock, K. (2015). The changing nature of city tourism and its possible implications for the future of cities. European Journal of Futures Research, 3, 1–8. https://doi.org/10.1007/s40309-015-0078-5

Chapuis, A., Gravari-Barbas, M., Jacquot, S., & Mermet, A-C. (2012). Dynamiques urbaines et mobilités de loisirs à Paris: Pratiques, cohabitations et stratégies de production de l'espace urbain dans le quartier du Marais." In Berthold, É. (Ed.), *Les quartiers historiques: Pressions, enjeux, actions* (pp. 43–65). Québec: Presses de l'Université de Laval.

Colomb, C., & Novy, J. (Eds.). (2016). *Protest and resistance in the tourist city*. London: Routledge.

Fuller, H., & Michel, B. (2014). "Stop being a tourist!" New dynamics of urban tourism in Berlin-Kreuzberg. International Journal of Urban and Regional Research, *38*(4), 1304–18. https://doi.org/10.1111/1468-2427.12124

Gotham, K.F. (2005). Tourism from above and below: Globalization, localization and New Orleans's Mardi Gras. International Journal of Urban and Regional Research, 29(2), 309–26. https://doi.org/10.1111/j.1468-2427.2005.00586.x

Judd, D.R., & Fainstein, S. (1999). *The tourist city*. New Haven: Yale University Press.

Kavaratzis, M., & Ashworth, G.J. (2007). Partners in coffeeshops, canals and commerce: Marketing the city of Amsterdam. Cities, *24*(1), 16–25. https://doi.org/10.1016/j.cities.2006.08.007

Maitland, R. (2008). Conviviality and everyday life: The appeal of new areas of London for visitors. International Journal of Tourism Research, *10*(1), 15–25. https://doi.org/10.1002/jtr.621

Milikowski, F. (2016, 27 July). In de greep van ijs en vastgoed: Amsterdam als koelkastmagneetje. *De Groene Amsterdammer*. Retrieved from https://www.groene.nl/artikel/amsterdam-als-koelkastmagneetje

Municipality of Amsterdam. (2015). *Stad in balans*. Amsterdam: Gemeente Amsterdam, Ruimte en Duurzaamheid.

Nijman, J. (1999). Cultural globalization and the identity of place: The reconstruction of Amsterdam. Cultural Geographies, *6*(2), 146–64. https://doi.org/10.1177/096746089900600202

Onderzoek, Informatie en Statistiek (OIS) Amsterdam. (1965–2016). Amsterdam in cijfers 1965–2016.

Retrieved from https://www.ois.amsterdam.nl/publicaties/

Pinkster, F.M., & Boterman, W.R. (2017). When the spell is broken: Gentrification, urban tourism and privileged discontent in the Amsterdam canal district. cultural geographies, 24(3), 457–72. https://doi.org/10.1177/1474474017706176

Terhorst, P., & van de Ven, J. (2003). The economic restructuring of the historic city center. In S. Musterd & W. Salet (Eds.), *Amsterdam human capital* (pp. 85–101). Amsterdam: Amsterdam University Press.

Terhorst, P., van de Ven, J., & Deben, L. (2003). Amsterdam: It's all in the mix. In L.M. Hoffman, S. Fainstein, & D.R. Judd (Eds.), *Cities and visitors: Regulating people, markets and city space* (pp. 75–90). Oxford: Blackwell Publishing

Urry, J. (1990). *The tourist gaze: Leisure and travel in contemporary societies, theory, culture & society*. London: Sage.

Zukin, S. (2008). Consuming authenticity: From outposts of difference to means of exclusion. Cultural Studies, 22(5), 724–48. https://doi.org/10.1080/09502380802245985

Contributors

Jaap Evert Abrahamse studied the history of architecture and urban planning. His graduation placement was at the Atelier parisien d'urbanisme, where he worked out a thesis on urban development in Paris. In 2010, he received his doctorate cum laude at the University of Amsterdam for his thesis *De grote uitleg van Amsterdam. Stadsontwikkeling in de zeventiende eeuw* (*Metropolis in the Making. A Planning History of Amsterdam in the Dutch Golden Age*). He is a senior researcher for the Cultural Heritage Agency of the Netherlands, publishing on the history of urban planning, architecture, infrastructure, and landscape.

Willem R. Boterman is Associate Professor of Urban Geography at the University of Amsterdam. His interests are in the social transformations of urban space, with a particular interest in intersections of class and gender. Current research projects focus on the relationship between gender, parenthood, and gentrification; consumption and distinction; middle-class politics in the city; and issues of school and residential choice across class and ethnicity and how these practices co-produce social and spatial inequalities in the city.

Len de Klerk is Professor Emeritus of Urban and Regional Planning at the University of Amsterdam. He has a background of twenty-five years as a planning officer in different municipalities, among others as deputy director of Urban Development in the City of Rotterdam. As a scholar, he has written books on the development of Dutch private and public urban planning practices in the nineteenth and twentieth centuries.

Jan Hein Furnée is Professor of European Cultural History at Radboud University (Nijmegen, The Netherlands). His research focuses on the history of urban leisure culture, consumer culture, tourism, and cultural participation and policy in The Netherlands and Western Europe since 1750. Recent publications: with Clé Lesger (Eds.), *The Landscape of Consumption. Shopping Streets and Cultures in Western Europe, 1600–1900* (Houndmills, UK: Palgrave Macmillan, 2014); with Peter Borsay (Eds.), *Leisure*

Cultures in Urban Europe, c. 1700–1870: A Transnational Perspective (Manchester, UK: Manchester University Press, 2016).

Robert C. Kloosterman is Professor of Economic Geography and Planning at the University of Amsterdam. He is also Honorary Professor at the Bartlett School of Planning, University College London. His research is guided by questions about how the social, economic, and cultural transition of advanced urban economies that gathered pace after 1980 has affected cities. He is on the editorial board of the *Built Environment* journal and is lead partner on the EU-funded CICERONE project on global production networks in cultural industries.

Susan Legêne is Professor of Political History in the History Department of the Vrije Universiteit Amsterdam, Faculty of Humanities. Prior to this, from 1997 to 2008, she was head of the Curatorial Department of the Tropenmuseum (Royal Tropical Institute) and Professor of Dutch Cultural History and Material Culture for the Royal Antiquities Society at the University of Amsterdam. Her research focuses on processes of inclusion and exclusion in colonial and postcolonial nation-state formation, exploring the impact of cultural canon formation through past academic research traditions and exhibition practices.

Clé Lesger is Associate Professor in Economic and Social History at the University of Amsterdam. His research interests include the economic history of the Dutch Republic, the organization of early modern trade, the retailing industry, and the spatial structure of early modern and modern Dutch cities.

Jan Nijman (Editor) is Distinguished University Professor and Founding Director of the Urban Studies Institute at Georgia State University and Professor of Geography at the University of Amsterdam. He was also the founding director of the University of Amsterdam's Centre for Urban Studies. His interests are in urban and regional geography and urban history, with a research focus on West Europe, South Asia, and North America. He also recently edited *The Life of North American Suburbs: Imagined Utopias and Transitional Spaces* (Toronto: University of Toronto Press, 2020).

Melisa Pesoa is an architect and PhD in urban studies, researcher and associate lecturer at the Department of Urban and Territorial Planning (DUOT-UPC), where she teaches at both the graduate and postgraduate level. Her research is focused on urban morphology, urban and territorial history, and cultural landscapes. She is responsible for the organization of the International Seminar in Urbanism held every year in Barcelona and co-editor of the journals *Identities: Territory, Culture and Heritage* and *Quaderns de Recerca en Urbanisme*. She held a postdoctoral position at the National Scientific and Technical Research Council in Argentina (2017–2019).

Karin Pfeffer is Professor of Infrastructuring Urban Features in the Department of Urban and Regional Planning and Geo-Information Management, University of Twente. Her fields of interest are the generation of actionable knowledge from different (spatial) data sources in urban areas and how spatial knowledge is used in urban governance. She has been actively involved in setting up a regional monitoring system for the region of Amsterdam that is widely used by policy makers and accessible to the public.

Fenne M. Pinkster is Associate Professor in Urban Geography at the University of Amsterdam and affiliated with the Centre of Urban Studies. Her research focuses on the geography of everyday urban life, exploring the dialectical and often ambivalent relationships between identity, belonging, and place and the ways in which residents experience, use, and appropriate urban space.

Joaquín Sabaté holds a PhD in architecture and economics and is the chair of Town Planning at the Catalonia Polytechnic University (UPC). He is vice-dean of the Barcelona School of Architecture and coordinator of its master's programs. He is also founder of the International Laboratory of Cultural Landscapes (MIT-UPC) and director of the journal *Identities: Territory, Culture and Heritage*. He has lectured in numerous European, Asian, and North and South American universities. His research focuses are the theories, methods, and tools of urban and regional design and the relation between heritage resources and local development.

Freek Schmidt is Associate Professor of Architectural History at the Vrije Universiteit Amsterdam. His latest book, *Passion and Control. Dutch Architectural Culture*

of the Eighteenth Century, was published by Ashgate in 2016. His research on the design, use, and appreciation of the built environment in the early modern and modern age makes use of insights of the history of art, culture and architecture, urban planning, and heritage studies.

Russell Shorto is the author of six books, including *The Island at the Center of the World*; *Amsterdam: A History of the World's Most Liberal City*; and, most recently, *Revolution Song*. He is a contributing writer at the *New York Times Magazine* and Senior Scholar at the New Netherland Institute in Albany, New York. From 2008 to 2013, he was director of the John Adams Institute in Amsterdam.

Herman van der Wusten is Professor Emeritus of Political Geography at the University of Amsterdam. He wrote a historical dissertation on Irish resistance to the political unity of the British Isles (1977) and studied international migration in a Moroccan-Dutch context. More recently, he published on international relations and EU affairs, on the role of cities in diplomatic practice, and on city-state relations.

Tessa VerLoren van Themaat is a freelance historian and exhibition maker. She graduated from the Vrije Universiteit Amsterdam in 2011 with an MA in history and a thesis focused on material culture and identity formation in the Netherlands. Since then, she has been working on various projects, including a research project about the protection of cultural heritage (VUA).

Over the past five years, she has also worked as a curator for the Amsterdam Light Festival, an annual exhibition of light art in the public space of the city centre.

Mark Warren is an architectural designer and urban historian working in San Francisco. He holds a master of architecture degree from the University of California, Berkeley, and a bachelor of arts in the history of art and architecture from Harvard University. He was granted a Fulbright scholarship to research the history of Barcelona's urban planning and development, with a focus on the changes of the past forty years.

Index

Page numbers in *italics* refer to figures, maps, and tables.